Praise for *Jarmila Novotná*

"A gracious and brilliant talent tells the captivating story of her life in the arts, set against the political upheaval of war and revolution, glamorous friendships with royalty, Hollywood icons, and the titans of the music world. This fascinating book has it all."—Wendy Lawless, author of the *New York Times* best-selling memoirs *Chanel Bonfire* and *Heart of Glass*

"Novotná's larger-than-life memoir has all the makings of a play or movie in Madison's elegantly readable compilation and edition. This first-person account is almost a who's who of twentieth-century politics and international culture as encountered by an extraordinary performer, personality, and patriot. As Ogden Nash quipped in a lyric entitled 'Very, Very, Very,' finally we can huddle with her memoirs, and '*boy!* What memoirs them was!'"—Kim H. Kowalke, President, Kurt Weill Foundation for Music

"A compelling narrative of how a prominent female artist navigates through major historical events, shaping her life, career, and persona according to shifting circumstances. It is both a remarkable historical document and an enjoyable read."—Claudio Vellutini, University of British Columbia

"Glamorous yet sensitive, Novotná believed and proved that any kind of music, any kind of art, can bring people together for the common good: to resist tyranny, to celebrate freedom, to heal, and to nurture. We've seen it proven over and over throughout history, but not all artists have been as bold and as brave as she was—to actually put into action her belief that music could transform. As I've made my way in opera, I've heard so much about this spectacular artist. Now, in her own words, she confirms the legends—with plenty of wonders and surprises along the way. Through her story, I, as well as countless other artists who are paying attention, can learn from her bravery and boldly carry on fighting through our art to transform the human experience!"—Joyce DiDonato, mezzo-soprano

"What a treasure to have the life of the great Czech soprano in her own words. Her rare combination of physical and vocal beauty, supported by her initial training as an actress, gave Novotná a dazzling versatility. Reading her detailed, candid remembrances, you enter an era when the classical arts were in full flower, when barriers between the opera house, popular music, the concert stage, Broadway, and Hollywood had yet to be erected."—Renée Fleming, soprano

"Even though I'm not a soprano, I've sung many of the roles that Jarmila Novotná made her own. I know just how challenging they can be, but she made them look easy; no wonder I admire her. One of the all-time greats, Novotná was a model of taste and artistry—and what a life she led, always at the center of the action, alongside the leading figures in the arts and politics of her time. There's something for everybody in this book!"—Susan Graham, mezzo-soprano

"A charming and informative memoir from a major opera singer. . . . The tale of a woman who never let anything stop her from pursuing her ideal of musical excellence."—Dan Callahan, author of *Vanessa: The Life of Vanessa Redgrave*

Jarmila Novotná

Jarmila Novotná

My Life in Song

Edited by William V. Madison

Foreword by Brian Kellow

UNIVERSITY PRESS OF KENTUCKY

Scholarly publisher for the Commonwealth,
serving Bellarmine University, Berea College, Centre
College of Kentucky, Eastern Kentucky University,
The Filson Historical Society, Georgetown College,
Kentucky Historical Society, Kentucky State University,
Morehead State University, Murray State University,
Northern Kentucky University, Transylvania University,
University of Kentucky, University of Louisville,
and Western Kentucky University.

Editorial and Sales Offices: The University Press of Kentucky
663 South Limestone Street, Lexington, Kentucky 40508-4008
www.kentuckypress.com

Unless otherwise noted, photographs are from the collection of George Daubek.

Library of Congress Cataloging-in-Publication Data

Names: Novotná, Jarmila, 1907–1994, author. | Madison, William V., editor.
Title: Jarmila Novotná : my life in song / edited by William V. Madison ; foreword by Brian Kellow.
Description: Lexington, Kentucky : University Press of Kentucky, 2018. | Includes bibliographical references and index.
Identifiers: LCCN 2018014279 | ISBN 9780813176116 (hardcover : alk. paper) | ISBN 9780813176130 (pdf) | ISBN 9780813176123 (epub)
Subjects: LCSH: Novotná, Jarmila, 1907–1994. | Sopranos (Singers)—Czech Republic—Biography.
Classification: LCC ML420.N85 A3 2018 | DDC 782.1092 [B]—dc23 LC record available at https://lccn.loc.gov/2018014279

This book is printed on acid-free paper meeting
the requirements of the American National Standard
for Permanence in Paper for Printed Library Materials.

Manufactured in the United States of America.

Member of the Association
of University Presses

Contents

Foreword

Although I never had the pleasure of experiencing the artistry of Jarmila Novotná onstage, I have always gained great sustenance from the warm, lyrical sheen and expressivity of her recorded legacy. I also recall her as a glamorous and aristocratic presence on the opera scene when I first came to New York City in the early 1980s.

Perhaps Novotná didn't possess what today might be thought of as a traditional "ear candy" voice, but as a singer, she possessed enormous reserves of communicative power and a remarkable sense of repose that enabled the listener to feel she was singing to him and him only.

In terms of her career path she was lucky to be able to work so much in the mid-twentieth century, when the U.S. musical scene did not make a point of polarizing the worlds of the classical and popular arts as it does today. A quick glance at the radio logs of the *New York Times* from the 1930s to the 1950s reveals an amazing confluence of brilliant performers, all thrown into the mix together. This was the bountiful atmosphere that helped Novotná to spring forward as a major vocal presence. From 1940 to 1956, she appeared steadily at the Metropolitan Opera, in roles ranging from Mimì in Puccini's *La Bohème* (her company debut) to Mozart's Pamina, Cherubino, and Donna Elvira, to Johann Strauss II's Orlofsky in *Die Fledermaus*. Opera and operetta were equally comfortable areas for an artist like Novotná; in 1934, she had enormous success in the title role of Franz Lehár's *Giuditta* at the Vienna State Opera. Once in New York, she distinguished herself in areas of the entertainment world that would be sadly off limits to today's most gifted opera and lieder singers. In 1944, she starred on Broadway in the musical *Helen Goes to Troy*, an adaptation of Offenbach's *La Belle Hélène*, for ninety-seven performances at the Alvin Theater. This was a production laden with impressive credits, among them director Herbert Graf, choreographer Léonide Massine, and the noted lighting designer Robert Edmond Jones. This was the level of work possible on Broadway in the 1940s. Novotná benefited from it, and Broadway benefited from her.

Helen, of course, was according to myth the world's most beautiful woman—and the role was no doubt authentically filled by Jarmila Novotná.

Even as an older woman on the social scene, her beauty, charm, and class were palpable. Older friends often explained to me the ways in which those same qualities made her a particularly illuminating Violetta in *La Traviata* at the Met; when Novotná sang the role, there was simply no way that Giorgio Germont could miss out on the fact that his son had fallen in love with a very rare and graceful creature.

Novotná also made a memorable impact in films—in two in particular: Fred Zinnemann's *The Search,* a 1948 post–World War II melodrama starring some fine actors, including Montgomery Clift and Aline MacMahon. Although Clift's definitive biographer, Patricia Bosworth, is right in her assessment that *The Search* skirts some of the essential horror of Hitler's final solution for the Jews, the movie still turned out to be a potent piece of work, and a project that elevated Novotná to an enviable status in Hollywood—especially given that she had come into the film world essentially as an outsider. Three years later, she gave a lively and spirited performance in the Mario Lanza vehicle *The Great Caruso,* a spectacular moneymaker for Metro-Goldwyn-Mayer in 1951. And she was a regular presence as a guest in television musical and comedy programs throughout the 1950s, magnificently bridging the worlds of "high" and "low" culture (terms that seem particularly reductive when describing the healthy entertainment atmosphere that existed at the time).

Whenever I think of Novotná and her singular accomplishments, I am oddly reminded not of another opera singer, but of a wonderful Golden Age film actress: Deborah Kerr. They shared a graceful, transformative quality that sprang from them naturally, and often lent astonishing dimensions to the material they were given to perform. They were both capable of catching us off guard emotionally with their coolly dispatched gifts. Like Kerr, Novotná never lost her ability to take our breath away, and didn't let us see quite how she did it.

Since I never felt that Novotná fully was recognized for her proper place in the pantheon of mid-century opera sopranos, it gives me great pleasure to salute my former *Opera News* colleague William V. Madison as he presents readers with this valuable document of her career.

Brian Kellow
New York City

Introduction

By reason of her beauty, her personal charm, a few accidents of fate, and above all her talent, Jarmila Novotná (1907–1994) occupies a singular position in history. It is doubtful we will ever see her like again; it is debatable whether we ever saw it before. A fervent Czechoslovakian patriot, she knew two of the country's musical titans of the previous generation: the soprano Emmy Destinn, her first voice teacher; and the composer Leoš Janáček. She made her greatest artistic statement with the *Songs of Lidice* (1942), recordings of traditional music dedicated to a Bohemian village obliterated by the Nazis; the diplomat Jan Masaryk accompanied her on piano. Novotná witnessed firsthand the birth of independent Czechoslovakia, the country's takeover by the Nazis, and then its fall to the Soviets. She was already a national heroine even before she was effectively exiled twice in succession, unable to return to her homeland even for her mother's funeral. But she lived long enough to make a triumphant homecoming to a free and independent Prague, where President Václav Havel received her with pride and bestowed on her the Order of Tomáš Garrigue Masaryk, one of the republic's highest honors, in recognition of her contributions to the development of "democracy, humanity, and human rights." In 1992, when the country divided into two independent states, the Czech Republic and Slovakia, Novotná grieved. In the aftermath of the Velvet Revolution, the Czech edition of her memoir, *Byla jsem šťastná* (I Have Been Happy), was a best seller.[1]

Born a tailor's daughter, Novotná would find herself dining with heads of state while she was still a very young woman. Marriage to a Czech baron, George Daubek, would bring her into even more rarefied circles: the Duke of Windsor was a favorite accompanist. As an actress, she would work with Max Reinhardt and Basil Rathbone in theater, and Louis B. Mayer would hound her for a movie contract. As a "crossover star," she would be the prized guest of Bing Crosby on radio as well as of Abbott and Costello on television, and an occasional visitor to Broadway; one of her final performances was in a musical adaptation of *Hans Brinker or the Silver Skates* for television, starring Tab Hunter in the title role. Cole Porter began writing *Kiss Me, Kate* with Novotná not only in mind but also seated beside him at the piano.

As an operatic soprano, she would become the favorite (one might even say the obsession) of Arturo Toscanini, and a fixture at both the Staatsoper in Vienna and the Metropolitan in New York, where she sang nearly two hundred performances between 1940 and 1956, a period often described as the Met's 'Golden Age.'

Through it all, she remained remarkably unaffected. Her father's customers would have included a number of society women, so that Novotná had a head start on the refined etiquette she would so quickly need. It was a democratic age, and as a little girl Novotná stood on the platform to greet the arriving train of Tomáš Garrigue Masaryk, who had worked passionately to ensure that Czechoslovakia would receive its independence in the aftermath of World War I. Later, after Masaryk's election to the presidency and following the launch of Novotná's career, he understood instantly that an attractive young soprano could serve as a first-rate cultural ambassador for the new nation. At Masaryk's recommendation, his government put her portrait on the 100-crown note.[2] But beyond the asset Novotná represented to his political interests, the president also took a warm, avuncular interest in the young singer and acted as her behind-the-scenes adviser; his son, Jan, became one of her closest friends. Perhaps most important, President Masaryk sought out Novotná's opinions, too, never snubbing her or condescending to her. At state dinners, the young singer spoke as confidently—and as tactfully—as anyone else, and those dinners served as a training ground for her later encounters with princes, kings, presidents, and captains of American industry.

Possessed of a pleasing vocal instrument, a slender, athletic body, and a face of uncommon beauty, Novotná was by all accounts a memorable presence onstage, as we can see for ourselves from her appearances onscreen. Her keen musical and theatrical intelligence made her one of the most sought-after performers of her time, even before Reinhardt and Toscanini refined her gifts. And Novotná's beauty was such that she even modeled occasionally, for Golden Opera Jewelry from the Deltah company in America, and in fashion houses in Austria; her photos appeared on cigarette cards in Germany.[3] Perhaps the most remarkable modeling gig came her way after she made headlines as the first Metropolitan Opera star to play a female character (Freia, in *Das Rheingold*) and a male character (Orlofsky, in *Die Fledermaus*) on the same day; a brewery promptly hired her for a newspaper ad, in which she declared that her "most thrilling day in opera" was when she sang *Rheingold* "and another opera . . . And afterward, you guessed it! I enjoyed another famous Rheingold—New York's Original Extra Dry beer."[4]

Yet her looks were not quite the trap they might have been. Everybody from Franz Lehár to L. B. Mayer seems to have wanted to view her as a sex siren, but that was a role she had no interest in playing in life. Mayer wanted to mold her in the image of a singing Greta Garbo or Hedy Lamarr, or a more exotic Jeanette MacDonald. She resisted his blandishments so resolutely that he began to refer to her by an abbreviated name: not "Madame Novotná" but "Madame *No.*" Lehár wrote the operetta *Giuditta* for her, and her aria "Meine Lippen, sie küssen so heiß" became her signature number, such that, decades later, house orchestras in Viennese restaurants still struck it up whenever she dined out. Yet the song is racy, the character of Giuditta an adulterous nightclub artiste.

> I myself do not know why
> As soon as men come near me
> They begin talking of love,
> And staring into my eyes and kissing my hand.
> . . . .
> But when the red light glows
> At the midnight hour
> And everyone strains to hear my song,
> Then the reason is clear to me:
>
> My lips, they kiss so hotly.
> My limbs are supple and white.
> In the stars, it has been written:
> "You shall kiss! You shall love!"[5]

Novotná was nothing like Giuditta—and nothing like Offenbach's Giulietta or Verdi's Violetta, or the characters she played in some of her European films in the 1930s, or the aristocratic vamp she played on television in *The Great Waltz* (1955). Her own role model was her mother, who also served as her chaperone in the early years. In life, Novotná wanted above all to remain a devoted Catholic wife and mother. When men like Toscanini and Montgomery Clift threw themselves at her—and they did—she ignored their indiscretions.

From the start of her career, critics acclaimed her, and it is telling that the only truly bad reviews she ever received were from Nazi-leaning newspapers in Germany in the early 1930s. They complained that a Czech singer had taken a job that might have gone to a German artist; they howled when she dared to sing German music in the Czech language—in Prague. Even these critics did not attack her fundamental artistry; their weapon against her popularity was the suggestion that it would be unpatriotic to hire her or to attend her performances. More often she dazzled the critics. Here is Olin Downes, writing in the *New York Times* about Novotná's first Violetta at the Metropolitan, in 1940: "No measure of the text, sung with the purest and most admirable Italian, lost its effect or failed to carry over the footlights. The word and the tone were indissoluble; the phrasing was that of the finest musician. Pathos was never overdone; by contrast the élan of her attack when she began the 'Sempre libera' made the pulse beat quicker, yet never lost the mood of the desperate gaiety of the condemned."[6]

Though audiences who saw her onstage are fewer today, I have known some of them and respected their opinions. "You really believed she was a prince!" enthused the widow of Jack Gilford, who played Frosch to Novotná's Orlofsky in *Fledermaus* at the Metropolitan. (Madeline Gilford then added pensively, "I guess she *was* a prince, or the wife of one, anyway.") Another friend praised the stillness and melancholy of Novotná's Mélisande while acting out her stage business, which my friend remembered in vivid detail from thirty years earlier—and then proceeded to mimic the sly sexiness of her Helen of Troy. Another friend who heard her often observed that Novotná offered her audiences "something very rare—music that aspired to the quality of poetry." Today, operagoers debate the degree to which mid-century operatic acting was merely "stand and sing" (also called "park and bark"); for her part, Novotná complained that *modern* opera singers did not know how to move, used too many gestures, and did not reveal the essence of the characters they played. Regardless, Novotná's dramatic ability clearly stood out from that of most of her contemporaries and earned her tremendous acclaim.

Novotná's reputation as a Broadway star might shine more brightly today had her greatest critical and popular theatrical success, *Helen Goes to Troy*, not fallen victim to two accidents of history: first, a heat wave that caused the show to close early, and second, the fact that original cast albums had not yet become de rigueur for Broadway musicals. Even a few years later, her work would have been better documented, precisely the kind of performance venerated by Broadway buffs. Scheduling conflicts prevented her from taking leading roles in the original productions of Kurt Weill's *One Touch of Venus* and Porter's *Kiss Me, Kate*, either (and surely both) of which would have rescued her definitively from the ranks of Broadway "might have beens."

To her earliest films Novotná brought not only her good looks but also a naturalness that, especially given how recently movies had turned to sound and how slowly acting turned away from an artificial, presentational style, now seems well ahead of its time.[7] In her memoir, she is critical of Max Ophüls' *Die verkaufte Braut* (The Bartered Bride, 1932), an adaptation of Smetana's opera.[8] Novotná objected to the film primarily because the director cut so much music and added so much spoken material to an opera she loved dearly from the first note to the last. The role of Marie (in Czech, Mařenka) would remain one of her favorites onstage; her performances of the opera during World War II would become an important demonstration of her love for her homeland and a rallying point for other Czechoslovakian-Americans; her performances in Prague, shortly after the war, were a national celebration.

Ophüls' *Die verkaufte Braut* is indeed more a testament to his artistry than to Novotná's, or, for that matter, to Smetana's. This is Novotná's fourth film, and while she is at ease, she is still learning how to act on camera. Under Ophüls' direction, the scene that demands the most from her character emotionally is more melodramatic than dramatic. In Smetana's opera, the heroine gets a tenderly mournful aria, "Ó, jaký žal" (Oh, what sorrow); in Ophüls' film, she gets something like a mad scene, as if that is the only response a soprano can give when she thinks her lover has betrayed her. The director's preference for wide shots denied her much opportunity to convey expressive subtlety in close-ups; Novotná felt physical constraints, too, since she was pregnant with her daughter, Jarmilka, at the time of filming. Nevertheless, this is a charming performance, as it should be. Ophüls' work is, by contrast, superlative. Taking liberties with the libretto, truncating songs, making extensive use of dialogue (including several scenes with the Bavarian comics Karl Valentin and Liesl Karlstadt), Ophüls opens up the material beyond its operatic origins, and in the process he creates a cinematic work, not merely a document of an opera. He films most of the movie outdoors, makes use of tracking shots, and imbues many sequences with frantic movement from the actors, beginning with the overture, which underscores swift-moving scenes of village life. Novotná's participation in the film, then, is significant, even beyond affording us a glimpse of one of her most celebrated stage roles.

Three years later, she appeared in director Karel Lamač's adaptation of Lehár's *Frasquita* (1934) that, again, is more movie than archival record.[9] Significant portions of *Frasquita,* too, were shot outdoors, and given that most Hollywood musicals at the time, and for decades to come, were filmed entirely on soundstages, Ophüls and Lamač can be seen as true innovators. While Novotna's Czech accent is perfectly appropriate to the Bohemian setting of *Verkaufte Braut,* it becomes exotic in *Frasquita,* in which her character initially conforms to a number of "Gypsy temptress" conventions.[10] Early scenes, set in a seaside village, find Frasquita casting seductive glances, brawling with another woman, getting arrested, dancing in a plaza—all the usual tropes, and yet performed with subtlety and flashes of vulnerability. We can see at once that Novotná has grown as a film actress, and Lamač, making greater use of close-up than does Ophüls, beautifully captures her performance. These early scenes set up the movie's subsequent romantic intrigues and Frasquita's surprising professional success—for this is not *Carmen,* but rather the rags-to-riches story of a young woman who becomes the star of a Parisian revue.[11]

Hollywood kept a close watch on European moviemaking in the 1920s and 1930s, importing stars such as Garbo and Marlene Dietrich, and it is entirely possible that MGM's Mayer saw one or more of Novotná's German-language films (it is certain that his scouts did) before he first offered her a contract, in 1937. His determination to engage her is easy to understand: she had become a natural screen actress. One can only speculate what might have happened if Novotná had accepted Mayer's offer. Movie stardom was by no means guaranteed. With European markets cut off during World War II, MGM could not maintain an audience even for Garbo, whose career came to an abrupt end. Novotná might have languished on the MGM lot—and hurried back to the Metropolitan as soon as her contract ran out. As it was, she resisted Mayer for fourteen years, relenting only to costar with Mario Lanza in *The Great Caruso* (1951).

Her best-known American film remains Fred Zinnemann's postwar drama *The Search* (1948), in which she sings only briefly, in her first scene. Thereafter, she relies on her expressive eyes and physicality to convey her character's weariness and despair. Her performance is so *visually* eloquent that it is hard to recall that Novotná's primary tool as an artist was her voice. She sometimes described *The Search* as "almost a documentary," with its location scenes shot amid the rubble of Nuremberg; many of the young children in the cast were indeed refugees. By the time of filming, Novotná had been able to return to Czechoslovakia a few times, to hear the wartime experiences of her family and friends, and to see for herself the vestiges of suffering and devastation. Thus she brings to her characterization her own sorrow at seeing some worst fears confirmed, and her own relief at seeing other fears denied. While even her memoir cannot entirely convey the degree to which Czechoslovakia's plight preoccupied her during the war, her performance in *The Search* gives us a clear sense of her true feelings.[12] Every word and gesture is authentic, and she thoroughly eschews the glamour that she and the Met so artfully deployed to promote her American career.[13] Novotná's affinity for children is manifest in many scenes (as it was between takes, she tells us in the memoir), and with the veteran actress Aline MacMahon she establishes a compelling on-screen relationship: by turns like friends, sisters, and mother and daughter.

Though Novotná and Clift appear together in only one scene, she won him over completely off-camera, and they remained friends, as did Novotná and Fred Zinnemann and his wife. Ivan Jandl, Novotná's young costar, won a special Academy Award for his performance, and throughout his childhood, he carried on a correspondence with his "little mother." By then, Czechoslovakia was already under Soviet domination, and Jandl's subsequent career did not—and was not allowed to—fulfill its early promise. In 1985, near the end of his life, he had a poignant reunion with Novotná, on which the Czechoslovakian press reported extensively.

During World War II, the Daubeks had by good fortune found themselves in the United States. George Daubek Sr. had been unable to take more than a small amount of money out of Czechoslovakia, and Novotná became the sole source of income for her family, receiving $600 per performance at the Met.[14] This was a substantial sum, and yet because she could sing at the Met only a few nights per week at most, it was not enough to maintain her family of four in the style to which they were accustomed. Thus, in addition to her operatic engagements, she took on lengthy recital tours, singing with local orchestras, music clubs, women's groups—virtually anyone who would have her. She became a favorite of Czechoslovakian-American organizations, which engaged her to sing all-Czech programs to benefit the Czechoslovak Red Cross (on which she served as chair) and other relief efforts. Again and again she crisscrossed the country by train, car, and airplane (a great novelty). As a result, Novotná saw more of her adopted home than most natives ever do, and she continued to tour widely even after her husband found employment as an executive with IBM. The tailor's daughter retained her practicality, and amid the constant travel she invented the garment bag—only to see it copied, down to the fabric she used, and patented by somebody else.[15]

As her singing voice matured, Novotná gravitated away from coloratura and lyric-soprano singing and toward operatic roles that are often sung by lyric mezzo-sopranos: Mélisande, Octavian, Cherubino, Orlofsky.[16] She also developed a different sort of recital, interspersing songs with stories about the people she had known and the funny things that had happened to her onstage. Reading the long profile of her in Lanfranco Rasponi's *The Last Prima Donnas,* and reading the manuscript of this memoir, I realized that the recital-cum-lecture tour was in a very real sense the first draft of this autobiography.[17] Indeed, all those portraits and stories are included here. She wanted to present a particular image to the public, one that was "lovely" and "charming" (her favorite English-language adjectives) and, above all, gracious. It seemed that the only people she was willing to disparage were Nazis and Communists. The sort of gossip and in-fighting that one may expect from a prima donna simply did not enter her conversation, and she expressed nothing but affection and praise for her colleagues. But the "lovely and charming" persona was not a false front, her son tells me, and even late in her life she employed tact and delicacy to avoid speaking ill of other singers: "Singing is so difficult, I wonder why anyone attempts it," she often remarked. When American editors (many of whom she knew socially) at commercial houses warned her that their readers had a taste for scandal and that in order to sell her memoir she would have to add "spicy" stories, she complained to the *New York Times,* "I was surprised. In Lotte Lehmann's book there is no sex. But that was many years ago. Now you have to go naked. What has happened to the world?"[18]

Novotná had hoped to work on her memoir with Rasponi, but his death in 1983 put an end to those hopes. Thereafter, Novotná worked for a year or so on the memoir, taking preliminary notes and drafting chapters on any available piece of paper, writing in English, Czech, or German, whenever inspiration struck her. When at last she was ready, and with the assistance of her granddaughter Jaji Packard, she compiled all these fragments into a unified English-language manuscript, the one American publishers ultimately rejected in the mid-1980s. Undeterred, Novotná translated her manuscript into Czech; the writer-researcher Jan Králik also prepared an extensive discography, filmography, and lists of theatrical and operatic roles that, revised and updated, form the basis of the appendix to the present edition. The overwhelming response from Czech readers in 1991 inspired Novotná to make a second attempt to find an American publisher. Initially, she thought of merely translating the Czech memoir into English, but she found this process frustrating. "I finished by writing a new book entirely," she told the *New York Times* a year before her death.[19] This "new book" is the manuscript from which I worked.

In writing her memoir, Novotná drew on a variety of materials that remain in the collection of her son, including private correspondence with her husband, business correspondence and contracts, voluminous photo albums, concert programs, and playbills. A few other documentary sources are worthy of mention. Despite her exile, Novotná managed to keep a number of scrapbooks, now in the possession of the Daubek family, and she consulted them frequently as she prepared her memoir. In the manuscript, she quotes at length from press clippings, particularly reviews of her performances. A meticulous record keeper, she also copied out and saved any letters of significance that she sent to others, and in her original draft she quotes in their entirety virtually every letter or telegram she received from President Masaryk and from Toscanini, without regard to the potential interest to readers. Because of copyright restrictions, I have paraphrased or described the contents of most of these letters. What is most important, really, is less what each man specifically said than the attitude toward Novotná that each man reveals. Masaryk is a benevolent, avuncular figure, Toscanini remarkably peevish and self-pitying.

Other correspondence, which Novotná surely would have quoted, too, has been lost. During World War II, first German and then Russian troops occupied the Daubek family estate, Liteň. Returning in 1946, Novotná assessed the condition of the property, her furnishings, and other belongings left behind, an experience she describes in detail in the memoir. While the bulk of her personal correspondence remained intact, she discovered that certain letters from luminaries such as Richard Strauss, Leoš Janáček, and Max Reinhardt had gone missing. She surmised that thieves, possibly soldiers or Communist officials, had pilfered those letters of greatest financial value. Even the mention of the Masaryk name was forbidden after Czechoslovakia fell under Soviet domination and Jan Masaryk died (very likely assassinated); letters from the Masaryk family would have been contraband, and so those letters survived. Her inquiries with the Communist government of Czechoslovakia received a pro forma bureaucratic nonresponse, but one that did suggest that the missing letters might have wound up in the National Archive. In 1990, Novotná herself searched the archive and found nothing.

The most important resource of which Novotná availed herself in preparing her memoir was her appointment books, in which she had diligently noted not only where she traveled and when, but also who attended which social functions with her. The original draft of the memoir thus employs a day-by-day approach that, even for a reader keenly interested in Novotná's life, defies patience. Similarly, the lists of names at dinner parties would hold little significance to most readers; in these lists, Novotná seldom offers any insights into her companions' characters, and she appears to have been motivated by the belief that these people would enjoy seeing their names in her book.[20]

In editing the manuscript, then, I have attempted to organize Novotná's account not by day but by tour or by season, and I have favored the names of people who are "characters" in this story (the governess Teta, the Masaryks, IBM's Thomas J. Watson Sr.); people who have been or are likely to be the subjects of biographies themselves (the Duke of Windsor, Dwight Eisenhower, Gabriele d'Annunzio); and people of particular prominence in the performing arts (Ezio Pinza, Sol Hurok, Fredric March). I have respected Novotná's fluent yet flavorful use of the English language, and I have added only a dozen or so sentences to this memoir. Most of these are what amount to punch lines to Novotná's humorous anecdotes. While she could get the desired laugh in performance during her lecture-recital tours by adjusting her inflections or expression, she had no real experience writing humor. She did most certainly want to amuse her audience, and I have tried to help her achieve that goal.

Her memoir, then, leaves the reader with what amounts to a detailed confirmation of the impressions Novotná made on me personally, from the moment I first heard about her to the moment we met. I found her as so many others had: brilliant, beautiful, captivating. She did indeed get the desired laughter as a response to her funny stories; and the charm she communicated in recordings, and even in still photos, she communicated even more directly in conversation.

I discovered Novotná on the recommendation of Lys Symonette, a musical mentor who had heard her many times: "*That* was an artist," Lys said, showing me a photo of Novotná in a magazine from the 1940s. Unable to believe that such a beautiful woman was not a chorus girl but an opera star, I bought one of her recordings, which featured her haunting account of "Měsíčku na nebi," Rusalka's song to the moon. Soon, I had purchased every one of her recordings I could find, and I read Rasponi's book. Still I wanted to know more. In the summer of 1990, I wrote her a fan letter, addressed to the stage door of the Metropolitan, where the staff are heroic when it comes to getting mail to the right people. Novotná replied, without a trace of the things one expects a diva to write to a young admirer: she moved promptly to the subject of her recent trip to Prague. "The enthusiasm and the happiness of the people are hard to describe,"she reported, scarcely eight months after Czechoslovakia had reclaimed its independence. She had attended a gala concert by her old friends Rafael Kubelík, Rudolf Firkušný, and Leonard Bernstein, and she had taken advantage of a meeting with President Havel to enlist his aid in the preservation of Antonín Dvořák's New York home. (She gently hinted that I ought to help, too.) Between the handwriting and newsy, intimate tone, her letter reminded me of those I used to receive from my elderly aunt—though my aunt never had the pleasure of informing me that Czechoslovakian astronomers had just named a planet after her.[21]

Not long after, my friend Catherine Karnow was asked to provide the photographs for a guidebook on New York. She wanted to shoot something that would represent the cultural richness of the city and the stature of the artists who live there. I suggested Novotná, and so I wrote to her again, explaining the project and giving her my telephone number. A few days later, I found the great lady's voice on my answering machine. We set up an appointment.

I wanted to bring a gift, ideally something with lips on it, a tangible echo of the restaurant orchestras that used to play "Meine Lippen" for her. The only items I could find were hopelessly tacky, so I settled on a rose—just one—and prepared to apologize for the fact that it was not silver, like Octavian's. I needed no apology, however, because Novotná understood the reference the second she opened the door and saw me. "Ach!" she cried, "you are der Rrrrrrrrosenkavalier!" She rolled the *R* until it became an elaborate confection: I could see that the word tasted good in her mouth.

She was wearing a Chanel suit, robin's egg blue, that I recognized as the one she had worn in a photo session for a cover story in *Opera News* the year before; the color was similar to that of her stationery. She wanted to know whether Cathy's family was Czech—"It's sometimes a Czech name, you know, Karnow"—and she fretted that my studies of language had not yet extended to her native tongue. I explained that I had flunked Russian in college. "Ach, Czech is much easier than Russian," she assured me. She loved her homeland, though she had spent most of her life in exile. Then, almost without warning, the Velvet Revolution had arisen, and Czechoslovakia was free. "And do you know, Václav Havel knows my work? Yes, he's a fan!"[22]

As Cathy prepared her photo equipment, Novotná told us stories, all of which you will find in this book. And as Cathy began to take the pictures, Novotná snapped into action. She moved heavy furniture around the room, to give us more space; she refused my help. I expressed astonishment: she was past eighty already. "Ach, it's easy," she said gaily. "When I was a girl, I was in the Sokol—you know, the Czech gymnastic society."

Cathy asked to get a few pictures of Novotná holding some sheet music. She trotted off to another room and emerged with "Voices of Springtime," then stood in the natural light of the window and glowed, with a natural light of her own, as she read the familiar notes.

And then she started to sing.

You couldn't say the voice was lustrous or seamlessly produced, but it was pitch-perfect and lovely, unforced and flexible, faint yet sweet and recognizably the voice I had fallen in love with, on records made forty and fifty years earlier. She sang the song twice over before we left. Cathy had succeeded in taking a series of striking photographs that her editors opted never to use.[23] But we had not thought to bring a tape recorder, so those pictures are the only record we have of Novotná's song.

"Voices of Springtime." A poignant choice of repertoire, though surely accidental. Novotná had reached the point in her life when she knew that more springtimes lay behind her than ahead. But springtime had lost none of its joy, and none of its charm.

On that autumn day in New York, Novotná had completed the first version of her memoir and was looking forward to its publication in Prague the next year. Consequently, our conversation was something like a cross between one of her recital-lectures and an author's reading. Because I failed to keep my promise to learn Czech, that afternoon would be, for more than two decades, my closest brush with her best-selling autobiography.

Until now.

William V. Madison
New York City

Dedication

I would like to dedicate this volume to my mother, Jarmila Novotná Daubek, who had always wished to have her memoir published in English here in the United States, her adopted homeland. The manuscript was stored away for over twenty years in one of many boxes I took possession of after her death, in 1994. As I pored over box after box of correspondence, scrapbooks, and photo albums, I began to understand how much of both my parents' lives had been entirely unknown to me. At times I felt like one of those mythological heroes who discovers his parents' legacy—and the wisdom that comes with it—hidden under a rock. My wife, Cathy, urged me to resurrect the manuscript of this memoir in particular, so that our children could learn more about their grandmother. The Czech edition of her memoir had been published, under the title *Byla jsem šťastná* (I Have Been Happy), but other than myself, no one in the family understands the language. My mother was a prolific writer, who wrote and rewrote until she was satisfied with her work. Even after discovering the complete English-language manuscript, I was unsure at first which version (among many drafts and fragments) it was. I am confident that the present version is the last, since it contains facts not mentioned in earlier drafts and covers events that took place not long before her passing.

I have always firmly believed that my mother's life story could inspire and greatly interest a broad spectrum of readers. My mother's roots were modest. She was blessed with incredible stamina and a talent and charisma that won over a large audience of admirers even when she was young—my father and many dignitaries among them. She spoke often of the four pillars of influence over her life: her husband; Czech president Tomáš Garrigue Masaryk; Arturo Toscanini; and Max Reinhardt. They were her supporters, teachers, believers, who allowed her to step away from her modest background and onto a world stage, not only as an entertainer and ambassador of goodwill but also as an individual who expressed her thoughts freely to presidents and to leaders of government and industry without fearing that she was out of place. Consequently, she was able to establish a philosophy of not allowing adversity, however calamitous, to prevent her from going forward in life. She never looked back at what could have been.

Dedication

This memoir would not have been published without Bill Madison's skillful editing. It was serendipity (and the Internet) that brought me to Bill. He had interviewed my mother in 1990 and subsequently published that interview on his blog; my daughter Tatiana tracked him down. His style of writing, his knowledge of the world of opera and music, and our subsequent meeting made it clear that he was the ideal person to bring my mother's memoir to life. Thank you, Bill.

Above all, I am grateful to my wife and to my daughters, Francesca, Antonia, and Tatiana, for their love and support, not only as I pursued this project but throughout our lives together.

George Daubek
Pound Ridge, New York

Prelude
Magic

Magic brought me to America.

I had worshiped Arturo Toscanini ever since I heard him conduct at La Scala in 1927, while I was studying in Milan. His unforgettable performances gave me insight into what is beautiful and important in music. At the time, I never dreamed that I would know the Maestro and sing under his direction.

In 1930, he came to Prague on tour with the New York Philharmonic Orchestra, and naturally I went to the concert. I still have the program from that concert.

Seven years later, the Maestro conducted *The Magic Flute* at the Salzburg Festival, and it was an indescribable joy for me when he chose me to sing Pamina.

Not long after, Toscanini asked me to come to New York. I told him how infatuated with him I had been, and to prove it I showed him my program from the Prague concert. He was pleased, and he signed it for me.

I was launching a rewarding career in the United States, especially at the Metropolitan Opera. It would be a long time before I saw my homeland again. I had to call on all my preparation, not only for my musical career, but also for my life.

1

Europe, 1907–1939

I was born in Prague, on September 23, 1907, into a wonderfully harmonious household, for my sister, Pavla, and I had understanding parents. My father, Josef Novotný, was a ladies' tailor with impeccable taste and a large clientele. Leftover scraps of silks and satins went into costumes for the friends who flocked to our home to act in the little plays I devised for our entertainment. Even then, I loved to immerse myself in theater, elementary as it was. As for singing, that inclination was with me from the time I was no more than three or four. When my sister, a year and a half older than I, said her prayers, I sang mine. Indeed, whenever there was an opportunity, I sang.

I was only seven years old when the First World War broke out, and my father was immediately drafted into the army. This was a very hard blow for us all, and my mother, Josefa, was left to take care of us children. She grew up on a little farm in Mníšek, a small town about three miles from Prague. During the war, when there was very little to eat, she went to the country and brought home whatever was needed, sometimes even a goose.

A wonderful woman, my mother loved music, and she used to say that music is as important to life as flowers in the garden, paintings on the wall, and food on the table. She insisted that my sister and I should learn to play an instrument. I took piano lessons, and my sister took up the zither; we both took French lessons, as well, in addition to the German we studied at school. How right and wise my mother was, for these lessons were an important preparation for my later life. Mother also saw to it that we had a very strict moral upbringing, and because Pavla and I obeyed her, our household remained always peaceful. However, due to the war, my father never joined us, until a day when Bohemia's destiny changed forever.

Situated in the center—I would almost say "heart"—of Europe, Bohemia was still part of the Austro-Hungarian Empire when the war began, yet we were brought up to appreciate its greatness. We studied our history, with its many memorable figures: Čech, the early Slavonic tribal leader who gave his name to what would become a nation; King Wenceslaus, about whom the Christmas carol was written; Libuše, who, according to legend, founded the city of Prague at the foot of the hill Vyšehrad and foretold its greatness; King Charles, who founded Prague University; and King John, who declared at the Battle of Crécy in 1346, "So will it God, it shall not be that a King of Bohemia flees from the battlefield." This glorious history came to a halt in 1620, when Bohemia fell under Austrian rule for the next three hundred years. We recalled that the Prussian chancellor Otto von Bismarck once said, "The Master of Bohemia is the Master of Europe." This was small consolation to a people as proud as the Czechs. We did not know that the terrible war would bring us the independence we craved.

When the war broke out, the legislator Tomáš Garrigue Masaryk left Austria-Hungary to begin a global campaign calling for the liberation of his homeland and the creation of a free, democratic, socially just republic. Masaryk and his associate, Dr. Edvard Beneš, founded the Czechoslovak National Council and conferred with U.S. president Woodrow Wilson, who expressly included the independence and unity of Bohemia, Moravia, and Slovakia among America's goals in the war. Then, in 1918, the Allies recognized the National Council as the de facto government of the new Czechoslovakia. From Páiladelphia, Masaryk issued a Declaration of Independence for the new nation in October 1918, and on October 28 that year, the Czechoslovak Republic was proclaimed in Prague.

I will never forget that day. Since the war began, my father had never received a furlough. Then he was wounded at the front, and after recuperating in a hospital, he was allowed to go home for two weeks. As if by a miracle, he returned to Prague on the day of liberation. When Father walked in and told us the war was over, we could hardly believe it. "You should go out to see for yourselves," he said. So my sister and I went down into streets overflowing with people, chanting and embracing. We ran home to tell our parents the news and to share our happiness. Father would never have to return to the war, thank God!

Masaryk was elected the first president of the Czechoslovak Republic by popular acclaim while he was still in the United States. He returned to Prague on November 18, 1918. There was great rejoicing and preparation for his arrival. The station in Vinohrady, where his train was to arrive, was renamed Wilson Station, in honor of the American president. The Sokol, a national sport and gymnastics organization, designated several of its members to escort President Masaryk, and the entire Vinohrady Sokol participated in this event. Pavla and I had been members of the Sokol since we were very young, and Father, who was very tall and good-looking, was chosen to be one of the escorts. He was proud of this his whole life long.

When the president arrived at Hradčany, the ancient castle where the kings of Bohemia reigned, schoolchildren assembled to greet him. Our school also took part in this ceremony, and we were among thousands and thousands of children who sang for Dr. Masaryk. When he appeared on the balcony, the jubilation was so immense that the voices of the crowd could be heard far, far down in the city. Of the many times my voice has brought me joy, this is perhaps the most memorable.

After the hardships of the war years, life assumed a more normal course. In school, we learned all the folk songs and dances, and often we were invited to other schools to perform. I often had to sing a solo for the children, although I was a rather quiet child. My teacher, Jarmila Brojova, confirmed this at the time, writing in my notebook: "The fragrant violet hides in the grass; every virtuous maiden has a modest heart." Miss Brojova was very musical, and I remained in contact with her until her death. When I turned sixty, she wrote to me with sweet memories. Miss Brojova recalled that her "darling doll" was a quick learner who made good grades, and that I was the fastest when we knitted socks for soldiers during the war. Already in fifth grade I had learned the role of Mařenka (in English, Marie) in *The Bartered Bride*. "You were simply the lark of the class," Miss Brojova said.

In junior high school, another teacher, Maria Mašková, recognized that I had a special talent, and before I was twelve years old, she took me to a singing teacher to ask her opinion. That lady, too, was impressed, but she warned against my starting too early to study.

Still, my love for music grew. My parents took Pavla and me very often to the National Opera. My favorite opera at that time was Tchaikovsky's *Eugene Onegin* because the role of Tatyana was so romantic. Soon I learned many soprano arias, which I sang at any and every opportunity.

On one such occasion, I was at a summer camp in Hronov Pod Radhostem. I was twelve or thirteen at the time. We often went hiking, and I would burst into song in the mountains. It was wonderful to hear an echo answering me. But one evening I was just a little late coming back to the dormitory. All the other girls had returned already, and the counselor asked me very harshly what had happened to me. "I do not think it is such a crime," I said.

"So you don't think anything of discipline?" he said. "You want to have your own rules, do you? Just to teach you, you will kneel now in the corner there for fifteen minutes, as a punishment." I was perplexed, ashamed in front of the other girls, and very hurt. Who knows? Maybe he just wanted to provoke me. He was tall, slender, and athletic, and he pleased me very much. But at this moment, my young love for him simply died!

I was still a member of the Sokol. The name means "Falcon," and the group's exhibitions of individual and collective gymnastic achievements were called the Sokol Slet, meaning "Falcon Flock." For Slavs, the Sokol Slet was what the Olympic Games were to the Ancient Greeks. In 1920, I took part in the Sokol Slet. I was one of some 80,000 participants from all over the world, and the stadium, which seated 100,000, was filled to the rafters. Twenty-seven thousand adults, 20,000 adolescent boys and girls, and 10,000 schoolchildren displayed their physical fitness in many, many events. By some lucky draw, I was seated in the first row among the 10,000, and I was so proud, I was sure that everyone looked only at me. With only one rehearsal, we performed our exercises. Later, we changed our Sokol dresses for traditional Bohemian costumes and performed folk dances.

Many Sokol groups offered cultural activities, as well, and the Vinohrady Sokol had its own choir and amateur theatrical group. I took part in several productions, and this really was my start. When I was fourteen years old, I sang the lead in an operetta called *Lucifer,* and later I performed in a more ambitious production, *Malérečka,* a play with songs. My partner was a young pharmacist, Jaroslav Gleich. He had a lovely tenor voice and later gave up his job to join the National Theater, where he became very well known. About a year later, when I was not yet fifteen years old, Jaroslav and I sang together in Smetana's *The Bartered Bride* for our Sokol. This experience proved valuable to me later on.[1]

I was also a member of the student choir, which was invited one year to sing Christmas carols at the municipal theater of the Vinohrady district in Prague. This proved fateful, because I became so entranced by being onstage that I begged my parents to let me perform in more plays. I became an "extra" and appeared in many productions, often playing a page because I was so slender. One day the actress Anna Baldová asked if I wouldn't like to become an apprentice at the National Theater, where her husband, Karel Hugo Hillar, was director. She told me she had already spoken of me to her husband. Another actress, Mila Pačová, encouraged me and even rehearsed with me my audition scene, from *Romeo and Juliet.* The miracle occurred, and I was accepted as an apprentice in 1922.

My apprenticeship proved to be good preparation for my later career. I had the opportunity to observe good actors during rehearsals, and soon enough I was given small roles to play. Not long after, I finished school and auditioned for the Prague Conservatory. Because I was so young, I was not accepted there. But no theater school could have given me better experience than I obtained at the National Theater, where I could appear on a real stage and get used to an audience. I played the page in Shaw's *Saint Joan,* the Actress in Pirandello's *Six Characters in Search of an Author,* and small roles in plays by such Czech playwrights as Arnošt Dvořák, Karel Čapek, and Julius Zeyer.

Moreover, the National Theater consisted, in fact, of two theaters, the Národní (the National) and the Stavovské (Theater of the Estates), in both of which opera and drama alternated. Mozart premiered *Don Giovanni* and *La Clemenza di Tito* at the Estates, and since the time of Smetana's directorship of the opera, performances there were given regularly in the Czech language.[2] Music was such an integral part of people's lives that Prague, though it had only a million inhabitants, also boasted a third opera theater, the German Opera House, for German-speaking audiences. These stages were my proving ground, the institutions that were so incredibly significant to my career as I matured.

A turning point for me came in 1923, when Emmy Destinn, the Czech soprano, returned to Prague to sing in a Sokol production of Smetana's *Libuše.* Because my father was still active in the Sokol organization, he took the opportunity to ask Mme. Destinn to audition his daughter: "She has nothing but singing on her mind," he explained. Destinn very graciously agreed, and two days later Father and I went to her hotel. Two black cats were lying near the piano, yet they weren't disturbed when I sang. I chose first to sing the song to the moon from Dvořák's *Rusalka* and then Tatyana's letter scene from *Eugene Onegin.* Mme. Destinn was very encouraging. She told me I had a good voice, and as long as she was in Prague, she would give me singing lessons. However, by this time she was internationally acclaimed and a great star of the Metropolitan Opera. So she urged me to find a local teacher as well, and she recommended Hilbert Vávra, a baritone with the National Theater.

I followed her advice and immediately started working with Vávra. We progressed so well that in October 1924, when I was seventeen, I gave my first recital, at the Mozarteum in Prague. The program consisted of lieder by Beethoven and Schubert, song cycles and arias by Smetana and Dvořák, and several folk songs, and I received good notices in the press. Within a few months, I would make my operatic debut.

In the spring of 1925, Hilbert Vávra arranged for me to sing Rosina to his Figaro in *The Barber of Seville* and Violetta to his Germont in *La Traviata* at a provincial theater in Louny, not far from Prague. A few members of the National Theater Orchestra participated in these performances, and when they returned to Prague, they gave the musical director, Dr. Otakar Ostrčil, a report of my success in Louny. Dr. Ostrčil auditioned me and offered me the role of Mařenka in *The Bartered Bride,* which I would sing on the afternoon of June 27, 1925. This did not give me much time to prepare, but luckily I had already sung the role with the Sokol in Vinohrady. All my friends from the Sokol came to hear me, so no wonder that I had a wonderful reception! But the rest of the audience and the press liked it, too.

Of course, I was still an apprentice in the drama division of the National Theater, and for the evening performance on June 27, I was scheduled to take the small role of Ziva in Zeyer's *Radúz and Mahulena.* This may seem odd, but I found nothing unusual in it, and I simply stayed in the theater after *The Bartered Bride.*

Dr. Ostrčil found my Mařenka satisfactory, and he asked me to sing Violetta on July 3, with Hilbert Vávra again singing Germont. The tenor Otakar Mařák, who was at that time internationally known, sang Alfredo. It seems that he resented having such a young girl for a leading lady, and he did everything possible to make the performance difficult for me. For instance, he upstaged me, so that I had to turn to him and sing to the back of the stage, rather than to the audience. There were many other unpleasantnesses, but rather than dwelling on them, I made up my mind always to be helpful to my partners. In a duet, or when I listened to another singer's aria, I always positioned myself so that my partner's voice could project easily into the audience. In this way, I learned a valuable lesson from Mařák.

Then it was time for vacation, though I could not sit idly, for I had quite a bit of work. I made my first film, *The Sun Worshipers,* in which I played a young woman unable to decide between two suitors. The plot bristled with complications, but unfortunately I don't remember much else about it! I could not guess how many more times I would stand before the movie cameras.

I also had many roles to prepare, since Dr. Ostrčil was pleased with my work and engaged me for several other performances. As soon as vacation ended, I would sing the Queen of the Night in *The Magic Flute.* Already I appreciated Mozart's genius, and Emmy Destinn used to say to me, "Anyone who can sing Mozart can sing everything, because his apparent simplicity requires the greatest control."

In performance, however, the vocal instrument is not all that requires control! I was a very slender girl, but the woman who sang Pamina, the

Queen's daughter, was much older and very buxom. It seemed to me that I must do something to change my appearance, or else nobody would take me seriously as this woman's mother. In opera, the dramatic power of the music allows an audience to suspend disbelief much more easily than in spoken theater, and we are often called on to accept, say, an Alfredo who is older than Violetta—or, nowadays, an Alfredo and a Germont who are of different races. So long as the singing is first-rate, we are not taken out of the drama. However, I suppose that I was already under the influence of the drama division of the National Theater, and so I took extra care with my characterization and credibility. The solution I came up with was to stuff my bosom with cloth, to make me look more imposing. Seeing myself in the mirror, I was not entirely satisfied—I didn't really look like Pamina's mother, but at least we might be related! I felt I had done everything I could.

The Queen of the Night has two important arias, one in each act of *The Magic Flute,* and both very demanding technically. I had hardly begun to sing my first aria when I felt the bundle of cloth in my bosom start to slide out of position. I had to keep singing, however, and could not make any adjustment: my "bosom" kept sliding until, by the end of the aria, I looked like an expectant mother!

In the next few months, I went on to Rosina in *The Barber of Seville,* Ariel in Fibich's *The Tempest* (in Czech, *Bouře,* after Shakespeare's play), Tatyana in *Eugene Onegin,* Jitka in Smetana's *Dalibor,* and further performances of *The Bartered Bride* and *La Traviata.* Though immensely busy, I was deliriously happy, especially when I received a splendid New Year's present, becoming a regular member of the National Theater on January 1, 1926. Now I was assigned to new operas, including Jaroslav Vogl's *Mistr Jira,* in which I sang the role of Lenka, and Otakar Zich's delightful *Les Précieuses ridicules,* after Molière's comedy. The story tells of two vain, pretentious girls who believe their suitors are too unfashionable to take seriously. The boys turn the tables, dressing their servants in magnificent outfits, then exposing them and humiliating the girls in front of their guests. It is interesting to see how this play inspires composers, and later, when I was a member of the Berlin Staatsoper, I sang in another adaptation, this one by an Italian, Felice Lattuada. In these operas, I didn't play particularly pleasant characters, but I relished the assignment, with its opportunities for comedy and drama.

As my repertoire grew, I also started to prepare a new concert program with Dr. Václav Stepan, a well-known composer. I performed several of his songs, as well as some by Leoš Janáček, the composer of *Káťa Kabanová* and

Jenůfa. Dr. Stepan told me that, through the Umělecká Beseda, or Society of Artists, he knew Janáček, and he asked whether I would like to meet him. And so at a dinner, I found myself sitting next to him. He had just returned from his first trip to London, where he had been highly acclaimed, and he was amazed by the sounds of the city. "Each city and country has different sounds," Janáček said, and he told me that he continually noted down the sounds and rhythms of streets, birds, waterfalls, and so on. "From the study of these diverse rhythms, I am able to shape a melodic arc," he said. "There must be an underlying tonality, but it must be kept fluid. I am learning from life, from nature, from people." What a treat it was to talk with him!

As you can see, my career did not leave much time for a private life. However, I loved to dance, and at dances I met a lot of young people, among them Prince Jiří Lobkowicz. In May 1926, he invited me to a ball hosted by the Narodní Beseda (National Club). Each year the club threw a ball in a different palace in Prague, and that year the Lobkowicz Palace had been selected. Because the prince needed to help in the preparations, he could not bring me to the ball. So he asked two friends to call for me at my home. One was an older gentleman, General Chmelar; the other was a very handsome man who introduced himself as Jiří Daubek. Together, we made our way to the palace.

I had never seen anything like this dreamlike setting, the lovely garden illuminated, and the rooms full of beautifully dressed people. I was already very well known for my success at the opera, and many people wanted to meet me, so I had a delightful time. I could have danced all night, but I remembered my mother, who was still very strict with me, even now that I was older. I had promised to be home not later than two a.m., and so—a little like Cinderella, perhaps—I had to leave the prince's ball. But I was less interested in the prince himself than in his friend. I asked Jiří Daubek to take me home, and on the way, he asked me for a date.

We agreed to meet the next Sunday, June 6. We drove to a country fair in the town of Průhonice, near Prague. He bought me a marzipan heart, which I cherished for many years to come. (I still had it the day we married.) That lovely afternoon came to an end, and unbelievable though it may sound, I returned to Prague for opening night of Weber's *Der Freischütz,* in which I sang the role of Ännchen. Amazing what one can do when one is young.

Many lovely afternoons would follow that first. I was in love for the first time in my life, and from then on I wanted to share every free minute with George Daubek. (George is the English equivalent of the Czech name Jiří, and it's the name he would use for most of his life.) But I didn't have much free time—I was also singing smaller roles, such as Frasquita in Bizet's *Carmen,* Camille in Charpentier's *Louise,* and many, many concerts and guest performances with the companies in Brno, Olomouc, Bratislava, Hradec Králové, and Prostějov. After summer vacation with my parents and sister in Yugoslavia, I was so suntanned that no amount of makeup could make me look like the sickly Violetta when we opened the season with *La Traviata.*

It seemed almost a scandal how little time I had to myself, but my new love consumed me. One day I was walking up the Narodní třída, the large street that leads to the National Theater, when I noticed George on the other side of the street. Immediately I signaled to him to cross over. "You tell me you are nearsighted," he said with a laugh. "How did you recognize me at that distance?" What a question! I would have recognized him anywhere.

George and his older brother, Josef—or Pepe, as we called him—were the handsomest men in Prague. Pepe was already married to Princess Olga Dietrichstein, who traced her ancestry to the Ruriks, the reputed founders of Russia who ruled that country until 1598. Her family lived in Prague in an eighteenth-century palace in Mostecká Street, just past the Charles Bridge, where they often hosted balls. At one such event, George introduced me to his mother.

Sometimes George found ways to be a part of my professional life. For example, in October 1926, the National Theater singers, orchestra, and chorus performed *The Bartered Bride* in Warsaw. The audience response on opening night was overwhelming, and my dressing room was filled with flowers. Afterward, the Polish government hosted a reception for the members of the National Theater. Although Czech and Polish are both Slavic languages with many similarities, it was lucky that I spoke French, which everybody spoke. But even before this excitement, the very first day I arrived in Warsaw, I was surprised to find George waiting for me when I got off the train. "I left Prague yesterday," he explained, "because I wanted to be present for your new triumph."

Back in Czechoslovakia that autumn, George wanted to show me Liteň, his country estate some twenty miles outside of Prague. It lay in rolling terrain, surrounded by woods, lakes, and fertile fields. George arranged for a little shooting party, my first. He also took me with him one afternoon to shoot a roebuck. As we arrived in the woods, he told me to be completely quiet. He took me to a deer blind, high in the crown of a tree. We climbed a ladder to the platform, where the view of the forest was breathtaking. Soon, on the other side of the clearing, a roebuck appeared. George shot him very neatly and said, "Now we can go."

I was a city child who had never seen such a thing before. "But why," I asked, "only one roebuck?"

George laughed. "We don't shoot them like hares!" he said. I saw that I had a lot to learn about hunting.

Later, when I was married, I learned to shoot. I tried my luck with clay pigeons, which wasn't at all easy, because they are thrown at very high speeds. When it came to real birds, such as pheasants and partridges, I just didn't have the heart to shoot them—so after a certain point I became just an onlooker.

Visiting Liteň meant another opportunity to spend time with George's mother, who invited me to join the family for Christmas. However, George and I had promised to spend Christmas Eve with my parents in Prague. George came to dinner that night, and then we went to midnight Mass. I can picture it now. It was snowing and very cold, but in the crowded church it was so cozy that I felt near to God. With the people I loved so near to me, I had a feeling of utter happiness.

Although my singing career was flourishing, I felt strongly that I needed more study, and I decided that I would go to Milan to look for a voice teacher there. Hardly had I made this decision than Franz Schalk, the director of the Vienna Staatsoper, came to Prague for a concert with the Prague Philharmonic Orchestra. He was a conductor of great renown, a protégé of Gustav Mahler who had conducted German operas at the Metropolitan and who (along with Bruno Walter) had been brought by Mahler to Vienna to raise the standard of conducting to undreamed-of heights. He was always looking for new singers, and when he came to Prague, he asked me to meet with him to discuss the possibility of an engagement with the Vienna Staatsoper. It was a wonderful opportunity, and of course very flattering, but I had already made up my mind, and I told him so. Schalk declared that my intentions were admirable, and he told me that he would give me letters of introduction—provided that I would promise to sing for him in Vienna when I had completed my studies in Milan.

It wasn't easy to make the director of the National Theater, Jaroslav Safarovic, understand my desire to take a break from singing. "Study?" he said. "But you already know how to sing!" At last we agreed that I would sing in new productions of *La Traviata* and *Falstaff* (in which I would play Nannetta).

Always before, *Traviata* was performed in modern dress, which I never really liked, and said so. For this production, we would wear nineteenth-century costumes, and for my gowns, I asked permission to order privately from my dressmaker, Hana Podolská. She succeeded beautifully, especially with the black-velvet gown with rhinestone embroidery that I wore in Act III. Not only did I wear this costume in Prague, but also later in Berlin, Vienna, San Francisco, Cologne, Buenos Aires, Rio de Janeiro, Santiago, and of course at the Metropolitan Opera. I wore the gown when I sat for my portrait, which is now part of the Metropolitan Opera Archives—and the gown itself ended its busy life there in 1983, when I donated it.

My Alfredo was Jan Berlík, with whom I had sung Violetta many times before. We understood each other perfectly, and the audience liked seeing us together. They called us "the Strong Duo"—close, perhaps, to the "supercouples" in popular entertainment in the United States today. For the premiere on January 16, 1927, we received wonderful reviews. The newspaper *Večer* wrote: "Glorious vocally, in acting and appearance is the Violetta of Jarmila Novotná. She is a real Violetta, *la vera* Violetta we know from the Dumas novel."

We repeated *Traviata* several times, along with *La Bohème, Freischütz,* and *Magic Flute.* At the same time, I was rehearsing *Falstaff,* and I gave a concert at Smetana Hall. There was so much to do in such a short time! *Falstaff* premiered on February 1, my last *Traviata* was February 10, and two days later, my mother and I left by train for Milan.

We went to a hotel on the Piazza del Duomo, which had been recommended to us. You can't imagine the noise! We couldn't open the window. Mother and I decided to stay there only as long as she remained in Milan with me. For the weeks I would be on my own, after Mother returned to Prague, we found a lawyer named Martinelli and his family, who agreed to rent me a room.

The next day I took a letter of introduction from Franz Schalk to Mario Sammarco, a famed baritone from La Scala, who Maestro Schalk believed would be a good teacher for me. I sang for Sammarco, and then he said, "Very lovely, very lovely. We shall study this role and that one."

"Yes, but I did not come to study roles," I told him. "I want to learn how to sing!"

"Oh, that will come anyway," Sammarco said.

This was not what I was looking for. I was very disappointed, and I asked my mother's advice. Franz Schalk had also given me a letter of introduction to Antonio Guarnieri, a conductor at La Scala, and Mother suggested that I speak to him.

We went to Maestro Guarnieri's hotel. He could not advise me without hearing me sing, he said, and he had no piano in his room. So he took me across the hall to his friends Maria Gay and Giovanni Zenatello. Maria Gay was a Spanish mezzo-soprano, quite famous for her Carmen, the role in which she made her Metropolitan debut in 1909, with Enrico Caruso as Don José and Arturo Toscanini conducting. She had married Zenatello, a tenor with the Boston Opera, in 1913; when I met them, they were managing the festivals at the Arena di Verona.

I sang one of Violetta's arias for Guarnieri, and before I finished I heard Maria Gay saying, "But she would be right, don't you think?" I didn't know what she meant, but as soon as I had finished, she asked whether I knew the role of Gilda in *Rigoletto.*

"No, I don't," I said. "Why do you ask?"

"We are planning to give *Rigoletto* at the Arena next summer," she said. "We would like for you to sing Gilda."

Once again I found myself explaining that I had come to Milan to study. "We know just the right teacher for you," Zenatello said, "but you must promise you'll come to Verona."

It was a miracle. Somehow, everything happened without any effort.

That evening, Mother and I went to see *Turandot* at La Scala, with Toscanini conducting. What an experience! We couldn't sleep the whole night. The next day, my mother left for Prague, and I moved to the Martinellis' apartment. This proved to be a very pleasant environment, and although I was in a foreign city, separated from my family for the first time, I did not feel lonely. The Martinellis had a daughter, Giovanna, about my age, and in the coming weeks she and I would socialize with her two brothers and their wives, going to Lake Como or the races, and getting to know other charming people as well.

Raffaele Tenaglia, the teacher whom the Zenatellos had recommended, lived just around the corner from the Martinellis. At first, my lessons with him were only a half-hour each day, since he didn't want to tire my voice in the beginning. He let me sing only scales, which I found rather dull.

I found plenty of excitement in the evenings, however, when I went to hear the operas at La Scala. The first week, I heard *La Bohème* and *Der Rosenkavalier;* the next week, *Lucia* with Toti dal Monte, which overwhelmed me. Then *Pagliacci,* with Aureliano Pertile, and dal Monte unforgettable again in *Rigoletto,* with Toscanini in the pit. When conducting, the long shadow of Toscanini's hands spread up to the ceiling, like a spirit embracing the whole opera house. To see and hear this perfection was the most important part of my studies.

Time seemed to fly, and now Maestro Tenaglia permitted me to sing songs by Scarlatti and Pergolesi. However, when I brought in the score to *Rigoletto*, he told me we were not ready yet, and I must be patient for another week or two. This schedule turned out well, because Easter came early that year. At the beginning of April, George came to Milan with the suggestion that we go to Paris for a week. I had never been to Paris, and I thought it a wonderful idea.

With its boulevards, its chestnut trees in bloom, and its beautiful shops, Paris seemed to me the most beautiful city in the world, although I didn't know very many great cities yet. George wanted to give me the best possible impression of Paris on this trip, and so he took me to the Louvre and the Comédie Française, to the Opéra and to Montmartre, and to the best restaurants. We also went dancing, and there was no end to the enjoyment. If I had even a tiny doubt before that I was in love with George, I was sure of it now. But our holiday had to end. George took me as far as Strasbourg in his car; then I boarded a train for Milan, and he continued back to Prague.

Maestro Tenaglia and I resumed my singing lessons, and we began at last to work on Gilda, as well as Lucia. He told me I was making excellent progress. But in June my mother accompanied me to Pesaro, where Maestro Guarnieri was to conduct several operas. Naturally, Guarnieri was too busy to work with me, but he asked me to sing for him, then told me that Maestro Tenaglia had led me the wrong way. "I advise you to study with him no longer," Guarnieri said. I was stunned, but he continued, "If you can meet me in Torbole in August, I will be able to spend more time with you, and I can correct the mistakes Tenaglia has made."

Mother and I returned to Prague, and in August, George drove me to Torbole, on the shore of Lake Garda. The lake is known for its incredible sapphire-blue color, and its waters are clear as crystal. I worked with Guarnieri every day, and at the end of my stay, he said, "Now I am confident that you will be a great success!" I returned to Milan for an audition with an impresario who signed me for the role of Adina in *L'Elisir d'Amore* at the Teatro San Carlo in Naples the next May. This made me very happy, and back I went to Prague, eager to practice what I had learned in Italy.

By now I had achieved an excellent reputation in Prague, such that President Masaryk grew curious to know whether the reports he'd heard about this young soprano were accurate. The morning after my first Gilda with the National Theater—opposite George Baklanov, who sang the Vendetta with the most inspired acting I have seen from any Rigoletto—I received an invitation to visit the President at Lány Palace. The government had purchased the Palace as a presidential summer retreat, but Masaryk preferred it to the formal, ancient Hradčany Castle in Prague. He made Lány his permanent home, and there he could indulge his love of horses and ride every day.

During my artistic career, I have met many famous people, and already I had begun to do so. Yet nobody ever made such an impression on me as President Masaryk, and nobody charmed me by his personality as he did. When he entered the room, I was thunderstruck, and yet his innate dignity and simplicity helped me to overcome my anxiety. At first I was unsure how I should talk to him, but I quickly discovered that he was interested in everything, and in any conversation he asked questions with such sincerity that it was easy to find the words to answer him. The president wanted to know what my future plans were, and I told him of my studies in Italy, my upcoming performances at the National Theater, and my plan to sing Gilda at the Arena di Verona that August. He advised me to continue to sing in Prague, but not too often, and to continue studying in Milan, because it would be unwise to interrupt my development at such an early stage. I explained that I had difficulty in finding good teachers in Milan. The family of the president's wife, the Garrigues, were all very musical, and Masaryk said he would ask his sister-in-law, Esperanza Garrigue, for advice.

Then he said, "Can your parents afford to finance your studies? I would like to help you in any way necessary." I accepted his offer gratefully, because my parents did indeed find my expenses quite burdensome.

After dinner that evening I sang some Czech and Slovak songs, while the president's son, Jan, accompanied me. I knew that the president liked a song called "Teče voda teče" (The water runs), but I asked what his favorite was. He answered that he preferred "Ach synku, synku" (Oh, my son, my son). In this song, a young farmer tells his father that he cannot finish his work because the plow is broken; the old man replies that he must repair the plow if he wants to be a good farmer. "This is why I like this song," President Masaryk explained. "If something is broken, it should be repaired."

Before the evening was out, Jan Masaryk made another helpful suggestion, inviting me to give a concert in London in January.

The party at Lány was something like a country weekend, and Mother and I stayed overnight. Early the next morning, I heard Mother moaning.

She had a terrible pain on the right side of her stomach, and I rang for a servant. Soon President Masaryk's daughter, Alice, came. Though she had studied medicine, she gave it up when it became clear how few opportunities for women there were in that field at the time, and she obtained her doctorate in philosophy. Still, she could see that Mother was seriously ill, and she called for a doctor, who diagnosed Mother with appendicitis. She was transported to a hospital near our home in Prague, and an operation was performed immediately. The appendix was perforated already. The president sent a get-well letter and a gift of champagne and caviar, making Mother very happy, and when I gave a concert on November 11, President Masaryk attended. I felt profoundly honored by my association with the president and his family, and it had only just begun.

Jan Masaryk was the Czechoslovak Minister to London from 1925 to 1938. His mother, Charlotte Garrigue, was American, and Jan had been chargé d'affaires in Washington before his posting to London. Delightfully witty and outgoing, he was completely different from his philosophical, intellectual father. Yet it was probably because of their differences that President Masaryk loved Jan dearly and called him "my ray of sunshine" when Jan was not there to hear him. In 1927, Jan married the daughter of the American industrialist Charles Crane, a great friend of President Masaryk. Their ways parted by 1932, but Jan would always say that Frances Crane Leatherbee was his only true love.

Jan was extremely popular in London, and Frances was known to be very selective in extending invitations to their parties. Naturally, everybody wanted to be included. Two days after my arrival, Jan gave a reception for Prince Paul of Yugoslavia, giving me the opportunity to meet members of two royal families, since Prince Paul's wife was the sister of the Duchess of Kent. The Prince of Wales (later to become the Duke of Windsor) attended, as did many British and foreign diplomats. With Jan at the piano, I sang several Czechoslovak folk songs, and this was very good publicity for my upcoming concert at Wigmore Hall one week later. Both the public and the press received me very well, and the *Times* wrote of my "fresh and vibrant soprano voice. . . . The spontaneity of her singing is very attractive."

As soon as I returned to Prague, the president asked me to give him a firsthand report. I was to come to Hradčany Castle at ten o'clock in the morning, but there was a heavy snowfall that day and my streetcar moved very slowly. I arrived a half-hour late, and I thought I would never outlive my shame. The president showed no sign of annoyance, however, and he listened with great interest to what I had to say about London and about his son's popularity there as the Czech envoy. But he had news for me, as well. His sister-in-law had recommended a voice teacher in Milan, Emilio Piccoli, whose most famous pupil was the tenor Tito Schipa. Then President Masaryk talked about art and about my studies. He recommended several books, and he urged me to learn languages, saying, "For every language you speak, you are a new person." As he spoke, his spirit and his pure, compassionate attitude were all but palpable. I was moved by our conversations, and his advice helped me along throughout my life.

Immediately I went to see Emilio Piccoli in Milan. From the beginning, I tried to follow his instructions, but I did not always succeed. Piccoli had a great sense of humor, and he was always ready with a quip when I fell short. Once, he described my staccato as "a cackling hen." This made me unhappy, of course, yet it also encouraged me to study more diligently—so much so that the next week he rewarded me with his photograph. Piccoli placed the greatest emphasis on correct breathing, which I had to practice at home as well as in the studio. He also encouraged me to develop absolute flexibility in the throat and neck, saying that the higher the tone that is to be sung, the more the throat must be widened.

To my surprise, President Masaryk wanted to know all about singing technique—he really was interested in every possible topic. He wrote back with a chatty letter, giving me a little news of daily life at Lány, and concluding, "You have your worries and I have mine, every business has plenty of it." He also enclosed a newspaper clipping in which Caruso had offered the "recipe" for a successful singing career: "Voice, 20 percent; perseverance and patience, 20 percent; practice and technique, 20 percent; personality, 20 percent; and luck, 20 percent." To this, the president added, "Therefore, 40 percent one's own effort, 40 percent from God, which is voice and personality; and 20 percent luck."

Not long afterward, President Masaryk wrote to urge me to seek out an Italian painter he had met, Mimi Bazzi, who was affiliated with the Brera Academy of Fine Arts in Milan. She proved to be a wonderful guide, showing me the Brera museum and all the important monuments and buildings in the city. Then, as I was getting ready to sing Gilda in Verona, President Masaryk wrote to ask what I was doing about costumes, then told me to "order for yourself everything you need, good quality and lovely-looking." His offer was really a great help, because the Zenatellos had told me I would need three dresses, high boots for the last act, and a blond wig: altogether quite expensive. Always compassionate, President Masaryk thought of everything.

That spring in Milan, I started to learn English and German at the Berlitz School, and I took piano lessons. I was as busy as could be, too busy even to accept invitations from the Czech consulate! But at Easter I went to Florence to meet George. We were enchanted by that lovely town, and we went from museum to museum, from church to church, overwhelmed by the wealth of art. After this jolly interlude, George went back to his work with a heavy heart, and I to mine—until July, when it was time to go to Verona.

As soon as I arrived, I went immediately to look at the Arena. I thought I would die. The immensity of it terrified me. How would anybody be able to hear me? The following night, *Turandot* was playing, and Zenatello gave me a ticket. The acoustics were so perfect that one could have heard a pin drop onstage! I did not stay in one place, but moved about, far from the stage, and still I could hear everything perfectly. After this performance, all my fears disappeared, and I started rehearsals with confidence. Really, my only worry was the terrible heat. It was over 104 degrees in the shade.

The dress rehearsal for *Rigoletto* went very well, and the day of the premiere, August 2, was at hand. As I was getting ready to go to the theater, there was a knock at my door. Two men I had never seen before entered. "We are coming to offer you our services for tonight's performance," they said.

"Oh, thank you," I replied. "I don't need anything."

"Yes, you do. We are the claque. You must pay us, and we will take care of the applause."

Now, paying for applause was very new to me. Then I thought, "If I pay, how will I know whether or not the audience liked me?" So I declined the offer, and the two men departed, furious.

When I got to the theater, the manager stormed into my dressing room, proclaiming that I should have consulted him before refusing the claque, and that I could have a disaster on my hands, because every other artist had paid. But the performance was about to begin, and there was nothing to be done about it.

Soon after Gilda's first appearance, she sings the aria "Caro nome." When I finished, thunderous applause greeted me, and people shouted to demand that I sing it again. At last the conductor gave me a signal, and I sang "Caro nome" a second time—but my knees were so shaky that I had to sing sitting down. Still, I was indescribably happy. I had proved to myself that I did not need anybody's "help," only my faith. For the first time in my life, I could not sleep at all that night, and I had to send for a sleeping pill in the morning. I took it right away, so that I would be able at least to sleep during the day.

The performance was "a thunderous personal success" for me, as the *Corriere della Sera* described it. I wrote to President Masaryk about the experience, and he wrote back to tell me that he had tried to send a telegram on opening night, but he had been confused: Were the *Amfiteatro* and the *Arena* the same theater? "I rejoice with you," he continued. "I can feel what it must have been when thousands applauded, and they did so quite obviously for your art and your personality, as there was nothing artificial about their enthusiasm"—by which he referred to the claque.

The next day, I went to meet my sister, Pavla, in Venice. We spent one day there, but it wasn't easy for two young girls alone, and all the time men would try to talk to us or call out "O, la bella bionda" as we passed. We returned to Verona, and I moved into the Boscochiesa Nuova. Because of the infernal heat, most artists stayed there: it is high in the mountains, just outside of town. The air was clean and cool there; I could take walks in the woods and sing like a lark, without disturbing anyone. Pavla and I didn't leave this ideal spot except when it was time for performances, when we could always catch a ride to the theater. Immediately after Pavla returned to Prague, George arrived. Still trying to escape the Veronese heat, we went to the town of Sirmione on Lake Garda, where we could swim and do a little boating.

For the first three performances of *Rigoletto,* Alessandro Wesselowsky sang the Duke of Mantua, but for the final three, Giacomo Lauri-Volpi took over the role. He had won acclaim since his debut in Rome in 1920, and he sang the Duke at his Metropolitan Opera debut three years later. It was a real joy to sing with him, and so my first Italian engagement ended very happily.

After my success in Verona, the opera houses in Vienna and Berlin wanted to engage me. Zenatello asked to be my agent, and he told me he had been approached already by Giulio Gatti-Casazza, the director of the Metropolitan Opera, who wanted to bring me to New York. I went to George to talk over these opportunities, and I was surprised when he said, "I have wanted to beg you to give up singing and marry me—but I see that you could never be happy without singing. Please, at least do not go to America. I don't want you to be so far away." I felt the same way, and so I asked Zenatello to decline Gatti-Casazza's offer.

Now George and I took a little trip to France, stopping first in Biarritz and St-Jean-de-Luz, where I went swimming and the high waves scared me to death. We crossed the Spanish border to San Sebastián, where we saw a bullfight, my first. I thought it a bloody sport, and I didn't enjoy it much. We went on to Bordeaux, where we dined at the famous restaurant Le Chapon Fin, where we ate and drank exquisitely. I even remember the menu: truffles in champagne, saddle of hare with potato croquettes, and a soufflé. For the first time in my life I became a little tipsy, and I danced all the way to the hotel that night. On the same trip, we visited the châteaux of the Loire. George wanted me to see as many beautiful things as possible.

I was sorry when this trip ended, but President Masaryk had invited Mother and me to spend a week with him in Slovakia at Topolčianky Castle, another presidential residence. On the train, we met Rudolf Firkušný, who was also invited to Topolčianky. President Masaryk wanted to promote young talent, and he was helping Firkušný much as he tried to help me. A former child prodigy and still quite young, Firkušný was a prize pupil of Janáček and had given his first concert when he was only sixteen. Now he laughingly confessed that on this trip he was wearing long pants for the first time in his life.

The evenings at Topolčianky were always filled with music. The first night, I had thought that I might sing and Firkušný might play, but the president surprised us: he had invited a Gypsy orchestra, and they played late into the night. Alice Masaryk was there, as was the president's other daughter, Olga Revilliod, along with her sons, Herbert and Leonard. Esperanza Garrigue had come from New York, and I had the chance to work with her a little. She was an accomplished musician and singing teacher.

The atmosphere was very stimulating, and President Masaryk indulged his wide-ranging interests and his wry sense of humor. One day, he arranged for an exhibition of modern furniture and architecture, and a leading architect came to display his proudest creation, a hypermodern armchair. The president scrutinized it from all sides, then sat down. But he stood up again in an instant. "I knew it!" he cried. "You make everything for the eye, but you forget that a chair is for another part of the body!"

I will never forgive myself for not keeping a diary and taking notes of my conversations with President Masaryk and the many interesting things he said. Fortunately I have a good many letters, full of his paternal advice. Some months after our stay in Topolčianky, for example, I returned to Milan, and the president wrote to urge me to take advantage of my stay by studying not only music but also art and architecture, to attend lectures or even university classes if I could. "It seems to me that such an education would benefit your singing and also your stage appearances and your acting," he said. "I trust you will find what will be best for you."

President Masaryk's letters were almost the only things I rescued when we left Czechoslovakia, and they are my dearest possession. Letter writing is really a lost art. I often ask myself why. Is it because we live in such a hurry? And yet most of the letters I have received are from people who could not be considered idle.

In Prague in the fall of 1928, I sang *Traviata, Rigoletto, The Bartered Bride,* and Tatyana in *Eugene Onegin,* as well as two concerts, for which my accompanist, Václav Stepan, and I prepared a well-balanced program, starting with arias by Monteverdi, Giordano, and Pergolesi; lieder by Schubert and Strauss; Fibich's "Dreaming Lake"; Dvořák's "Biblical Songs"; and Novák's "Oh, Bottomless Sea of Love." I rounded out the program with a group of Czech and Slovak songs, some beautifully arranged by Dr. Stepan himself. Then came many encores, but the audience would not leave until I had sung "Sempre libera" from *Traviata.*

Then it was time for me to return to Milan and to learn the role of Adina in *L'Elisir d'Amore.* On my way, I stopped off in Vienna to meet with Franz Schalk. We agreed that I would make my debut with the Staatsoper in *Rigoletto* on January 5, 1929.

In Milan I resumed my acquaintance with Guarnieri's friend Medea Colombara. She knew Gabriele d'Annunzio very well, and she suggested that we visit him at his home in Gardone.[3] I was anxious to meet the famous poet, many of whose books I had read already. He fought with spectacular bravery in the air force during World War I, for which he was given the title Duke of Nevoso. Naturally I also knew of his relationship with the great actress Eleonora Duse, which he depicted in his novel *Il Fuoco* (The Flame of Life).

I don't know exactly what I expected d'Annunzio to be like, but I cannot describe my disappointment when I met him. A small, bald, rather ugly man, he wore an admiral's uniform when he greeted us in the garden. But over lunch, he started a most animated conversation, and I began to forget all his shortcomings. He had such a command of words—it was said that he invented words, by which he enriched the Italian language.

We discussed the power of personality. Charm, d'Annunzio said, is the elusive quality that men and women have tried to analyze and describe for centuries. Physical beauty had little to do with it; history provides many instances of people who lacked beauty, yet whose attractive personalities changed the world. A striking example was Voltaire, who, though physically almost repellent, drew others to him through his brilliant intellect and irresistible personal manner. Of course d'Annunzio himself was doing something quite similar as we talked!

The poet concluded that charm is an inner quality that shines forth and that attracts those who come within its sphere. Though no single quality defines charm, several qualities when added together can always be found in charming people. For example, they possess enthusiasm, even over the smallest things in life, which the French so aptly describe as *joie de vivre*. Probably the most important quality is a sincere interest in people, in what they say, think, and do. Humor, of course, is an indispensable quality. "Focused attention can be felt like a magnet," d'Annunzio said, "and it may be used to draw us out, so that we talk about our innermost feelings." The voice is an important tool, "but silence," he added, "can be wonderful, too." Many of the attributes of charm can be learned and developed, and many of them must be, if we are to function at all successfully in the modern world as effective individuals. The cultivation of charm is the duty of all who wish to give their lives distinction.

We also talked about theater. D'Annunzio had seen me at Verona, and because he knew that I wanted to be as good an actress as a singer, he talked about Duse, who was the first to present many of his plays. The key to her acting, he said, was extreme simplicity, so that no matter how she restrained her emotional power, it had a tremendous effect. He especially praised her portrayal of Dumas' lady of the camellias—perhaps realizing that already I often had played Verdi's version of the same character, Violetta in *La Traviata*.

D'Annunzio's airplane from the war had been preserved in the garden, and his house was like a museum, almost overflowing with beautiful objets d'art. As all the windows were made of stained glass, it was rather dark inside, and when he showed us his bedroom, we saw that he slept in a coffin with black-velvet covers. "This way," he said, "I will be prepared for my final hour." He was known to be a great ladies' man, and I wondered how anybody could share that bed with him!

I returned to Prague for Christmas. It was freezing cold, and after having grown accustomed to the milder climate in Italy, I caught influenza. I was incapacitated by a high fever and had to cancel my debut with the Vienna Staatsoper. But as soon as I had recovered a little, I had to fulfill my commitment to the company, and so I sang Gilda in Vienna on January 19. I was well received, and Schalk wanted to offer me a contract. Sick as I was, this was hardly the time to discuss a contract, so I asked him to let me postpone making any decisions.

To recover completely from my illness, George suggested that we go to the mountains. With skiing gear we left for Spindelmühle in Riesengeberirge in northern Bohemia. My first attempt on skis was not very successful. I went with a guide, but he was always ahead of me and seldom looked back to see how I was doing. As we passed a high slope, I felt as if my skis were pulling me toward it. Surely this was the result of my fear, but my feet kept turning toward the danger. So I simply stopped and took off the skis. But this was very unwise: my feet disappeared in the newly fallen snow. At last the guide noticed that I was no longer following him. He had to pull me out of the snow, and once I'd put the skis on again, he held me so that we could ski downhill together. We moved faster than the devil, and George—a very good skier who was far ahead—was already worried about us. Still, the exercise and the mountain air helped me to recover completely.

I had remained in contact with Medea Colombara, and in fact I arranged for her to sing Madame Butterfly at the National Theater in Prague. She suggested that we visit d'Annunzio again, since she was scheduled to sing at a nearby theater that winter. We took the train, and following Medea's success, we spent the night at d'Annunzio's home in Gardone. The next day, I found myself in the library waiting for Medea, and I began to read a book called *Contemplazione della Morte* (Contemplation of Death, by d'Annunzio, 1912). I was so absorbed in my reading that I didn't hear d'Annunzio come in. Suddenly he was standing behind me and groping me under my skirt. However, because the weather was so cold, I was wearing heavy woolen long johns. D'Annunzio gave me a wicked smile and said, "Ah, I see you are very well protected." Thereupon he gave me the book, inscribing it "To the blond flame of life, contemplation of death. Gabriele d'Annunzio."

I returned to Milan to continue my studies. The time flew, and in May I went to Naples to rehearse *L'Elisir d'Amore* at the Teatro San Carlo. What a lovely city! The windows of my hotel room faced Mount Vesuvius, with the beautiful sea below. I could hardly wait to go swimming, but the next day when I mentioned this, everybody thought that I was crazy! Nobody in Italy would go swimming before June or July, they told me, though it seemed to me that May was a much more sensible time of year.

But I had no free time at all when rehearsals began. I did not mind this, because to listen to Tito Schipa singing was such a great delight. At the dress rehearsal, it seemed he sang more beautifully than ever before, and I was so entranced that I forgot to sing during our duet. I just stared at him in admiration.

Later, when we had no more rehearsals, Schipa invited me to go driving with him. As he drove, he sang popular songs like "Torna a Sorrento," "Addio, mia Bella Napoli," and "Funiculi, Funicula." Oh, what a wonderful concert, just for me! Everything was so romantic and beautiful that, if I hadn't been so much in love with George, I might have done something foolish. Luckily, Schipa was happily married, and when his wife arrived from Rome, she and I became good friends, and the three of us went to Pompeii together.

L'Elisir was a great success. The critics called me "the incomparable, exquisite Jarmila Novotná" and said that I "conquered everybody, even the blind and the deaf, because the blind can hear her and swoon with desire at her sweet voice, and the deaf can see her, like Botticelli's Primavera come to life onstage as Adina."

I returned to Milan to continue my studies, but in June I received a letter from President Masaryk's office asking me to come to Prague and sing at a reception for Fuad, the King of Egypt. President Masaryk and all the state dignitaries attended this command performance at the Egyptian Embassy. I sang "Ah, fors'è lui" from *Traviata* and Rusalka's song to the moon, as well as some Italian songs. Afterward, when I was presented to King Fuad, he surprised me by speaking to me in Italian. "You sing the language so perfectly," he said, "that I thought you must speak it, too."

We had a long, delightful conversation. The king planned to spend a few days in Karlsbad, and he invited me to join him there. I was to sing *The Bartered Bride* at the National Theater the next day, but I agreed to come to Karlsbad the day after.

My mother and I took the train and arrived about eleven o'clock. There at the hotel was Jan Masaryk, who had been dispatched from London especially for the king's visit. Jan wasn't expecting us, and when I explained that the king had invited me, he said, "Oh, the king isn't feeling well today, and no one has seen him." But he agreed to announce me, and ten minutes later he came back with word that the king would receive me. So my mother and I went up to his rooms. There was no sign of any illness at all, and the king and I enjoyed another lively conversation—though I must say he looked a little disappointed when he saw that I had come with my mother!

Later that summer, I sang two concerts at the well-known summer festival at the Kursaal d'Ostende, where I met the Russian bass Fyodor Chaliapin and his daughter, Marina, whom I saw often in the years to come. Chaliapin was a tall, handsome man with a ready smile. His voice had unique quality and power, but mainly he was an ingenious actor. In the program for his concerts, he listed and numbered his whole repertory of arias and songs; then, when he was onstage, he would announce the number of the piece he wanted to sing. I asked him why, and he said that he preferred to sing whatever suited his mood best at the moment.

My time in Ostend offered the chance to go swimming in the North Sea. I would change into my bathing suit in a little wagon stationed directly on the water line. In those days, people did not sunbathe, lying for hours on the shore, and most people did not try to get a suntan. On the contrary, we would dip in the water, and then cover ourselves to escape the sun. The trip also gave George and me an excuse to explore the cities of the Netherlands, as well as Brussels. George wanted me to see some of the famous museums, such as the Rijksmuseum in Amsterdam, with its works by Rembrandt and Van Gogh and its other fine Dutch paintings.

My success as a mere twenty-year-old at the Verona Festival had brought me many offers. In addition to Schalk, who wanted to bring me back to Vienna, Bruno Walter wanted me for the Charlottenburg Opera in Berlin, also known as the Städtische Oper. I also had a serious offer from Otto Klemperer, the director and chief conductor of the Kroll Opera, the second house of the Berliner Staatsoper. I decided to see Klemperer. Making my way through meter-high snow on the streets of the German capital, I auditioned for him, and with the approval of the Intendant, Heinz Tietjen, he immediately offered me a contract to start September 1, 1929.

At the time, I did not speak perfect German, so before I left Prague, I engaged a companion, Mrs. Perko, a very nice widow. This was really George's suggestion, because, he said, it was a good idea to have someone near to help you guard your privacy. He was right, and Mrs. Perko proved helpful on several occasions. Through an agent, I found a very pleasant apartment with a family named Markiewitz, in Prager Street. I found this amusing, because "Prager" in German is the adjectival form of the name Prague.

Berlin was a fascinating place to live. I don't think there was another city in the world so alive with artistic activity. It was a brilliant, cosmopolitan, avant-garde center of the visual arts, literature, and music. Until its virtual destruction in World War II, Berlin was the second largest city in Europe and the political, financial, commercial, and cultural center of Germany. In the legitimate theater, Max Reinhardt presided over four or five houses, and his productions were a marvel to behold. Wilhelm Furtwängler led the Berlin Philharmonic, and all the great artists of the time performed there: Pablo Casals, Emanuel Feuermann, Chaliapin, Alfred Cortot. In operetta, Franz Lehár's *Das Land des Lächelns* was a hit, starring Richard Tauber. And there were three opera houses: the Städtische Oper (City Opera), led by Bruno Walter; the Staatsoper Unter den Linden, led by Erich Kleiber; and the Kroll, where Klemperer reigned beginning in 1927.

Together with the conductors Alexander Zemlinsky and Fritz Zweig, Klemperer opened the Kroll as the second house of the Berliner Staatsoper. With its own ensemble of singers, chorus, and orchestra, the Kroll under Klemperer presented traditional repertory, as well as modern operas by composers such as Arnold Schönberg, Paul Hindemith, Ernst Krenek, and Igor Stravinsky. Because of the diversity of the repertory, the Kroll was considered the most exciting and most important opera theater in Berlin, and I was very happy to be singing there.

On Monday, September 2, I arrived at the Kroll. Klemperer said that he hadn't yet decided whether I should sing *Rigoletto* or *The Magic Flute* for my debut. Meanwhile, the director Gustaf Gründgens was preparing three modern one-act operas: *Angélique*, by Jacques Ibert; *Der Arme Matrose* (The Poor Seaman), by Darius Milhaud; and *L'Heure Espagnole*, by Maurice Ravel. Klemperer suggested that the role of Concepción in *L'Heure Espagnole* might interest me, and so I attended the rehearsals. It was fascinating to watch Gründgens with the singers, because this was the first time I had seen a stage director with a concept of the opera as an entire dramatic work and a clear sense of each character.[4] Rose Pauly, who was to sing Concepción, was also singing Strauss's Elektra at the time—a role in which I heard her several times, and in which she had no peer. When Pauly had to miss a rehearsal, Gründgens asked if I could replace her for the day. I was happy for the chance to work with him. But this one rehearsal was enough to persuade Gründgens that I was ideal for the role of Concepción and that only I should sing it.

And so I made my debut in *L'Heure Espagnole*. The critics described me as an important addition to the Kroll ensemble, and soon afterward, Max Reinhardt asked to meet with me.

I went to Reinhardt's office at the Deutsches Theater. He was very friendly and not very tall; he had deep blue eyes and graying hair. His voice was soft, just like his handshake. "He has never done anything in a hurry," I thought.

"I am producing *Die Fledermaus*," Reinhardt said. "Would you be interested in singing Rosalinda?" I don't know why he wanted a change, because

Maria Rajdl, who had been singing the role, was excellent. But I had just joined the Kroll Opera, and I was sure that Klemperer would not let me work at the Deutsches Theater so soon. At least I could tell myself that I had met the great Max Reinhardt! The father of a Golden Age of German theater and the founder of the Salzburg Festival, he was a great innovator—and a master of spectacular scenery and crowd scenes. I would have loved to have worked with Reinhardt right away, but I had to wait until the right moment came.

Besides, I was quite content at the Kroll Opera. In fact, we seemed like one big family. Klemperer personally selected all his artists, and we learned and grew together in performance, with each singer playing the same role in every performance throughout the run, something that today is almost impossible. Apart from *L'Heure Espagnole,* I was to sing three other operas, all of which Zemlinsky conducted: *The Bartered Bride, Rigoletto,* and *Madame Butterfly.*

Then Klemperer assigned me the role of the Queen of the Night in *The Magic Flute,* which he conducted. He was in every respect a giant, and everyone was a little afraid of him. Soon enough, I understood why.

During one performance, I returned to my dressing room after my first aria, and there I found a basket waiting. It contained a black kitten, and my dresser did not approve. "Black cats bring bad luck," she warned. Soon, some of my colleagues stopped by to admire the kitten, among them Käthe Heidersbach, who sang Pamina, one of the most wonderful sopranos of the time and a darling person. Käthe enjoyed playing with the kitten so much that she forgot that to make her next entrance, and as the stage crew didn't find her in her dressing room, the performance came to a halt. Klemperer was furious and made Käthe pay a 300-mark fine—which I helped to pay, as I felt somehow responsible. I never found out who sent that cat.

On December 30, the Kroll unveiled a new, updated production of *The Bartered Bride,* in which I sang Mařenka. I wasn't very happy with the staging, but this was a joyful assignment nevertheless. The *Berliner Tageblatt* gave me an excellent review ("the loveliest Mařenka in the world . . . the State Opera scarcely knows what a great catch they have scored"), President Masaryk wrote to congratulate me, and it was decided that, in recognition of my contributions to Czech music, my portrait would appear on the new 100-crown bill. I sat for the artist Max Švabinský, and a year later, the new bills came out.

Early in 1931, I began to rehearse a new role, Tamar in Ernst Krenek's *The Life of Orestes.* The vocal part was written strangely, very low at the beginning and then coloratura in the highest range. I didn't know how I would be able to endure this torture. Klemperer, who was conducting, was not helpful. On the contrary, he could at times be terribly sarcastic, as he was in commenting on my work during one rehearsal. I burst into tears. Probably meaning well, he brought me a glass of water and said, "Drink this, it will calm you." But this made me only more anxious, and after the premiere, I lost my voice. I thought I would never be able to sing again, but my doctor ordered complete rest, no singing, no speaking out loud. Slowly, my voice came back, and I began to work with a new teacher, Frederick Husler. With his guidance and encouragement, I sang better than ever. Heinz Tietjen evidently agreed, and he offered me a contract for the next season at the Kroll, as well as inviting me to sing *Traviata* at the Unter den Linden.

Unexpectedly, I had the opportunity to sing with Berlin's city opera, the Städtische Oper (now called the Deutsche Oper Berlin), at its theater in the suburb of Charlottenburg. The soprano who was to sing the Queen of the Night was ill, and Bruno Walter asked me to replace her. It was short notice, and I didn't even know the staging. But in most productions the Queen of the Night simply stands to sing her arias, so I was sure that everything would be all right. When I got to the theater, I discovered that for my first aria I was to be seated on a bit of scenery painted to look like the moon, suspended high in the middle of the stage. I had to climb up to reach it in the darkness, and once I was seated, the "moon" began to sway. It was a miracle that I could sing at all!

The life of an artist isn't always a bed of roses. Often there are many more thorns than the audience may be aware of. But I always loved rehearsals for a new opera, the preparations, the way an idea grows like a tree in the spring: at first only a few green leaves before it bursts into full bloom. To feel the stage under one's feet, to breathe the air of the theater, is so different from the outside world—and yet it is real life to those who are born to it.

The *Traviata* at Unter den Linden featured an excellent cast: Helge Rosvaenge as Alfredo and Heinrich Schlusnus as Germont, with Erich Kleiber conducting. I liked singing with Rosvaenge very much, not only for his voice but also for his excellent acting. Kleiber was a very agreeable, relaxed man who put everyone at ease.

I was to sing Violetta very often, and it became my preferred role for many reasons. What did I know of the character the first time I sang *Traviata,* when I was only seventeen? Yet through some curious, inexplicable inspiration, I made the part believable to the audience and the critics. Only a few other roles offer such a showcase for every facet of a soprano's talent. Vocally, the role is very demanding, and dramatically one must be a good actress to make Violetta believable. Last but not least, the soprano's appearance plays an important part. Today more than ever, audiences expect a singer to convey the reality of the character in a compelling way; only in very few instances do they accept a great voice alone. Undoubtedly the finest gift an artist can bring to the stage is personality, an inborn understanding of the human dimension of the dramatic situation, and the ability to interpret a character so believably that audiences are carried away.

President Masaryk's eightieth birthday on March 7, 1930, was the occasion for many celebrations. In Berlin, the Czech ambassador, František Chvalkovský, hosted a reception and asked me to sing a few songs. There I met Albert Einstein, an enthusiastic music lover, who confessed that he played the violin not well but with great passion. I also met Cardinal Eugenio Pacelli, who became Pope Pius XII nine years later; and the painter Emil Orlik, who asked me to sit for a portrait and who had been recommended to me by President Masaryk himself. ("He knows how!" the president wrote to me.)

To celebrate Masaryk's birthday in Prague, the Männergesängsverein (German men's choir) and the Czech Philharmonic Society invited me to sing Beethoven's Ninth Symphony, with Zemlinsky conducting. The men's choir usually performed in German, as you might suppose, and I learned the soprano part in German for this occasion. But when we arrived in Prague, we discovered that the mezzo-soprano knew her part only in Czech. Zemlinsky decided that the women soloists would sing in Czech, and the male soloists and chorus would sing in German. Nobody, however, could have foreseen the consequences. When Zemlinsky and I returned to Berlin, the newspapers there declared war on us, especially me, saying that since I preferred singing in Czech, I should stay away from Germany. Zemlinsky, they said, had no place in a German opera house. Tietjen suspended us both for about a week, until he learned that we were quite innocent in the whole affair and had not intended any anti-German political statement whatever with our concert. So we were reinstated, and at my next performance, I received a tremendous ovation. On the whole, this incident seemed to provide us with good publicity, and I became even more popular in Berlin.

Offers came from all sides: films, recordings, and musical comedy, in addition to my operatic engagements. When a man came to my apartment and identified himself as a journalist, it seemed natural (if flattering). Only after we had concluded our "interview" and he had left did I realize that he had stolen a little gold powder box that had been lying on my desk. Mrs. Perko had been out at the time, and I got angry with her: if she had been with me, I felt, this unfortunate incident might never have happened.

Despite my popularity, I myself was not satisfied with my singing. I still believed that Krenek's *Life of Orestes* had done damage, and my high notes did not respond in the way to which I was accustomed. I sang more performances of *Rigoletto,* this time with Iso Goland as my father—not quite on the level of Baklanov, perhaps, but very good. As I sang, I felt as if I had lost head resonance. If I had taken a long rest immediately, then I might have remedied the problem. But my busy schedule left time only for very short intervals of relaxation, seldom more than a weekend or an afternoon. Most of all I loved going to Berlin's famous zoo, the Tiergarten, where I used to watch the bees, whose hives were exposed behind a plate of glass; and baby crocodiles struggling to emerge from their eggs.

At the end of May, Lauri-Volpi came to Berlin, and we had a pleasant reunion. He sang a few performances of *Aida,* and he was scheduled to sing a concert on June 3. He asked me to sing with him, and I accepted with pleasure. I performed a few arias, and with Lauri-Volpi the duet from the end of Act I of *La Bohème.* He performed several solo arias, and it was a great pleasure just to listen to him.

Apart from concerts, I sang about sixty operatic performances that year, adding to my repertoire Rosina in *The Barber of Seville,* and another world premiere, *Die glückliche Hand,* by Arnold Schönberg. After my experience with the Krenek piece, I never would have consented to another modern opera, but this one lasted only twenty minutes and I was only acting; I didn't have to sing a single note. I also made my first movie in Germany, *Brand in der Oper* (Fire in the Opera House). I had only one scene, in which I sang Olympia's aria from *The Tales of Hoffmann.* But Gustaf Gründgens played Mephistopheles, and I thought that such distinguished company would mean that my film career was off to a good start.

That summer I vacationed with my parents in a house we sometimes rented on the Berounka River, near Prague. My father was a wonderful companion, always full of jokes, and all the children from the neighborhood used to come to hear his stories, of which he was master. My mother was an excellent cook, and I adored her apricot dumplings. I remember one meal when, after a good-sized portion of beautifully crispy goose, I ate about ten dumplings in one sitting. In that setting, I could forget about my weight and enjoy myself. George built a little cabin nearby, and we had the most delightful time swimming, fishing, and entertaining the many friends who visited. Such relaxing times gave me strength to return to Berlin and the hard work, challenges, and rewards of the coming season.

Making my next film, an adaptation of Carl Millöcker's *The Beggar Student,* was a pleasure in many ways. This operetta contains many charming melodies to sing, and my costars were Hans-Heinz Bollmann, a well-known film actor; Trus van Aalten; and Hans Yaray, a very handsome young man who later became a great star in Vienna. But because the Kroll would not release me, I often worked at the movie studio until late afternoon, only to sing Rosina, Violetta, or Mařenka that evening. This was very taxing, and again my voice started to suffer. Other people didn't seem to notice the difference when I sang, and I was becoming very popular. But I felt miserable. I knew there was something wrong.

Today, after many years of experience, I understand that I began much too early to sing such an enormous repertory, without sufficient technical preparation. I had a naturally well-placed voice, but I would advise every young singer to study rigorously for several years and not to give in to the temptation of performing in public until the vocal technique is secure. I worked on technique all my life. I found good teachers who helped me along, and with time I met the goals I set for myself. But if I had followed the kind of advice I am offering here, I would have spared myself quite a lot of anxiety.

My new popularity meant invitations to social engagements in Berlin, and at the salon of Dr. Prof. János Plesch, I met Albert Einstein again. This time I was less bashful, and we had the most delightful conversation. President Masaryk sometimes wrote to complain teasingly that I wasn't singing in Czechoslovakia often enough, though I continued to return to sing for his birthday concerts, and in fact I sang in Prague as often as I could. He told me he understood that, at this point in my life, my international career must take precedence.

In Berlin, I continued to take on new roles. I sang Cherubino in a charming *Marriage of Figaro,* with Gründgens as stage director. Klemperer conducted, and by this time I had gotten used to his overwhelming personality. Although he was best known for his Beethoven, his Mozart was so delicate, with astonishing beauty and style. Immediately after *Figaro,* I sang Madame Butterfly. With Zemlinsky conducting, Hans Curjel directing, and László Moholy-Nagy's atmospheric designs, this was one of the great hits of the season. The American tenor Charles Kullman made his debut as Pinkerton, and the famed critic Alfred Einstein wrote that he "displays real tenorial brilliance," while noting that the ovation for me "would not end, and she deserved it."

My success as Butterfly led to an invitation to sing Puccini's Manon Lescaut at the Unter den Linden, with Leo Blech conducting. He insisted that the singers look directly at him at all times during performances, though this was contrary to all my principles of good acting. To be believable, I had to look at my partner when I addressed him. Blech had a habit of writing little notes after each performance, to inform singers of certain mistakes and to remind them to sing a particular passage correctly the next time. One night, I received a note saying, "Everything is in perfect order, except that you forgot to look at me. But I know what to do. I will disguise myself as Klemperer, and then I am sure that you will watch me." Everybody knew that we were afraid of Klemperer.

Manon Lescaut was beautifully staged. Manon's boudoir was done in gold lace, and I wore a gold lamé dress, with only my face and a white wig for contrast. I was sorry that I couldn't see the effect for myself, but George told me it was breathtaking. I received excellent reviews, for example from the *Berliner Morgenpost,* which said that my voice "reflects the nature of the character, sweet and helpless. . . . [In the more parlando passages,] she expends less breath in extended phrases, thereby appearing childlike and leading to moments of most convincing intimacy. . . . In Act II, even her coquetry [seems to] wear a halo."

Even though I didn't always watch Blech in the pit, he liked my singing well enough to offer me the role of the Queen in Meyerbeer's *Les Huguenots.* Gründgens directed, adding some telling touches. As I sang "Ô, beau pays de la Touraine," a very difficult aria, I had to play with a ball, synchronizing the bouncing of the ball with the coloratura passages—no mean feat. The *Berliner Anzeiger* described my performance as "charming . . . in all the art and prowess of her voice and deliciousness."

When I had a few days off, I sang a concert in Brno. As usual in Czechoslovakia, I sang in Czech. And once again, German newspapers sympathetic to Nazism complained. On April 2, 1931, for example, *Der Tag* wrote of my "tactlessness," accepting "good German money" to sing at the Staatsoper and yet singing German music in my native language; my experience with the Beethoven Ninth, the year before, should have taught me a lesson, the critic said. "If Novotná is such a fervent Czech," the critic concluded, "we recommend that she be given the opportunity to become so completely"—that is, to be fired from the Kroll and to go back to Prague. "Can it be that there is no German replacement for her?"

The *Deutsche Zeitung* wrote, "What can the German public think, when it hears such outrageous news about the appearance of a member of the Berliner Staatsoper in Czechoslovakia? Jarmila Novotná knows how to play the outward role of a harmless artist, and hides behind her mask a miserable chauvinism while openly demonstrating against German values." The *Deutsche Zeitung,* like the *Münchner Neueste,* demanded that the Kroll not renew my contract.

This was too much, even for the Germans. Another newspaper, *Der Montag am Morgen,* ridiculed the whole affair: "Beware! Nasty tricks menace us! The singer Jarmila Novotná, Czech by birth, member of the Berliner Staatsoper, equipped according to international standards with a first-class voice box . . . has not shied a second time from singing in Czech in concert in her native land. The Siegfrieds of all types cannot contain their outrage." If the Kroll were to dismiss me, the critic wrote, then "with her, it is hoped, may also be stamped out the highly treasonable opera composer W. A. Mozart, who openly set music to librettos in foreign languages"; he also suggested that "foreigners who enjoy German employment [who use] their mother tongue even beyond our borders [be] charged with high treason and summary exile." Given the political atmosphere at the time, I wondered how the critic dared to write such scathing satire.

Despite the controversy over my concert in Brno, Max Reinhardt asked me to sing the title role in Offenbach's *La Belle Hélène.* It took some juggling to work out a schedule that would allow me to sing at the Staatsoper and yet be available to rehearse and perform the Offenbach. Even after discussing the matter with Reinhardt, Heinz Tietjen decided that the Kroll couldn't entirely release me and that I would have to sing at least once a week with the company. This would be quite a challenge, since my repertoire at the time included *Manon Lescaut, Butterfly, Rigoletto,* and *Traviata.* Yet I was so eager to work with Reinhardt that I would have agreed to anything.

When I arrived at the first rehearsal, on May 19 at the Kurfürstendamm Theater, Reinhardt was surrounded by many assistants. There was a hush, and nobody dared to talk to him. I just seized my courage and went up to him. "Herr Professor," I said, "I am happy that I can be your Helen."

"If I were Paris, I would give you the apple, instead of giving it to Venus," Reinhardt answered. The ice was broken, the rehearsal began, and a completely new horizon opened before my eyes.

Reinhardt emphasized that nothing was lost onstage: the audience noticed every detail, which conveyed its effect. For him, the effect must be gauged not in terms of acting, but as life. He abhorred empty gestures, and in his books he noted each movement he wanted from us. In the mornings, his assistants would work from Reinhardt's notes, and most days he did not appear at the theater until about two o'clock, after we had taken a quick lunch break. Once Reinhardt joined us, the real work started. He corrected the scenes that we had prepared for him, but he had a magical way of injecting life into every character, just by asking for a particular vocal inflection from us. When he wasn't satisfied, he would play the part for us. Soon we were able to portray the character the way he prescribed, and we found something enormously encouraging and inspiring when he was satisfied with our work. When we performed a comic scene well, he could laugh so heartily that he was really the best possible audience.

Reinhardt found his conductor, Erich Wolfgang Korngold, indispensable. Born in Brno (part of the Austro-Hungarian Empire at the time), Korngold was a wunderkind who had produced operas while still in his teens, and whose most famous opera, *Die Tote Stadt,* had its simultaneous premiere in Hamburg and Cologne when he was only twenty-two. Later, Reinhardt took Korngold to Hollywood to make *A Midsummer Night's Dream,* and he went on to a successful career writing film scores, as well as operetta adaptations for Broadway. Korngold was a thoughtful and agreeable conductor, and to watch him was an inspiration, because he enjoyed every minute as much as we did.

La Belle Hélène premiered on June 15, 1931, and the next day, the *Berliner Tageblatt* wrote that "Reinhardt makes of Novotná . . . a human, a female, an Offenbachian female, with all of the desires of this species, in a way one never could have imagined." What I learned from Reinhardt I was able to apply later to my other roles. When, after my first Metropolitan Opera *Traviata,* the critics compared me with Duse, it was due only to Reinhardt.

My work pleased Reinhardt, and he asked me to give up the opera altogether and to dedicate myself to the legitimate stage. "I can make the greatest actress out of you," he promised. But I knew that I would miss out if I gave up opera, and I told him so. He told me he was directing Shakespeare's *Twelfth Night* in Salzburg that summer, and "at least you must play that," he said. But I had to refuse.

The reason was simple.

By now George had given up his demand that I put a stop to my career, but he didn't want to wait any longer for us to marry. He sent me a lovely poem in Czech, which translates as follows:

Happiness, what is happiness?
Happiness is roaming together, avoiding the ugly and base;
It is knowing you are not alone in snow and sleet and bad weather;
It is looking into another's eyes and warming yourself in the glow—
Happiness is knowing deep in your soul how to love.

Who could resist?

We married on July 16, 1931, in the church of Pana Maria pod Řetězem, on Malá Strana in Prague, near the palace that belonged to George and his brother. We were careful to keep the ceremony a secret, because by now I was so popular that we had reason to believe that half the city would come to see "our Jarmila" get married. Only a few family members and friends were present, and after a brief reception at the palace, George and I left immediately on our honeymoon. We stayed at St. Raphael on the French Riviera, in an apartment with a large terrace that overlooked an orange grove, and beyond it the sea, where the setting sun played on the surface in all its brilliant colors. It was so beautiful that we stayed on the terrace all evening, and even asked that our dinner be served there. Only my next engagement in Ostend—an annual affair now, because of my repeated successes there—could take us away from that lovely scene.

We returned to George's family home at Liteň on August 2. George was astonished to see that the fields were already harvested: it had been an exceptional year. His mother, the most wonderful woman who ever existed, prepared a great reception for us, covering the front gate with flowers and arranging for girls and boys in folk costumes to greet us.

Soon I got used to a new way of life. The estate boasted two houses: the château, where my mother-in-law lived; and a baroque one-story house, where George and his brother had lived as young men. George and I decided that we preferred to live in the baroque house whenever we were at Liteň, and after our honeymoon we found that George's mother had supervised all the preparations, making the house most comfortable. Although it had its own kitchen, we took our meals at the château with the rest of the family.

The main house was always full of guests, especially on weekends, when George liked to host shooting parties. With a group of about eight of the best shots, it wasn't unusual for the men to bag two thousand partridges and pheasants in a single day. We would assemble for breakfast at 7:30, and an hour later we would be crossing the fields. It was easy to make our way through fields that had been harvested, but potato fields required fancy footwork that, over the course of an entire day, could prove to be exhausting. We looked forward to dinner and relaxation in the evenings, which were very much part of the appeal of these parties.

Then Max Reinhardt sent me a telegram, asking me again to play Olivia in *Twelfth Night,* this time for a "one-time performance" in Salzburg that somehow would be repeated in Vienna and Berlin. I knew I could not accept, and wired him my reply. Only two days later, I received a second telegram from him, now speaking of the possibility of a film, too, and underscoring that my participation would build interest in my work among foreign audiences. The project would take only ten days, Reinhardt said, and there was no reason George could not join me.

I tried several times to reach Reinhardt by telephone, but without success. At last I wrote him a long letter, explaining my situation in detail—as well as my gratitude to him for thinking of me, and my regret at being unable to participate. It was simply a question of timing, because George really had made his peace with my career. This was something that even President Masaryk understood, much to my surprise: he said as much in a letter I received around this time, offering congratulations and the wish that "Mrs. Daubek will not overshadow Miss Novotná."

Even as I began a new chapter in my life, so Germany was entering a new era. Curiously, one of the first signs was the closing of the Kroll Opera, with a performance of *The Marriage of Figaro* on July 3, 1931. Officially, budget considerations led to the closing, but in fact it was a political act, and it signified the growing power of the Nazis, who took over the whole country only eighteen months later.

At first, however, only the setting of our performances changed: I continued to work with most of the same colleagues, but now at the Staatsoper Unter den Linden. Beyond that theater, Max Reinhardt once again made a tempting offer. This time, he wanted me to sing Antonia in *The Tales of Hoffmann,* and he made arrangements with Heinz Tietjen to permit me to participate in a long run. Tietjen even released Leo Blech for the initial performances, but later George Szell took over as conductor. This was the first time that I had sung under Szell's baton, though I had heard him often at the German opera house in Prague. He gave remarkable performances of both classical and modern works, in which he always endeavored to conform completely with the composers' wishes.

I loved the part of Antonia, and so did Reinhardt. One day we were rehearsing, but we had not gotten to my scene when six o'clock arrived. Reinhardt told me to go home, and he would telephone if he needed me. I had my dinner and went to bed around ten o'clock. Then, at eleven, the telephone suddenly rang: "The Herr Professor would like to run through the Antonia scene." So I jumped out of my warm bed, quickly dressed, and went to rehearsal, which lasted until twelve-thirty in the morning. Can you imagine anything similar today? Yet we were so happy to work with Reinhardt we would have agreed to any time at all.

The *Tales of Hoffmann* production was really spectacular. In the Venetian scene, Giulietta and Hoffmann glided smoothly on a gondola under bridges on a giant revolving stage. On opening night, however, the gondola's prow collided with a teetering bridge, broke off, and plunged not into gentle waters but onto the hard wooden floor of the stage! Still, the overall illusion was so powerful that the audience in the Großes Schauspielhaus, all 3,500 of them, remained unaware of the mishap. And yet the critics observed that the Antonia scene was the most impressive of all because of its simplicity, its lack of tricks, and its concentration on the essence of the music, "especially the singing of Jarmila Novotná," which the *Berliner Tageblatt* described as a "heavenly rising and falling voice . . . this sound echoing on in the ears of all who heard it, this sound that cannot fade away." In this production, different singers took the roles of each of Hoffmann's lovers (although many years later, in Vienna, I took all three soprano roles, as the composer intended), with Göta Ljungberg as Giulietta and Adele Kern as Olympia; George Baklanov sang the Villains, including an especially powerful Dr. Miracle.

The long run of *Hoffmann* encouraged Reinhardt to bring *La Belle Hélène* to the Großes Schauspielhaus. But in the meantime, I returned to sing several concerts in Prague. In Berlin, I sang a gala celebration of Haydn's two-hundredth birthday under Erich Kleiber, as well as my usual operas with the Staatsoper. Then in April 1932, we brought *La Belle Hélène* to the Unter den Linden. For the subtlety of this production I preferred the intimacy of the Kurfürstendamm. However, we had a new Menelaus, Max Hansen, much younger than his predecessor, Hans Moser. Thus Hansen played not an old Menelaus but a young one who simply could not satisfy Helen's desires. This approach proved to be effective and funny in a fresh way.

After the premiere, Reinhardt invited everybody to dinner, at which Marlene Dietrich was also present. Whether she was jealous of my success or of my seating—at Reinhardt's right hand, while she sat far from him—I don't know. But she snubbed me in a way that was really ridiculous, and even today I laugh when I remember it.

It was an exciting time. Bruno Walter invited me to sing a few concerts with him, featuring Mahler's Fourth Symphony and any arias I preferred. I signed a contract for a film adaptation of *The Bartered Bride*. And I learned that I was expecting my first child.

I had accepted the offer to make *The Bartered Bride* because I thought that the traditional peasant dresses would hide my pregnancy. I didn't tell anyone about my condition, though at several points during filming, during takes and retakes, I worried about getting tired. In the opera, the character of Vašek disguises himself as a bear, and Mařenka runs from him. In the film, however, they used a real bear, who was kept in a cage between takes. After a few takes, somebody decided to have some fun by feeding the bear. As the fellow put his hand through the bars, the bear tore his hand. This caused great consternation, and it was decided that the scene would not be reshot. Was I relieved!

Although Max Ophüls, one of the best directors of the time, was in charge, he retained very little of Smetana's beautiful music, and he greatly changed the story. For example, the character of the hero, Jeník (or Hans, in most German-language productions, including this one), was transformed from a farmer's son to a postilion, riding from town to town; Mařenka (or Marie) became the daughter of the town's mayor.[5] Unfortunately, I did not get to read the script until we started shooting, and then it was too late to protest. The opera is so beloved by Czech people that I knew that they would not approve of the changes made in the movie, and I was right: Ophüls' movie was never shown in Czechoslovakia. As things turned out, I didn't see the movie until 1939, in New York City, at a theater on Eighty-Sixth Street where German films often played. The cast did include some fine performers, including the excellent baritone Willi Domgraf-Fassbaender, with whom I sang very often at the Staatsoper; and the famous comedian Karl Valentin.[6]

At the end of July I returned to Liteň. Though I had been married for a year by this time, I hardly knew George's home because I had been away so much. At harvest time, George's family observed a lovely old custom, inviting the farm workers to the château for a celebration. Young people dressed in folk costumes, and we danced with everyone. The festivities then continued at a local inn until very early in the morning.

Liteň was a real country farm. We had many horses, cows, and prize hogs, which George bred. A funny old man looked after the hogs, and when I first met him, he said to George, "You know, a man is the head of a family—but a woman is the neck." (That is, the wife supports the husband.) There were four thousand acres of forest, two thousand acres of fields, a brewery, a distillery, and many ponds. George took care of all of this, so he was kept quite busy. I usually slept late in the morning and fetched him at noon from his office. In the heat of summer, we often went to our cabin on the river for a swim. Despite her age, my mother-in-law often went with me to the river, to be nearby in case something happened to me and the baby. This kind of consideration showed what an exceptionally lovely woman she was, not only very beautiful but also the kindest lady I knew. We lived in perfect harmony.

On Sunday, September 25, around noon, I started to have labor pains, and George and his mother took me to a clinic in Prague, where my doctor was waiting for me. Around nine o'clock that evening I gave birth. George always said he hoped we would have a little girl, "because they are so much nicer than boys," but I probably hoped for a boy. I know this because, when the doctor told me, "It's a girl," I apparently answered, "It doesn't matter!"

Two days later, the Archbishop of Prague, Cardinal Kaspar, came to the clinic to christen the child Jarmila Theresa, after Saint Theresa, whom he revered. We nicknamed her Jarmilka, or "little Jarmila." The Cardinal invited us to visit him and his mother at the Archbishop's Palace. The reason he wanted us to meet his mother, he explained, was that she had told him he was born with a full head of hair. He didn't believe her until he saw that our Jarmilka also had a big tuft of hair, so he wanted his mother to see the baby. Naturally we visited them on our way to Liteň, where I remained with the baby. Everybody was very happy.

Because Berlin remained the center of my professional life, George and I engaged a registered nurse to look after the baby in Liteň. Milada Feilerovà effectively joined our family as soon as we met her at the maternity clinic; we nicknamed her "Teta," which means "aunt." Because the baby was so young, we also engaged a wet nurse, a very nice woman from Slovakia. My mother-in-law supervised every aspect of the baby's care, and of course George was there too. This freed me to continue to perform in Germany, though I returned to Liteň as often as possible.

Reinhardt came to me with the idea of my playing the part of Beauty in Hugo von Hofmannsthal's *Das große Welttheater* (The Great World Theater, after Calderón's play *El gran teatro del mundo*). I hesitated for the simple reason that Beauty is a speaking part, always played by an actress. At that moment there were many unemployed actors in Berlin, and I also reminded Reinhardt that the nationalistic newspapers in Germany had declared war against me, as a Czech. "I have a remedy," Reinhardt said. A young composer, Mark Lothar, had written all the background music for the play, and so Reinhardt commissioned him to write two coloratura arias for Beauty. "Now no actress can play the role!" Reinhardt said. "I need a real opera star, so if you do it, nobody will object."

However, the Czech composer Jaromír Weinberger, best known for his opera *Svanda the Bagpiper* (in Czech, *Švanda dudák*), begged me to sing the leading part in an operetta he had just written, *Frühlingsstürme* (Spring Storms). I informed him that I couldn't stay with his production later than the beginning of February, when rehearsals would start for *Das große Welttheater.* Weinberger accepted my conditions, and *Frühlingsstürme* premiered on January 20, 1933. His score contained lovely melodies, but the book was not of the highest quality. Nevertheless, the show was a hit, and my leading man had to repeat his aria three times, always with fresh variations.

He was Richard Tauber, and this would be the first of many times I sang with him. He was a wonderful colleague, very proper, agreeable, always the first to arrive at rehearsals, and indefatigable in his work, repeating and repeating a song until he was satisfied that he had achieved his desired effects. His voice had such a special quality that, even today, when one hears a recording, his timbre is immediately recognizable. It was a pleasure to sing with him, but after fifteen performances, I had to leave *Frühlingsstürme.*

I returned to Liteň for just a week, but while I was there, I had a call from Gustaf Gründgens. "You must not perform *Das große Welttheater,*" he said. "Call Reinhardt and cancel immediately!" To this day I wonder how much he already knew about what was happening. (Who was his informant? Göring?) At the time, however, Gründgens gave no explanation for his curious request, except to say something about other actors going hungry. I explained that Reinhardt and Lothar had made Beauty a challenging musical role, and that I couldn't cause trouble for Reinhardt by canceling only a few days before rehearsals started. Though he still seemed agitated, Gründgens had to accept my position. But this wasn't the end of the matter.

I returned to Berlin to join in the preparations for the *Welttheater,* and on the day of the dress rehearsal, the telephone rang. Gründgens was on the line. "Don't you know that the Reichstag is burning?" he asked.

Yes, of course, I knew of the fire, just the night before—February 27, 1933. The radio and newspapers talked of nothing else that morning. The fire had been put out, but the investigation—so-called—continued.

"Nobody is allowed to pass the building," Gründgens went on, "and the theater is very near it. I will take you there, since I can obtain the necessary pass." I was grateful for his help, and we arrived at the theater without any difficulty, after he showed his papers to the authorities. The play went on, but Reinhardt could not know, when he took his bow on opening night, that he would never return to Berlin.

This was really the beginning of the end.

Bruno Walter had asked me to sing the soprano solo in Mahler's Fourth Symphony with the Berlin Philharmonic on March 19, but only two days after the Reichstag fire, the *Völkischer Beobachter* published an article, emphasizing that Walter and Mahler both were Jewish, and attacking me personally as one who had "repeatedly stirred up public outrage." According to the *Beobachter,* I had "evoked lively condemnation in all German-minded circles for her totally unnecessary singing Beethoven's Ninth Symphony in the Czech language in an appearance in Prague. The justified attacks against her by the Berlin press might almost have caused the singer to be banned from the company of the Berlin Staatsoper. Now she emerges once again in a symphonic concert under Bruno Walter. This collaboration is indeed a defiance of nationalistic Germany." About ten days before the concert, Bruno Walter called me and said that, because the *Beobachter* had revived the story of the Beethoven performance in Prague, he feared that protestors would disrupt our concert. "Would you be good enough to agree to a cancellation of your contract?" he asked. I found this very strange, but I answered, "If you wish, then naturally I will comply."

But Walter's effort did nothing to appease the *Beobachter.* Only a few days later, the newspaper wrote again about the affront to the German nation, the conductor Bruno Walter Schlesinger (his full name), and "another Jew, Gustav Mahler." The concert's directors, the agency of Wolff and Sachs, removed Walter and asked Richard Strauss to present a different program.

Day by day the atmosphere became more disagreeable. I made yet another film, *Die Nacht der großen Liebe* (The Night of Great Love), opposite Gustav Fröhlich, the popular star of Fritz Lang's film *Metropolis,* before

I returned to Prague to sing at the National Theater I was very glad to add Carolina in Smetana's *Two Widows* to my repertory (though for me *The Bartered Bride* will always remain his crowning achievement). In work after work, Smetana's music somehow manages to capture the essence of the Czechoslovakian spirit, both in its lightheartedness and in its tragedy. Thus *Two Widows* was in more ways than one a homecoming for me. Yet almost immediately, my international career would turn away from Berlin forever—and toward Vienna instead.

My happy association with the Vienna Staatsoper began with a call from Otto Klemperer and a performance as Butterfly on June 17, 1933, during the Festwochen. Klemperer was very proud of bringing me back to Vienna, and almost immediately he began trying to tempt me with such offers as a lieder evening. "Don't get frightened," he added in a note to me, "but I would like to write a musical film for you. May I—or, better question—*can* I?" Unfortunately, the film never materialized, but Clemens Krauss, the director of the Vienna Staatsoper, asked me to return in the fall.

Krauss told me that Franz Lehár had written an operetta called *Giuditta,* and the composer's cherished dream was to see it produced at the Staatsoper. Until my arrival, Krauss said, he had found no one capable of playing the leading role: only if I would consent would he produce *Giuditta.*

Though I was flattered, I answered that I must see the score first, and I had quite a number of other engagements scheduled. These included another Czech film, *Song of the Lark,* after the play by Jaroslav Kvapil, and a series of performances in Prague: my first *La Bohème* in my hometown, with President Masaryk in attendance; plus *Onegin, Traviata,* and *Two Widows.* I also took a long vacation in Liteň, which seemed like another world that I had grown to miss terribly. The house was again full of people, but George and I interrupted our summer leisure for a few days to see Reinhardt's production of Goethe's *Faust* in Salzburg. We were too late to see the premiere or the second performance, but this turned out to be quite lucky, because both performances were interrupted by torrential rains and had to be transferred hastily from the Felsenreitschule to the Festival Hall. The night we attended, the weather was perfect, the performance unforgettable, the summit of Reinhardt's art. This was my first visit to Salzburg, and the town enchanted me.

Reinhardt still wanted me to play Rosalinda in *Die Fledermaus,* and he came with an offer for a production in French, which would open in Paris in the fall. This interested me very much, and without knowing the exact date of the premiere, I accepted. Reinhardt then turned over the contract negotiation to his agent, Herald Leonidoff, but he and I had difficulty coming to terms. Leonidoff claimed that my requirements were unreasonable for just one performer in a large cast and a small theater; he went so far as to tell Reinhardt that I had turned him down, whereas I really was waiting only for a response to my counteroffer. Reinhardt was beside himself with worry, sending many telegrams to beg me to come to Paris to negotiate face-to-face. Finally I agreed to come, and as Reinhardt hoped, Leonidoff and I came to terms that I could accept: not only about money, but also about my costumes, the difficulty of singing two performances per day on certain days, and so on.

Although I spoke French fluently, I knew that French audiences found it difficult to accept anybody with a foreign accent. And an accent I had for sure! Reinhardt's assistant, Francesco von Mendelssohn, the composer's great-grandson, proved a great help to me in learning the role, because he spoke French perfectly—something that not all of Reinhardt's assistants could claim.

Lotte Schöne was an admirable Adele, and the rest of the cast were all French actors. My partner was Jules Berry, one of the most acclaimed French actors of his generation.[7] But I found it disconcerting that he did not learn his lines correctly, and he was apt to improvise from time to time. This was difficult at first, but I got used to his methods. I could answer his improvised lines in such a way that not even Reinhardt noticed that we did not stick to the script.

Korngold conducted, and Grete Wiesenthal, a well-known Viennese dancer, choreographed. Her work was the hit of the evening, representing a true apotheosis of the waltz. She even taught me to dance the czardas! Nevertheless, George jokingly told me that I needed more of the true Gypsy spirit, and after the final dress rehearsal he insisted on taking me to a famous Hungarian nightclub in Paris. I was tired, but I must have profited by the experience, because one critic described me as "a stunning revelation, especially remarkable in the Czardas." The critic of *Le Petit Parisien* wrote, "Mme Novotná, who played Rosalinda, deserves the highest praise for her mastery of the vocal stage. Her voice is pure, supple, with a fresh timbre. In this artist one finds the musician who with equal ability reveals the vivacious waltz and the passionate Czardas. In the latter she was dazzling."[8]

La Chauve-souris, as the French call it, was a great success, and it was striking to see Reinhardt set aside his usual reserve when Cécile Sorel, the celebrated French actress, came to see us: he greeted her like a queen. The French actors' guild requested a special performance just for its members. The date was set for December 19, the day after my last scheduled performance. Naturally Reinhardt wanted to present his production as advantageously as possible, and he did not want the special performance to be the occasion of the debut of the soprano who was to replace me. This put me in a terrible situation, since I already had my train ticket and had planned to leave for Vienna at 5:00 p.m. I simply could not tell Reinhardt this, so instead I told him I was sick. Two of his assistants came to my hotel to beg me to reconsider, and finally I agreed.

Secretly, however, I planned to sing only the first two acts (including the Czardas), and then to say that I was too ill to continue. On the day of the performance, I played Act II as if I were really unwell. In spite of this, the Czardas received a long ovation, so the act ran much longer than usual. Backstage, I told everyone how miserable I was to be unable to finish the performance. Then I dashed to a nearby street, where George's nephew, Josef Bromovský, waited in a taxi with all my luggage. I got to the station just as my train was pulling out. I thought I would die. Luckily, there was another train leaving for Vienna later that evening, and I was able to meet Franz Lehár the next day, exactly as Clemens Krauss had arranged it for me.

I was afraid that Reinhardt would be angry if he found out about my deception. Some time later, however, he told me that, after the *Fledermaus* performance ended, he had called my hotel to find out how I was feeling. The hotel told him that I had checked out, and he realized what had happened. "I always knew that you were a great actress," he said with a laugh, "but to put me off the way you did, you are greater than I thought!"

At last I met Franz Lehár, a most amiable man. He played *Giuditta* for me and said that he had always thought of me in the title role while he composed his operetta. (Perhaps this is why Krauss said he could imagine nobody but me in the part!) I took the score with me to Liteň and started right away to learn it; rehearsals began in Vienna just after Richard Tauber and I opened in *Butterfly* at the Staatsoper. Tauber was to co-star with me in *Giuditta* as well. Our rehearsals were really a joy, and we felt none of the nervousness that sometimes accompanies the launch of a new work.

Giuditta isn't as easy to sing as some of Lehár's other works, and the music assigned to Giuditta can be very taxing. In Act II, there is a very dramatic scene that some newspapers compared to *Elektra*. Tauber's character takes lighter music, but for my character there was also a hit song, "Meine Lippen, sie küssen so heiß" (My lips, they kiss so warmly). After the premiere, this song was heard all over Vienna, and whenever I walked into a restaurant, the house orchestra would greet me by playing it.

We rented a little *palais* in the Salmgasse. My sweet little Jarmilka came to stay with me, along with her nurse, Teta. We also brought an excellent Czech cook, my maid Adele, and a butler, Jan Jelínek. This meant we were very well prepared to entertain, which pleased George, who often joined us. For the premiere on January 20, 1934, my mother-in-law also arrived. Her three sisters lived in Vienna; the oldest, Anna Foregger, was the grandmother of Audrey Hepburn (still a little girl at the time).

It is difficult to describe the success of *Giuditta*. We had to sing it almost every day, very unusual in an opera house, and I rarely got to sing anything else, apart from one *Butterfly* and a *Rigoletto* with the tenor Alfred Piccaver. In the midst of this heavy schedule, I caught a cold and realized that I would have to cancel *Giuditta* on February 12. Lehár telephoned frantically, because the performance was completely sold out, but there was nothing I could do. On February 11, Lehár and Tauber arrived at my home, but they could see at a glance that, no matter how much I hated to disappoint them, I was miserably sick. So Tauber turned to our little Jarmilka, who was two. "Come," he said, "I will sing for you, so that you can say when you grew up, 'Tauber sang for me alone, only for me.'"

That night, we were awakened by the sounds of distant shooting. A revolution had broken out between the government and angry, unemployed workers. The skirmishes lasted for three days, with many casualties. Naturally in this atmosphere the opera remained closed, and there was no question of my singing in *Giuditta,* regardless of my health. But over the next several months, tensions persisted between the Christian-Democratic national government and the Socialist city government; the Nazis began to organize the young, and on July 25, a group of ten Nazis assassinated the chancellor, Engelbert Dolfuss. Political unrest seemed to be everywhere. During a brief break from the Staatsoper, I sang in Prague at President Masaryk's reception for the French foreign minister, Jean-Louis Barthou, on April 6, 1934, where the minister and I enjoyed a pleasant conversation, and he told me he had seen me in *Fledermaus* in Paris; on October 9 that same year, Barthou and Yugoslavia's King Alexander were assassinated in Marseille.

Yet we continued to work, not as if there were no troubles in the world, but rather as if these troubles would pass.

Due to the success of *Giuditta*, the Atlantis Film Company approached me for an adaptation of another Lehár operetta, *Frasquita*. We started filming in June, first at the studios in Vienna, where all the musical scenes were prepared and conducted by Lehár himself. The outdoor scenes were filmed in and around Dubrovnik. For one such scene, I was on a boat, with the camera placed on another boat just in front of me. Suddenly, the sea became agitated, and the boats began to rise and fall. It was terrible to have to look toward the camera while my boat moved in its own directions, and I became seasick. "Cut, please!" I yelled. We tried again the next day, when luckily we had no waves.

A month later, I went to Paris to make another film, *La dernière Valse* (The Last Waltz), with music by Oscar Straus. Production lasted two months, because we made not only a French but also an English version. My costar was Jean Martinelli, a young and good-looking actor from the Comédie Française. His mother was a well-known singing teacher, so we had plenty to talk about. George's cousin Trixy Ruston was with me, and George came to Paris when he could, so we often went to the theater and opera.

Movie offers continued to come in, and when I got home in October, there was another letter from Lehár as well. Really, for the moment I didn't want to accept any engagements of any kind, but that was easier said than done. Following the success of *Frasquita,* the same studio wanted to start as soon as possible on a new film, *The Cossack and the Nightingale.* The script, an elaborate and rather amusing espionage story, called for location shooting in Greece and Egypt, and I could not resist the wonderful opportunity to visit these two countries. In December, we began shooting interior scenes at the Rosenhügel Filmstudios in Vienna (where I was also singing *Traviata* and *Madame Butterfly* at the Staatsoper), with director Phil Jutzi; the handsome Ivan Petrovich played the Cossack of the title. Then we were off to Greece. George came along for the trip, and we enjoyed it immensely. On days when I wasn't needed on the shoot, we visited museums, the Acropolis, and the Parthenon, which impressed me as a perfection of dimension and beauty. We also visited Mycenae, and I found myself standing in Electra's room and on the very spot where Agamemnon was murdered. After such an experience, it was difficult to look at Strauss's *Elektra*—or even Offenbach's *La Belle Hélène*—in quite the same way.

The day after Christmas, the whole company departed for Egypt on a perfectly equipped Italian boat, which took us first to Crete and then to Rhodes, with time for sightseeing in both places. The trip to Alexandria lasted two days, and on the first day we had such bad weather that the boat seemed to dance from one side to the other. That night I made the mistake of leaving open the window in my cabin, and a big wave came crashing in, soaking me as I lay in my bed. But the next day the sun came out, I sat on the deck to dry out, and we all had a good time.

After landing in Alexandria, we continued to Cairo and then, after nightfall, to an exquisite hotel called the Mena House. We were not prepared for what we saw the next morning when we looked out. There were the Pyramids right before us, as if we could reach out and touch them! The beauty, the simplicity, the majesty of the Pyramids overwhelmed me, and I was pleased to learn that they would be part of the scenery in our film. However, shooting them exposed us to the weather, and one day we had a taste of a real sandstorm. There was no way to escape it! Everyone's eyes, nose, and mouth were full of sand, and in a mere second all the cameras were unusable. We had to send them away to be cleaned, and we took advantage of the break to visit Luxor-Thebes-Karnak. I marveled at the glories of the ancient temples, which really should be seen at different hours to appreciate their richness. We also visited the Luxor museum, on every step of which sat a snake charmer. Even in my dreams, for nights to come, I saw snakes dancing before my eyes.

With calmer weather and refurbished cameras, we returned to Giza and completed the shoot, returning by the Italian boat to Venice, where we were greeted by a most unusual and very beautiful sight: the city covered in snow in the morning light.

After a short break I packed for Vienna again, taking with me Jarmilka, Teta, the cook, the butler, and a maid. We found a very comfortable apartment this time, in the Opernstraße, directly across from the artists' entrance to the Staatsoper, which was very convenient for me. We enjoyed that winter in Vienna very much. We went to several balls, and the luncheons and dinners we threw were the talk of the town—everyone wanted an invitation! I must say that social duties do not make the life of an artist any easier, and I remember Reinhardt's warning me against getting married: "An artist must be free, and marriage brings so many of its own demands, that there surely will be conflicts." Well, maybe he was right, but the compensations of family and home must be accounted for, as well. No matter how much work I had, I was happy.

And I did have work that season: a concert with the Philharmonic Orchestra, and performances of *Bohème, Traviata,* and *Butterfly* before we resumed the run of *Giuditta.* We began rehearsals for *The Bartered Bride,* with Richard Tauber as Jeník, and conducted by Josef Krips. This was the first time I sang under Krips' baton, and I found the experience delightful. He was most inspiring, always in good humor, and his smiling face gave everybody confidence. He always said, "All music is singing, and that which is not singing, is noise." The production had its premiere on February 27, and it was so successful that we repeated it many times.

Two new roles awaited me as well. The first was Fiordiligi in *Così Fan Tutte,* with Felix von Weingartner conducting. I asked Dr. Weingartner whether I could bring my little daughter to the final dress rehearsal, because she loved Mozart's music above all else. She was a little over two years old then, and she told us that Mozart was "so happy, light, and quick." Weingartner agreed, and after the rehearsal he asked how Jarmilka had liked the performance. "Oh, Mama danced so beautifully!" she replied. It took me a long time to make her understand that I was a singer, not a dancer, but perhaps Lothar Wallerstein's stage direction, emphasizing graceful movements from everyone in the cast, had given her that impression.

This production served more or less as a preparation for the next Salzburg Festival, where I would repeat the role of Fiordiligi, reprise the Countess in *The Marriage of Figaro,* and introduce the second of my new roles, Octavian in *Der Rosenkavalier.* I found Octavian to be a real challenge, something very different from what I had done so far in my career.

As I see the character, he is a youth in his late teens, very much in love, and very definitely the aristocrat. In the eighteenth century, young Viennese noblemen were encouraged to accept the patronage of older women in order to polish their manners. So even when Octavian is dressed as a chambermaid, he must never offer even a hint of burlesque. In preparing for the role, I found that the best teacher or stage director is often life itself. To be sure that I really looked like a boy, I observed young men to study how they moved, what their posture was like, and how they used their hands. Once, however, when I was pursuing these "studies," I got into a silly situation, when a young man mistook my attention for an advance on my part.

My first Octavian, among so many through the course of my career, was in Vienna on June 23, with a marvelous cast: Lotte Lehmann as the Marschallin, Adele Kern as Sophie, and Fritz Krenn as Baron Ochs. Josef Krips conducted. I could not have asked for a more auspicious role debut.

I was scheduled to sing *Rosenkavalier,* as well as *Così Fan Tutte* and the Countess in *The Marriage of Figaro,* at Salzburg later that summer. However, the morning after George and I arrived at the Österreichischer Hof to begin our stay in Salzburg, he received a phone call to inform him that his brother, Pepe, just forty-seven, had suffered a severe heart attack. George left immediately for Pepe's home in Brněnec, where he found his brother unable to speak, yet alert and showing with his eyes that he recognized George and was glad to have him at his side. Pepe died just a day later, on the eve of my *Così* premiere. I managed to get through opening night, then hurried to Pepe's funeral the next morning—then back again to Salzburg by August 9, for the *Rosenkavalier* premiere.

George loved his brother very much, but he rejoined me in Salzburg as soon as he could. Almost immediately, we switched from the Hof, in a busy part of town, to a small hotel in a quieter neighborhood. However, for both of us, worldly affairs continued to intrude on our private grief: my performing commitments, as well as social obligations. In Salzburg we encountered a number of interesting people, including Francesco von Mendelssohn and his sister, Eleonora, the great-grandchildren of the composer Felix. Though their father and other family members had gone into banking, both Francesco and Eleonora had inherited a talent for music, he playing cello, she piano. (The goddaughter of Eleonora Duse, she was also a well-known actress.) Eleonora was staying that summer in a castle owned by her ex-husband; she had rented half of the property to Raimund von Hofmannsthal, the son of *Rosenkavalier*'s librettist, Hugo von Hofmannsthal. Raimund's wife at the time was the former Alice Astor.

All of these distinguished people were terribly nice, and we could hardly refuse a generous invitation, but they seemed neither to know nor to care whether they were throwing an intimate lunch (which is what George and I expected) or a large party, with many people coming and going (which is what we got). Nobody was introduced to anybody else, and both the luncheon and a subsequent evening party lasted several hours, much too late for me, in particular, because I had to sing the next day. At last, George and I slipped out unnoticed, or so we thought, until we were preparing for bed and heard a knock at the door of our hotel room. Alice von Hofmannsthal stood there with two enormous dogs. She apologized to us for not seeing us off earlier. When she had left, I said, "Perhaps we should have stayed at the Österreichischer Hof after all," and George and I promised each other to decline any further invitations if we possibly could.

Two days later, Eleonora came to us, exclaiming, "Maestro Toscanini is coming this afternoon, and you must come also!" Goodness, who could resist that? I had never met the great conductor, and so George and I accepted. We reached Eleonora's garden just as Toscanini and his wife, Carla, arrived. As we all took the staircase to a reception room, Eleonora rushed ahead, took a painting from the wall, and thrust it into the Maestro's hands. "Please take this token of thanks for joining us here today," she said.

Toscanini was taken aback: this was a beautiful painting of Venice by Guardi. "I cannot possibly accept!" he protested, but Eleonora insisted.[9]

She was a passionate creature, always in love with somebody, and (it was rumored) quite in love with Toscanini himself. She died quite young in New York City, reportedly a suicide. I shall always be grateful to her for introducing me to the Maestro, who would have such an important influence on me.

The last *Figaro* closed the festival, then opened the Staatsoper season two days later. The very next day, I performed *The Bartered Bride* again with Tauber, and with Krips conducting, and I rounded off this busy schedule with a quick trip to meet with Bruno Walter in Prague, who was conducting there. He asked me to sing the role of Euridice in Gluck's *Orfeo ed Euridice* at the Vienna Staatsoper. I agreed, and with a few weeks free—finally—I retreated to Liteň, where I learned the score with an accompanist.

Working with Bruno Walter was a delight, and I found him unique among conductors, because he seemed to love every note of the music. He wanted to inspire in us the same enthusiasm, and in this task he succeeded mightily. For those first performances of *Orfeo* in the fall of 1935, Kerstin Thorborg, the excellent Swedish mezzo-soprano, took the title role. She not only sang beautifully, but also acted the part very convincingly. The production also benefited from the dance sequences, choreographed by Margarethe Wallmann.

That season I worked for the first time with several conductors with whom I would go on to perform many times. The first was Victor de Sabata, in a concert with the Prague Philharmonic, and he invited me to sing again with him when he returned to Prague the next year. This was the start of a very nice friendship. Critics sometimes compared him to Toscanini, and with good reason. He possessed great imagination, and I remember a performance of Ravel's *Boléro* when the audience went wild.

Again with the Prague Philharmonic, but in London in November 1935, I sang for the first time with Václav Talich, the first Czech conductor to earn an international reputation. For our concert, I won praise from the critic of the London *Times,* who called me "an extremely accomplished singer [who] also commands the beauties of simplicity" and "an artist who adds an attractive personality and appearance to a voice as clear as it is rich." While in London, I met with Sir Thomas Beecham to discuss my appearing at Covent Garden—and with the producer Alexander Korda, who wanted to cast me in a film.[10]

London welcomed me warmly whenever I performed there, though some critics seemed to believe each time that I was making my local debut. After a concert with Richard Tauber at Queen's Hall in the fall of 1935, the critic of the *Daily Telegraph* called me "unheralded," and said that our duet from *Butterfly* "gave final proof that the winning of a reputation overnight does occasionally happen outside the pages of a novelette"—though he was aware of my career in Austria, describing me as "already . . . the idol of the Viennese, no mean judges."

As my career became more and more truly international, I was called on to appear at more and more diplomatic events, and I realized that the early invitations from President Masaryk had given me a good education. In the summer of 1935, Austria's president, Wilhelm Miklas, awarded me the title of Kammersängerin. (The closest English equivalent is "court singer," and it's still considered a great honor, long after the imperial court came to an end.) Dr. Edvard Beneš invited me to sing at a special concert in Geneva for the League of Nations, of which he was president (as well as Czechoslovakia's foreign minister, at the time).[11] At that concert, on September 20, 1935, Rudolf Firkušný performed, and at the ball that evening I danced with the Aga Khan and with Maxim Litvinov, the Soviet foreign commissar—men whose roles on the world stage could hardly have been more opposite.

Returning to Vienna in December, I attended a concert, beautifully conducted by Maestro Toscanini. After the performance, I went backstage, where he suggested that we meet again before he left, so that he could discuss a possible engagement for me in Salzburg. George arranged a dinner with the Toscaninis, as well as another couple, the Polish ambassador and his wife. Even before dinner, Toscanini asked me to sing Pamina in *The Magic Flute* with him in Salzburg, in the 1937 season. Of course I told him that I would adore singing with him; he warned me that nothing was settled yet, but he wanted to plan ahead. I was in seventh heaven.

That year we celebrated Christmas with the family in Liteň, and it was an especially happy time, because our Greek trip had meant missing out the previous year. George and I prepared something special for our daughter. We had a beautiful Christmas tree in the living room, which was on the ground floor. As we assembled to exchange presents, a servant brought in a little Shetland pony directly from the terrace. Jarmilka was so flabbergasted that she started to cry with happiness, and that night she had a fever. She was so excited, but after a good night's sleep, everything was all right.

She was a "lucky child," as we say, born on a Sunday, and she had everything a three-year-old could dream of. She had two dogs, two Angora rabbits with red eyes, and a pair of pet roebucks in the garden. Unfortunately, the male roebuck became vicious when he grew up and started rutting; we had to return him to the nearby woods. Once Jarmilka saw some peacocks and decided that she wanted them. We gave her two beautiful birds, but they made such ugly noises that we had to give them away.

When Jarmilka was about four years old, I sang again with Victor de Sabata, who visited Liteň several times and played piano for her. He even gave her a little instruction, and she caught on very quickly. From then on, I found her trying to play with her little fingers what he had taught her. She later took piano lessons, and played very well, and her appreciation for music grew as she did.

The life of a child can be greatly enriched by integrating music with work in other fields. I firmly believe that every child should be taught the elements of music, early and accurately. I am aware that music lessons often necessitate financial sacrifices for a family. But it is money well invested, and it returns the best kind of interest: a knowledge that no one can take away from the child.

Do not worry if the child shows no great talent. I am sure that everyone who studied a musical instrument, or took voice or dance lessons, grows to adulthood with an appreciation of music more profound than that of the person who did not study at all. Music is our children's heritage. Give them every chance to understand and to learn it. Encourage them. Through music, a child experiences his or her innermost self, tastes the joy of creating, and enters into a world of beauty. Today, perhaps more than ever before, children need to know this other side of life. Music is the best recreation in the world.

1936 began with some unusual repertory for me. First, the conductor Felix von Weingartner asked me to sing all three heroines in *The Tales of Hoffmann,* as well as the mute role of Stella, with Lothar Wallerstein directing. Having sung Olympia and Antonia already, I had to learn only Giulietta. Still, it was a great challenge to sing all three roles in the same evening, and I was pleased when the press was favorable. One critic wrote, "The charm of the doll, the seduction of the Venetian adventuress, the tragedy of the singer Antonia . . . Jarmila Novotná, with all the intensity of which she is capable, has portrayed each vividly in sound, in gesture, and at last through her own beauty in its versatile variations."

In April I began rehearsals with Bruno Walter for Hugo Wolf's *Corregidor.* Walter put the blood of his soul into his conducting, and achieved what the great lieder composer, in his pathetic and helpless way, probably aimed at. The score has something especially lovable about it, but I found it too lyric for a large operatic stage. At least I was given the beautiful song "In dem Schatten meinen Locken" (literally, In the shadow of my locks of hair) from the *Spanisches Liederbuch,* which Wolf incorporated into the opera. This song is one of the treasures of the lieder repertoire. I also had to dance a fandango, to the delight of the audience. My partner, singing the role of Tio Lukas, was Alfred Jerger, not only a very good singer but also an extremely gifted actor. Gunnar Graarud sang Corregidor, and Kerstin Thorborg sang the small but impressive part of his wife, Mercedes. I adored singing with these artists.

For Salzburg that year we were lucky to find most agreeable accommodations, a house owned by our friend Count Alois Auersperg in the Hellbrunner Allee. We had only to bring our servants; otherwise, we found everything we needed, and we had room enough to invite guests to stay with us.

My first assignment was again the Countess in *The Marriage of Figaro,* and two days later we premiered *Così Fan Tutte.* Felix von Weingartner conducted both performances. We all liked his work quite well, but his performances always lasted longer than those of any other conductor in the pit, because he favored very slow tempi. To sing "Porgi amor," the Countess's aria from Act II, was a real breath exercise.

In this opening aria, the Countess bemoans the fading of her husband's love, praying that his affections return to her—if not, she would prefer to die. Similarly, in her other great aria, "Dove sono," she speaks of moments of love now lost. I see the Countess as a faithful, loving wife, and yet she also receives, with no displeasure at all, young Cherubino's adoration. I find this delightfully human. At the end, when she forgives her philandering husband, his plea ("Contessa, perdona") marks a turning point that leads to a real apotheosis of all that is good and decent in the human heart—and all that is beautiful in Mozart's music.

What is the secret of Mozart's music? It is its extraordinary emotional diversity. The singer must be able to express what Mozart clearly put into his music. Take for instance the two arias for the Queen of the Night. These are not only technical showpieces, they are expressions of heartbreak and entreaty in the first, and fury and vengeance in the second. The singer must have these emotions at her command, or else she is miscast in the role. It is not an easy task to sing Mozart well, but how rewarding!

When we began rehearsals for *Orfeo ed Euridice,* I brought Jarmilka to rehearsals. When she saw me lying on the stage, she began to cry and yelled, "Don't do anything to my mommy!" The performance, with Bruno Walter, was critically acclaimed, and the conductor Václav Talich sent me a lovely note afterward, telling me that he now understood how wide-ranging my talent was and concluding, "I bow to you in deep admiration."

On August 11, we gave *Corregidor* again, with much greater success than in Vienna. After the performance, I attended a party hosted by Max Reinhardt at Leopoldskron, with several remarkable guests, including Elliot Roosevelt, Jack Warner, and the playwrights Felix Salten and Ferenc Molnár.[12] The great cellist Emanuel Feuermann and Princess Marie-José of Belgium, an excellent pianist, played a duet as if they had been concertizing together all their lives.

What a treat that was, and yet I preferred the intimate affairs at Leopoldskron, when only a few people from theater and the arts were present, and the after-dinner conversation sparkled. Reinhardt was never a great talker; he preferred to listen, which is also a great art. A man named Rudolf Kommer helped him to arrange these "soirées monstres," as he called them. Plump, almost hairless, with deep-set, wise eyes and mocking lips, Kommer was always the heart of the company. He had a dry wit and seemed to know everybody; Reinhardt's son Gottfried called him his father's "*maître de plaisir.*"

Jack Warner was not the only person from Hollywood in Salzburg that season. MGM had tried earlier to sign me to a contract, and now, during the Festival, the studio sent Robert G. Ritchie to persuade me. However, I simply didn't want to go to America. I showed Mr. Ritchie around Salzburg and obtained invitations for him to some of the loveliest homes, but my response was still no. He tried another, personal approach, and I think he was rather surprised when he failed. He had been closely linked to the MGM star Jeanette MacDonald, and in his way he was a pleasant, good-looking man. But it was all too naïve to think that he could succeed with me. Not long afterward, I met with Alexander Korda, who once again insisted that I film a screen test for him—and I once again refused. If making a movie could be done in such a way that I would not be separated from my husband and little daughter for an extended period, then I was happy to consider it. But otherwise, I preferred to concentrate on my singing.

Among other engagements in the fall, I returned to London for a concert at Queen's Hall and a great many social occasions. These concluded with a fancy-dress ball, hosted by the Austrian ambassador, after my concert. I didn't know what to wear, but Jan Masaryk lent me a beautiful folk costume, and it was a sensation. Of course, as things turned out, he and I had to perform a few Czech folk songs for the guests. Once again we were happy to play "cultural ambassadors" for Czechoslovakia.

Immediately after Christmas, George and I returned to Milan, where I was to make my debut at La Scala, singing Alice in *Falstaff,* with Victor de Sabata conducting. The critic of the *Corriere della Sera* described me as "a singer of very worthy theatricality and vocal line," one "who aroused the most lively appreciation from the audience." De Sabata was also conducting *Tristan* and some other operas that season, and he invited George and me to several rehearsals. At one rehearsal, George and I sat in the first row, right behind him. Something went wrong in the orchestra, and de Sabata seemed to explode. But he paused, and I heard him softly saying to himself, "Stai buono, Victor" (Be good, Victor). Then he continued without making any further remarks. I wondered what Toscanini would have done.

The day after my debut, George and I were pleased to meet Alma Mahler and her husband, the writer Franz Werfel, who, having written *Verdi: A Novel of the Opera* (1924), was now preparing a second biography of the composer.[13] Alma was a fascinating woman, possessed of intelligence and sparkling personality. Together we lunched at the restaurant Biffi, which was their favorite spot; they were very good friends with de Sabata as well. George had to leave soon after, but while I remained in Milan I was able to visit Raffaele Tenaglia and Emilio Piccoli, as well as Felice Lattuada, whose opera I had sung, and other acquaintances I had made during my earlier stays in the city.

In the spring of 1937 I sang for the first time with Jussi Bjoerling. Together in Vienna, we performed *Bohème* and *Butterfly,* and I found him a very agreeable partner. I always enjoyed singing with him, and I was delighted when he sang Rodolfo to my Mimì at my Metropolitan Opera debut a few years later. Once again at the Staatsoper I sang the heroines in *Hoffmann,* and this time something funny happened. I had the habit of checking all the props on stage before every act, to make sure that everything was prepared; this way, I could devote all my attention to my performance, without worrying about any other matters. And so, just before Act II began, I checked all the props, then returned to my dressing room to wait for my call. Unfortunately, the stage manager had seen me onstage, and thinking that I had remained there, he rang up the curtain. Through my dressing-room door, I heard the first bars of the Barcarolle. I ran as fast as I could, but it was a very elaborate set, representing the terrace of a Venetian palazzo. I should have glided slowly down a long staircase, but the Nicklausse had started singing already. Instead of losing precious time, I chose a shortcut, not realizing that I was walking right on the waters of the Grand Canal. The audience had a good time laughing.

I also sang *Rosenkavalier* and *Traviata*, in which Anton Dermota made his debut as Alfredo; in later years, he became the Staatsoper's leading tenor. Richard Tauber and I repeated *Giuditta* several times, as well as *The Bartered Bride*. When I look in my diary, I see that almost daily George and I had social engagements, and we went to museums and the theater quite often.

I was very lucky that Teta was still with us, after more than four years working as Jarmilka's nurse. Teta never asked for a vacation, though I offered many times to find a temporary replacement so that she could visit her many relatives in Moravia. She was perfectly happy just to take off the occasional afternoon to visit her brother, a well-known physician in Prague. I just cannot imagine what life would have been like without her, and she became even dearer to us when we left for America.

As the season continued, I sang my first Pamina in *The Magic Flute*, with Josef Krips conducting. Maestro Toscanini had declared that he wanted to see the Viennese production before he conducted it in Salzburg, and so President Miklas invited him to join him for the premiere. This performance was on a Sunday, and so we had an early curtain, seven o'clock. But something strange happened. Seven o'clock came and went, and yet we didn't start. Seven-fifteen, and still nothing. We thought perhaps Toscanini was late. But no, he and President Miklas were sitting in their box. Then, at seven twenty-five, the curtain finally went up. What had happened? The principal flutist had forgotten about the early curtain!

The next day, Toscanini told me that he had enjoyed the performance and that he was glad I would be his Pamina. For that premiere, we had a marvelous cast, with Helge Rosvaenge as Tamino and Alexander Kipnis as

Sarastro. Also that season, I had the great joy of singing my beloved Tatyana in *Eugene Onegin,* under Bruno Walter's direction. Walter also conducted a *Marriage of Figaro* at that year's Maggio Musicale festival. I sang Cherubino in the Teatro alla Pergola, a delightful setting for this opera. The theater's proportions are so perfect that in these lovely surroundings the transparent quality of the music became more evident than ever. Bruno Walter became the medium that breathed new life into the proceedings, and our cast included Mariano Stabile as Figaro and Mafalda Favero as Susanna. It was unforgettably beautiful, and thanks to our success, I was asked to return the next year to sing Antonia in *Tales of Hoffmann.*

One social engagement from that Florence season stands out: a luncheon given by Countess Carolina Rasponi, whose son, Lanfranco, later became an important press agent in America, with all the most prominent opera stars under contract—including me. After the premiere of *Figaro,* many other members of Florentine society came backstage to greet me, and the mayor of Florence asked me to see his gardens, reputed to be the most beautiful in Florence. I promised to come the next evening. George joined me, expecting to see some of his own Florentine friends, but no, we were quite alone with the mayor. I could see from his face that he was quite surprised to see me with my husband. He maintained his composure, however, and asked his sister, the Contessa della Gherardesca, to serve tea. It was really funny.

George and I made a quick trip to Venice on the way home, but soon enough I was off to England for a private recital, then a return to Vienna for another performance of *Orfeo ed Euridice.* Then I took a short but well-deserved vacation at Liteň before the start of the Salzburg Festival on July 15.

Those of you who have visited Salzburg know what an enchanting place it is. The many lakes, large and small, look as if the Creator provided mirrors in which the lovely countryside could admire itself, and the atmosphere is delightfully serene. One dresses informally, in simple peasant dresses called dirndls, low-heeled shoes, and nice loden capes in case of rain—and even the rain there has its charm.

We again rented Count Alois Auersperg's house, and Jarmilka, almost five and increasingly interested in music, asked me to allow her to come to some rehearsals. There were plenty of rehearsals for her to see, because I had a heavy schedule in the 1937 Festival: Octavian in *Rosenkavalier,* Euridice in *Orfeo ed Euridice,* Cherubino in *Marriage of Figaro,* a concert in the Dom (where I sang a psalm by Czech composer Anatol Provazník), and Pamina in *The Magic Flute.* Rehearsals for *Magic Flute* started right away.

I must confess that we all were a little apprehensive, since we knew that Toscanini wasn't easily satisfied. I needn't have worried. I found that he clearly explained his wishes, and if we followed them, then he was among the easiest, nicest conductors I had known. The first rehearsal passed so pleasantly that we looked forward to the next one.

Maestro Toscanini was small. He had a beautiful face with a moustache, and his eyes were crowned with heavy eyebrows. Though he was very nearsighted, he never wore glasses. But when he looked at you, his eyes were penetrating. The stories of his temperament are countless, but just as easily he could be the most understanding, gentle man. To the men of the orchestra, he spoke half-German, half-Italian, usually in a low voice. But when there was a mistake, he reprimanded the guilty and sometimes roared in desperation. Even at such times, the men loved him, and, seeking his favor, they played better than ever.

At heart, Toscanini was a man of the theater, and it was a great joy to see all the characters come to life under his direction; he brought out moments of magic in every performance. I remember especially the Three Boys, who are often sung by women, but Toscanini chose instead to cast members of the Vienna Boys Choir. The sound and their appearance were just heavenly. The rest of the cast included Helge Rosvaenge as Tamino, Willi Domgraf-Fassbaender as Papageno, Julie Osvath as the Queen of the Night, and Alexander Kipnis as Sarastro.

What was the secret that made everyone try to give his best to Maestro Toscanini? What did he demand of us? Above all, precision, but not only technical precision: our music had to be animated spiritually. And melody reigned above all, like Heaven over the Earth. Toscanini sang along with the singers and the orchestra from beginning to end, and he demanded the clearest diction, whether we were singing or speaking. *The Magic Flute* contains a great deal of spoken dialogue, and though it seems incredible, he knew every word by heart. When I asked how it was possible for him to learn the text, though he didn't really speak German, he answered, "That's the wisdom of age." Not of old age, I would say, but of eternal youth! If the world were still ruled by gods, he would have to be the God of Music. But he was that anyway.

The performance received rave reviews, and Maestro was very happy. As a reward, he sent me a photo, and a few days later a brief letter with what he insisted was a better photo, and the promise of a still-better photo yet to come.

The schedule of rehearsals and performances was quite intense. Luckily, we didn't need a full orchestra rehearsal for *Orfeo,* because we had just sung it in Vienna, and Bruno Walter rehearsed us with piano only. *The Marriage of Figaro* required quite a lot of rehearsal, because we had a new cast, this time under Walter's direction. Now I sang Cherubino, with Ezio Pinza as Figaro, Mariano Stabile as the Count, Aulikki Rautawara as the Countess, and Esther Rethy as Susanna. Several newspaper critics wrote that they had never seen on any stage such an ensemble of beautiful people, especially the three women.

I adored singing Cherubino, whose liveliness and constantly changing moods appealed to me enormously. His adorably innocent sensuality brings mischief and a gay spirit to the atmosphere. Mozart had a musical sense of gesture and a consideration for stage timing unusual even among the finest composers. In Mozart, an interlude is not simply an interlude. It is usually a cue for the performer to move or react in a particular way, and an alert actor can easily guess what the composer had in mind. Under Bruno Walter's loving direction, all the aristocratic loveliness of the music came to life, and with each performance I found, or let's say I improvised, some new details. This was great fun. For instance, in Act II, when the Count bursts into the Countess's room, Cherubino must hastily put on his coat. At one performance, I put the coat on backwards, so that when I put my arms in the sleeves, I couldn't move them. The audience laughed and enjoyed this bit, and Herbert Graf, our stage director, used it in later productions as if it were his idea.

After my concert in the Dom, I invited the composer Anatol Provazník to a lunch that George and I gave for Maestro Toscanini and Max Reinhardt. I was told that this was the first time these two geniuses had met privately. I am really sorry that I didn't keep a guestbook, with their signatures. But I do have a photo of Toscanini and Reinhardt as a souvenir of our party.[14]

Reinhardt invited us several times to Leopoldskron, and one day he called to ask me to come by that afternoon, because someone wanted to meet me. That guest was Louis B. Mayer, the head of MGM, who was in Salzburg for only one day. He very much wanted to discuss a contract with me, and he wanted to show me MGM's latest movie with Jeanette MacDonald and Nelson Eddy, to let me see for myself what the studio could do for me. However, the only copy he had brought was in Budapest, and Mr. Mayer invited me to meet him there as soon as possible. I had to sing *Rosenkavalier* the next day, but then George and I drove to meet with Mr. Mayer, Bob Ritchie, and two lawyers.

The film, *Maytime,* was indeed quite lovely, and the offer more attractive than I had expected: a five-year contract, beginning at $1,000 a week, and after two years, my salary would go up. Five years was a reasonable amount of time, Mr. Mayer explained, because the studio would see a return on the investment put into publicity for me; MGM would not want to pay to make me a star and then see me go to another studio after only a year or two. I was concerned about leaving my family for such a long time, but Mr. Mayer agreed to give me three months' leave every year to come back to Europe. One other condition stipulated that I would be at the disposal of MGM at all times, which would mean that I could accept no opera engagements. That was the hardest part to swallow, and I told him I would have to think it over. George and I talked it over, and then I returned to Mr. Mayer and said, "I am sorry, but my answer is no."

We returned to Salzburg; the final performance of *The Magic Flute* was August 31. I could not realize that this would be Toscanini's farewell to the Festival—as well as my own. Though Hitler's occupation of Austria was still several months away, already many artists were looking toward America. Reinhardt had already transferred his activities to Broadway and Hollywood, and when I returned to Salzburg, he urged me to accept Mr. Mayer's offer.[15] Naturally I trusted Reinhardt's judgment, and now I began to question my decision. I wrote to Maestro de Sabata for his advice. He replied with confidence that my contract would not constrain me as much as I feared, and he believed in the power of film as an art form; the principal consideration, he said, should be my family's welfare.

With these things in mind, George and I returned to Liteň, just as the death of President Masaryk was announced. Jan Masaryk invited us to Lány, where the president was lying in state. He took us to the bedroom where his father had died. "Father died as harmoniously as he lived," Jan said. "His death was serene, like his life. It was like a solemn symphony that proceeds from rousing *fortissimo* to *piano* and to *pianissimo.* I am glad that he wasn't aware of his final struggle. He already needed a rest, even this last and eternal rest." I found it revealing that, even at such a time, Jan expressed himself in musical terms.

On the night table lay a bunch of violets, the last flowers on which President Masaryk had set his eyes. Jan gave them to me, saying, "The president liked you very much, and certainly he would have wanted you to have these."

George and I attended President Masaryk's funeral, September 21, 1937. All the diplomats and other dignitaries assembled at Hradčany Castle in Prague, and on a lovely, sunny day, we sat in the courtyard for the parting ceremony. Then we drove to Lány for the burial. All along the route, people waited and wept openly. The president truly had been a father to the nation.

Two days later, I celebrated my thirtieth birthday.

Around this time, I received a letter from Heinz Tietjen, who was still intendant at the Berliner Staatsoper. He asked whether I would like to sing again with the company, but as I was fully booked for the rest of the year, I promised to let him know later. To tell the truth, I found it a very delicate question, and I spoke about it with Edvard Beneš, who by this time was president of Czechoslovakia. He said he had nothing against my singing in Berlin, and that I might even help to improve the political situation between the two countries. So I wrote to accept Tietjen's offer, and we agreed that I would sing *Rosenkavalier, Traviata,* and *The Bartered Bride* in February 1938.

I traveled a great deal in the next several weeks, going to Vienna to *The Magic Flute* as well as two *Bohème* performances with Jan Kiepura, a sympathetic partner and a great favorite of Viennese audiences. In Amsterdam, I sang Octavian under Erich Kleiber, a flexible conductor with a genuine Viennese spirit. This was a special Festival performance of the Concertgebouw Orchestra, and we were informed that there would be neither a prompter nor a page to send us onstage. This didn't bother us at all, although each artist came from a different opera house: I from Vienna; Viorica Ursuleac, the Marschallin, from Munich; Erna Berger, the Sophie, from Berlin; and so on. But each of us knew her part so well that we had no problems, and in rehearsal—only one on the stage and one with the orchestra—everything went well.

Then came the performance. Act I had ended, and I waited in my dressing room for Act II to begin. It seemed a very long intermission, but I knew that Queen Wilhelmina was to attend. Perhaps she is receiving in her box, I thought. I had completely forgotten that I wouldn't be called to the stage when suddenly someone opened the door and yelled, "Mme. Novotná, they've started—you should be onstage already!" I hurried as fast as I could, too late to make the full effect of my entrance but present, at least, to sing the first line of the Presentation Scene, "Mir ist die Ehre widerfahren" (The honor falls to me). Then I realized that, in my haste, I had forgotten my sword, which I would need for the fight with Baron Ochs later in the act. But I couldn't leave the stage.

What to do? When the Majordomo started to make an exit, I approached him, whispering, "Bring me my sword from the dressing room." Luckily, he understood, and a little while later, a window stage left opened just a little, and I could see someone standing there with my sword. I had to remain in place stage right, however. I waited until Octavian gets angry with Ochs and sings, "Hinaus, hinaus, und kein Adieu" (Get out, get out, and no farewell). With these words, I went to the window as if to get a breath of fresh air. I got hold of the sword, and I was saved. I hoped no one noticed, and in fact Kleiber said nothing afterward about my difficulty. But the next day the queen sent me a large box of orchids—along with a papier-mâché sword.

On that same trip, I briefly met the former kaiser, Wilhelm II, who lived in nearby Doorn, following his abdication at the end of World War I. What sort of omen this might be, as I prepared to return to Berlin, I did not know.

We celebrated Christmas and then spent two weeks in St. Moritz. I took skiing lessons, and Jarmilka tried her luck sledding with dear Teta, but the greatest fun we all had together was a ride in a horse-drawn sleigh. However, I came down with what was later diagnosed as influenza, and by the time I got to Berlin, on January 27, I felt quite miserable with fever. I had to cancel *Traviata* and sang *Rosenkavalier* only a week later, and then *The Bartered Bride.* Among some critics, my reception was as warm as it had been during my first seasons in Berlin, and H. H. Stuckenschmidt wrote in the *B.Z. am Mittag,* "The beauty of this woman can dominate an entire opera not merely through her appearance, her voice, or the bounty of her musical taste. It is the sum of all these values and moreover the wonderfully human quality, the self-contained simplicity which permits no theatrics, which possesses the charm of youth without cosmetic, and a natural spirituality which gains its most noble and varied expression through acting. . . . It is inconceivable to think that our great Staatsoper might ever again do without this artist." Over the next several weeks, I returned to Prague and sang a concert at the Salle Pleyel in Paris, making my way back to Vienna, where I sang *The Bartered Bride* with Tauber once again, and another *Giuditta* on March 7. Then came the fateful evening of March 11. That night I was to sing Tatyana in *Onegin.* Even before arriving at the theater, I sensed restlessness in the air. We knew that Austria's chancellor, Kurt von Schuschnigg, would deliver a radio address, and during the first intermission we were able to hear it. Schuschnigg aimed to strengthen the country internally, resisting Hitler's attempt to unite Austria with Germany. Violent riots had broken out as a result, and so that evening, during our first intermission, Schuschnigg declared that there would be a plebiscite on Austrian independence. By the second intermission, we heard reports that Schuschnigg had resigned. We didn't have to wait long to see what would befall Austria. As we emerged from the opera house, hordes of German soldiers were already marching through Vienna. Schuschnigg had been arrested, and the Nazis would hold him prisoner until his liberation by American troops in May 1945. (In 1947, he settled in the United States. I met him in St. Louis, where he was a university professor, in 1952.)[16] The Anschluss had begun.

On March 12, George and I drove to Semmering, an hour or so south of Vienna, where my mother-in-law was staying. On the way, we passed hundreds of trucks filled with German soldiers on their way from Linz, where, it seems, they had been massing in anticipation of the takeover. George's mother decided to leave immediately for Czechoslovakia, and we drove first to Vienna, where I was scheduled to sing *Giuditta* March 15 and 17. But on March 14, Hitler made his entry into Vienna, and the Staatsoper canceled the performances. Because I was contracted with the Staatsoper as a guest artist, we were able to leave the next day for Prague, where I had two engagements.

In retrospect, it seems strange that I returned to Vienna, performing *Bohème, Rosenkavalier,* and *Butterfly,* exactly as planned. Except for German soldiers everywhere, the city seemed to have returned to normal. After another brief trip to Czechoslovakia for performances in Prague and Plzeň, I was back in Vienna by April 19, singing *Rigoletto, The Magic Flute,* and *Traviata,* all in one week. Then—still as if little had changed—I proceeded to Florence.

I brought Jarmilka with me because I believed that, at five-and-a-half years old, she was ready to see the beautiful Tuscan capital. Teta was with us as well, so that the two could sightsee or amuse themselves as they pleased while I was busy rehearsing Antonia in *The Tales of Hoffmann.*

During this time, Hitler paid a state visit to Mussolini in Rome, and they both came to Florence. All along the motorcade route, building façades were whitewashed, and loudspeakers were installed. For a few days, the welcoming committee tried out the sound system, playing recordings of crowds cheering, "Evviva Mussolini! Evviva Hitler!" Something went wrong, however, and when it came time for the two leaders' drive through the streets, the loudspeakers didn't work, and though crowds dutifully lined the streets, a stony silence prevailed. Suddenly the loudspeakers worked again, but one heard only a fragment of the recorded cheers: "Evviva Musso—" before the sound went dead again. *Muso* in Italian means "snout" or "muzzle," but unlike the English word, this "muzzle" can mean "loudmouth." Someone in the crowd began to laugh, but he caught himself quickly. Surely he realized that he could be punished harshly. I did not attend the gala performance at the opera that night.

George arrived for the last performance of *Tales of Hoffmann,* and we left for Capri, which we found enchanting. We returned to Liteň by car, driving through Bologna and Rimini—very much the sort of trip we had grown accustomed to taking. Despite the political changes, we still pursued our plans and went about our daily life more or less normally.

However, when I prepared to return to Vienna for a gala performance of *Rosenkavalier* on June 14, I had a very disagreeable experience. As the train arrived at the Czech border, the customs officer asked me to get off the train and to take all my luggage with me. I protested, to no avail.

By now everything in Austria was under German control, and the officer was German. His men went through all my belongings, even reading fan letters that I had just received and hadn't even opened yet. Then the officers ordered me into a special room, where a female attendant stripped me. Naturally, she didn't find anything, but just as she finished, I heard the whistle of the train as it departed for Vienna. I dressed as fast as I could and prepared to take the next train back to Prague. "I will never return to the Staatsoper," I told the customs officers, "and I will hold you responsible." I never found out what they were looking for, though I did not imagine it had anything to do with me personally.

I should have taken this incident as a pretext to stay away from Austria altogether. However, when I got home to Liteň, I called the Staatsoper, told them of my humiliation, and said that it would be impossible to return to Vienna without a safe-conduct pass. The very next day, a man from the Austrian embassy personally delivered such a pass, and with it I left again for Vienna. All the German bigwigs attended our *Rosenkavalier* gala. As soon as I had completed my contracted performances, I left for good.

A short time later, I left for Scandinavia, beginning with Stockholm: one concert in the outdoor auditorium Grona Land (which means "Green Land"), and the next day a radio concert. As always on my travels, I liked to explore as much as my schedule permitted, and so I spent a full day walking around this elegant and sophisticated port city, deserving its nickname "Venice of the North" for its network of waterways. While on one of my walks, a car passed me, and I recognized Greta Garbo and Leopold Stokowski. I hadn't met either of them yet, nor even seen them up close, so this was quite a sensation for me. My next stop was Malmö, where George joined me, and we proceeded to Båstad for two days by the sea. I was surprised to discover the Swedes' habit of swimming in the nude, a huge contrast to Italy at the time, where not only women but also men were required to wear bathing suits that covered the entire torso. *Tempi passati!*

We went on to Copenhagen for two concerts at the famous Tivoli Gardens, then back to Sweden for a final concert in Gothenburg. I was glad to board the train home immediately after the concert ended: I was pregnant again, in my fifth month, and all this travel tired me. Why did I agree to the tour in the first place? Well, it is very difficult in the midst of one's career to refuse certain engagements, and besides, concerts are not as demanding as staged operatic performances. Furthermore—I enjoyed it.

We returned to a crisis in Czechoslovakia. Britain's Lord Runciman had come to mediate a dispute between the government and Konrad Henlein, the Nazi Party leader in the Sudetenland. During the fortnight of negotiations, George and I were on the periphery, because Jan Masaryk attended the talks and asked us to invite two members of the British delegation to spend the weekend with us in the country. Under orders from Berlin, Henlein refused to cooperate with the Czech government, and by the end of August, Runciman returned to London without an agreement. This failure heightened a certain anxiety in the air, although in many ways life went on normally for us.

On September 4, 1938, while George and his friends went off on a shooting party, I heard a radio broadcast in which Hermann Göring described President Beneš as "a little *Knirps*" (a derogatory word for a little fellow—perhaps the best English equivalent would be "shrimp") and belligerently threatened to show him who held real power. When George came home, he and his friends and I talked about Göring's broadcast, and we agreed that it was rather alarming. In these circumstances, Beneš could not remain silent, and some sort of escalation seemed inevitable. Because I was pregnant, George and I agreed that it was best for me to leave the country, in the event that Germany declared war. I decided to go to London, and our friend Inge Lazansky, who had many good friends in England, would meet us there. Jarmilka, her nurse, and I were hardly the only ones fleeing the country, and we shared our train compartment with Mrs. Tomáš Bata, wife of the shoe manufacturer.

We checked into the Goring Hotel (of all names) in London, where Inge found us on September 15. She knew so many people that immediately we had many social engagements, embassy luncheons and weekends in the country. All this sounds very gay, but it was really a somber time. The fate of Czechoslovakia hung in the balance, and everyone discussed the situation wherever we went. Hitler had launched violent attacks on Czech authorities in the Sudetenland, and on September 15, at the very moment Neville Chamberlain arrived at Berchtesgaden to meet with Hitler, Henlein delivered a proclamation demanding that Germany annex the Sudetenland. Lord Runciman, back in London, persuaded Chamberlain that only capitulation could prevent Hitler from launching a full-scale invasion of Czechoslovakia. With the Germans and Italians, the British and French drew up terms, called the Munich Agreement, which they insisted that President Beneš accept without amendment. He refused, but on September 30 the Great Powers signed the Munich Agreement and forced their decision on Czechoslovakia. President Beneš promptly resigned. It was a dreadful situation.

That same day, an English friend from the embassy in Prague arrived, telling me that he was one of the last people allowed to leave the country, and that Czechoslovakia was fully mobilized and ready to fight. He brought with him a letter from George, who had been drafted as an officer and was unsure when he would be able to see us again. This of course made me very anxious and unable to sleep, and the next morning at about nine o'clock, my labor pains began. This in itself was alarming, because my doctor in London had advised me that I would not deliver yet for another month. I hurried to the clinic, and early in the morning on October 1, our son was born. He was tiny, weighing not even five pounds. But he was so perfect, and I was happy.

The next day, I telegraphed to Liteň with the news. I also wrote a long letter, in which I described my baby's beauty and perfection in such a manner that the family teased me about it long afterward. Two days later, Teta brought Jarmilka to see the baby, and our daughter took immediate possession of her brother, as if he were a new doll to play with. Teta energetically intervened, but in any case, the nurses allowed the baby out of their hands only for a short while. Because he was so little, he required special supervision at first.

So far from home, and with communication so difficult, I did not know when our family would be united. Thus it was a wonderful surprise when, on October 5, I heard a knock at the door—and there was George! He had received a week's leave, and on October 12 we had our son christened at a nearby church. Little George Sebastian Jan Josef Remigius Daubek's godfathers were Jan Masaryk and another friend, George Schicht. But his father had to return to Czechoslovakia the same day. I intended to join him there soon. Like so many others, I hoped that the annexation of the Sudeten might satisfy Hitler, and the rest of Czechoslovakia might remain independent.

Our friends George Schicht and his wife, Lene, urged me to stay with the children at Buckhurst, their estate, and I gratefully accepted. Their two sons, still quite young, took Jarmilka to play in the enormous gardens, where wild ducks, pheasants, and stags were kept not for shooting but for their sheer beauty. Every weekend, the Schichts invited friends to visit, and we stayed with them for almost a month. I left only a few times on short trips to London, chiefly to acquire a passport for my son. Robert Hadow, our good friend, took care of it, and the Foreign Minister, Lord Halifax, signed it himself. Inside was a photo of Georgie when he was just five days old; he still keeps it as a souvenir.

I also dined with Alexander Korda, who once again insisted that I make a film with him. Like the offer from MGM, Korda's proposal had begun to seem less unlikely, but I replied that I could do nothing for now, because my most important duty was to my baby.

As we prepared to make our way back to Czechoslovakia, Teta and my children and I stopped off in London, where Jan Masaryk invited us to stay at the embassy for a few days. We attended a concert by the Czech Philharmonic Orchestra at the Albert Hall, conducted by Václav Talich, as well as several parties, concluding with a luncheon also attended by George and Lene Schicht. I thanked them again for their help, and that same evening we left for home.

When we arrived back at Liteň, there was much rejoicing. My dear mother-in-law had invited my parents, my sister, and her husband, and they all admired little George, who even as a baby always smiled. My parents had bought a villa in Radotín, not far from Prague, where they grew fruits and vegetables in the garden and raised hens and rabbits (a stroke of luck because later, during the war, they would have enough to eat). Life seemed to resume its normal course. Even so, I was especially happy to receive a telegram from Maestro Toscanini, inviting me to sing *Traviata* with him at the New York World's Fair in May 1939. I accepted immediately.

As soon as the directors of the National Opera in Prague heard that I had returned, they invited me to sing Dvořák's *Rusalka* with the company. This was a wonderful assignment and, though I had sung Dvořák's songs and Rusalka's aria to the moon, a new role for me, as well. A fairy tale of a water sprite in love with a human prince, *Rusalka* was very little known outside

Czechoslovakia in those days. The score is romantic, filled with infectious rhythms, sensitivity of feeling, and great passion. Now, as I looked ahead to my debut in the United States, I remembered how consequential to Dvořák's career were the three years he spent teaching at the National Conservatory in New York, where he wrote his celebrated "New World" Symphony, incorporating the musical idioms of tribal cultures, Negro spirituals, and folk songs of European settlers. I asked Alfred Holeček, an excellent pianist who accompanied me in my recitals, to come to Liteň to help me prepare *Rusalka,* and I immersed myself in the exquisite melodies that characterize this work. After one performance each of *The Bartered Bride* and *Onegin,* I sang *Rusalka* for the first time on January 27, 1939. Oh, how I adore this opera!

But just three days later, George's niece, Mia Bromovska, and I departed on what we called my Balkan Tour, with stops in Belgrade, Zagreb, Bucharest, and Ljubljana. In Zagreb I was very pleasantly surprised to receive flowers and a congratulatory note from Milka Ternina, a great soprano who had sung with the Metropolitan Opera and was also the teacher of Zinka Milanov, soon to be a Metropolitan star in her own right. In Bucharest, Mia and I attended a traditional, very colorful Romanian wedding. We also received a large jar of caviar, on which Mia and I gorged ourselves on the train to Ljubljana. After breakfast, lunch, and dinner of caviar, we still had leftovers! I worried that the rest wouldn't keep, so I gave the jar to the train conductor—much to George's disappointment when he met me a few days later at Cannes.

We had come there for two performances of *The Marriage of Figaro* at the Théâtre du Casino Municipal in Monte Carlo, where I sang Cherubino with a wonderful cast: Mariano Stabile, Tancredi Pasero, Aulikki Rautawaara, and Margit Bokor. We enjoyed a rousing success. Little did we know that these would be the last performances that Bruno Walter would conduct in Europe before the war. He already had a French identity card, he told me, and he was departing soon for America.

Before my own departure for New York, I accepted an invitation from the Czechoslovak National Council to sing at a benefit on March 3 for the organization National Assistance to Refugees, under the patronage of our newly elected president, Dr. Emil Hácha. With performances from the violinist Jan Kubelík, the pianists Rudolf Firkušný and Alfred Holeček, and myself, this concert was not announced as a memorial for President Masaryk, though it was scheduled just days before his birthday, March 7. The audience clearly understood this as an occasion for an outpouring of feeling for our late president, and the concert became a spontaneous demonstration of national pride.

Again with Mia Bromovska as my companion, I left for New York two days later. We stopped in Paris so that we could send our luggage on to America, but I discovered that one trunk was missing—unfortunately, the one that contained my *Traviata* costumes. I called George, who made inquiries and learned that the trunk had been confiscated by the German authorities at the Czech border, though he didn't know why. He promised to send the trunk along as soon as possible, but by the time Mia and I got to Le Havre, it had not arrived. My first transatlantic crossing was a rough one, but at last the *Ile de France* arrived in New York late on March 14. We spent the night on board, disembarking in time to hear the horrible news: Hitler had invaded Czechoslovakia. My first glimpse of the Statue of Liberty was spoiled by the realization that my own country's liberty was lost.

I feared for my family, but luckily the next day I was able to reach George by telephone—a miracle, really. He reassured me that everyone was all right, and that, because we lived in the country, the German occupation had changed daily life very little so far.[17] Then George urged me to finish my obligations and come home as soon as I could.

That very afternoon I went to see Maestro Toscanini at the Hotel Astor, where he lived, and the next day we met with David Sarnoff, the president of NBC; and John Royal, a vice-president at NBC who also managed a subsidiary, the RCA Victor record company. They were the sponsors of the Maestro's performances at the World's Fair, including not only *Traviata* but also *Falstaff* and a few concerts. A new hall was being built at the fairground, and Sarnoff and Royal recommended that the Maestro inspect the facilities whenever he found the time.

Shortly thereafter, we began rehearsals at the Hotel Astor. It was an unforgettable time. Though I had sung Violetta more often than any other role, I discovered new meaning under Toscanini's tutelage. He showed me how Violetta weeps, and despite his lack of singing ability, he made the passage "Dite alla giovine" heartrending.

While in New York, I made contact again with Lanfranco Rasponi; also Mrs. Murray W. Crane, who had heard me in Salzburg, invited me to perform privately for friends at her home. There I met Mrs. Otto Kahn, the widow of the well-known Wall Street millionaire, who had backed Reinhardt's *The Miracle* (in 1924) and who had rescued the Metropolitan Opera at the height of the Great Depression. On other occasions I met such New York personalities as Grace Vanderbilt and Mr. and Mrs. Samuel Barlow, as well as Countess Mercati, the Duchess of Westminster, and the French writer André

Maurois, who had seen me in *La Chauve-souris.* I became good friends with the delightful and lively Mrs. Charles Marshall, who after her husband's death married Vincent Astor and became known universally as Brooke Astor. Through Rudolf Kommer, I met—at the same time—Anita Loos, Claire Booth Luce, and Anita Louise. Kommer must have worked hard to get these three "Looses" together. A few days later, he presented me to S. N. Behrman, the playwright; and to Laurence Olivier, who enchanted me with his knowledge of music.

I found the Americans so hospitable that, from the very first day, I felt at home. There was something to do almost every day. Yet perhaps the most memorable social event was an intimate celebration of Maestro Toscanini's seventy-second birthday, in the company of his wife, son, daughter-in-law, and daughter. I was grateful to be included in this family gathering, the Maestro was in a very good mood, and it was a lovely evening.

I also laid some important groundwork for my American career, when Marks Levine of National Concert and Artists Corporation, another NBC affiliate, agreed to represent me, during a meeting in David Sarnoff's office. At the same meeting, Sarnoff contracted me to sing at a concert that would open the World's Fair, on April 30.

But Maestro Toscanini still had not seen the new hall, and a few days after I signed with NCAC, a group of us (as well as Olin Downes, the music critic of the *New York Times;* and Samuel Chotzinov, head of musical supervision at NBC) accompanied him to the fairground. The Maestro seemed quite satisfied with the large, modern building—until an airplane flew overhead, followed almost immediately by another. Of course the planes made a terrible noise, but a representative for the fair told Toscanini that nothing could be done, not even during performances: They could not stop traffic at the New York Municipal Airport (which today is called La Guardia).

Two days later, Toscanini told me that, after great deliberation, he had decided to cancel all his appearances at the fair. However, he felt responsible for me, because he had invited me to New York, and so he promised to introduce me to Edward Johnson, the general director of the Metropolitan Opera. Once he had secured an appointment with Johnson, the Maestro asked me to meet him at the Hotel Astor, and together we walked the few blocks to the opera house.

What I didn't know was that, following a dispute with Johnson's predecessor, Giulio Gatti-Casazza, Toscanini had vowed never again to set foot in the Met. That was in 1915. He had broken this promise only once, in order to conduct a concert by the orchestra of La Scala in 1920. Nineteen years later, with me at his side, he returned to the Met for only the second time.

As we entered Johnson's office, the Maestro greeted him with a cry of "Lei è stupido!" (You are stupid).

"Why do I deserve that?" Johnson asked with a laugh.

"Why didn't you engage Novotná a long time ago?"

"We wanted her already in 1928," Johnson replied, "but she refused. Gatti-Casazza himself made the offer, after hearing her at Verona."

Toscanini said, "And what will you do now?"

"Sign her right away!" Johnson answered. This satisfied Toscanini, and I was overwhelmed. I called George immediately to tell him that I had signed for one year at the Metropolitan.

I had several days still to spend in New York, and so David Sarnoff invited me to attend some performances at NBC, including a lovely concert with the NBC Orchestra, conducted by Bruno Walter; and Gian Carlo Menotti's *The Old Maid and the Thief,* which was delightful. Finally, on April 30, I sang as scheduled for the opening of the World's Fair, on an NBC radio broadcast: "Sommi dei," from Handel's *Radamisto;* Haydn's "Cupid's Arrow"; and "Depuis le jour" from Charpentier's *Louise.*

The next day, Mrs. Crane hosted a party in my honor, inviting many people from the musical world. Edward Johnson was there, telling me that my contract was ready to sign. Olin Downes from the *Times,* Virgil Thomson from the *Herald Tribune,* Samuel Barber and Gian Carlo Menotti also attended, among many others, making this a very important evening for me. Mrs. Crane also took the opportunity to discuss with me my plans for Jarmilka's education while I was in New York. She was on the board of the Dalton School, and she assured me that Jarmilka would do very well there, despite the fact that she spoke no English. Dalton was a progressive school, Mrs. Crane said, where teachers lavished the kind of individual attention on the students that would bring my daughter along very rapidly.

So, when the *Ile de France* left New York Harbor on May 13, I felt satisfied that I had arranged a great deal for my future—even though I hadn't sung Violetta at the World's Fair.

George was waiting for us in Le Havre when the ship landed. I worried that the German occupation would have brought drastic changes to Czechoslovakia, but in Liteň life continued in ways that seemed normal. I was overjoyed to see the smiling face of little George, who was now eight months old. Jarmilka adored him and cared for him like a mother. I enjoyed fourteen beautiful days of relaxation before returning to the National Opera for *Rusalka,* which I repeated in Plzeň a few days later. The director of the Pilsner Brewing Company heard me there, and the next year, he marked my Metropolitan debut by sending me a basket of bottled beer instead of flowers. In June, I sang *Butterfly, Two Widows,* and *Traviata* in Prague, little knowing that these would be my last performances there for a long time.

I had been asked again to sing at Ostend, and I decided to bring the children with me. Since the Germans took over, it had become more difficult to obtain permission to travel. I told no one that I planned to leave for New York in September; I simply asked to take my children and their nurse with me on vacation by the seashore. I received permission, and set out with a great deal of luggage, including an entire trunk filled with orchestra parts that I would need for my concert. Separately, I sent ahead the large trunk that contained my costumes.

We set out from Plzeň, but soon our train came to a stop. Two other trains had collided near Mariánské Lázně (Marienbad), blocking all other traffic on the line. We were told to get off our train and to board another train some four hundred meters away, which would take us to our destination. This was indeed very difficult. Teta took the baby in a bassinette, while I tried to manage little Jarmilka, who was not yet seven years old, and three suitcases—not counting the trunk filled with the music. The terrain was uneven, and I saw that I would need help with the luggage. At last I found someone, and we boarded. But when I counted the bags, I saw that the trunk with the music was missing.

I explained to the conductor that I could not proceed to Ostend without my music, but my protests were to no avail. Not knowing what else to do, I marched to the front of the train and stood in front of the locomotive, announcing that I would not budge until they found my trunk. People grew angry and yelled at me, but my behavior yielded the desired fruit. Somebody retraced our steps and found my trunk in a ravine. Whoever had started to carry it had thrown it away because it was so heavy.

It was a relief to arrive in Ostend, and the festival that season featured several excellent artists who were also good friends, including Nathan Milstein, the violinist, and Erna Sack, the coloratura soprano. George met us, and Jarmilka's French tutor, Mlle. Céleste Sova, helped Teta with the children. I sang four concerts in total, then George and I went on to Scheveningen for *The Marriage of Figaro,* with Bruno Walter conducting and a cast that included Alexander Kipnis as Figaro and me as Cherubino, on August 31.

The next morning, we expected to see reviews of our performance in the newspapers. Instead, we saw the horrible news that Hitler had invaded Poland. Like lightning, the thought flashed through our minds: this means war. George and I hurried back to Ostend, where the children were waiting for us.

We decided that Teta and the children should leave with me for America. George wanted to return home, to care for his elderly mother; as soon as the situation had grown quieter, he said, he would follow us to New York. I surprised myself with my answer.

"No, no, my darling," I said. "You will go with us, and then, if things quiet down, you can return to Czechoslovakia. But now I will not go alone." He tried to reason with me, and told me we would talk more the next day.

I am not superstitious. But that night I had dreamed of a large, stately building, in the entrance of which stood George. I was already outside, and I beckoned to him to follow me. He hesitated, and so I took his hand to pull him out. In that moment, the building collapsed behind him.

The next morning, I told George about my dream, which seemed prophetic. The building was Czechoslovakia, and he must come with us, I said. At last he agreed, and we all drove to Brussels to ask the American consul for visitors' visas for him, Teta, and the children. (I still had my visa, from my trip in the spring.) The consul told us he would have to get clearance from the U.S. embassy in Prague, but he would try to let us know as quickly as possible.

We returned to Ostend, but when England declared war on Germany on September 3, our nervousness mounted. We returned to Brussels on September 5, but only on September 7 could the consul deliver the necessary visas. Jarmilka's French tutor left for Vienna, and George booked passage for the rest of us on the *New Amsterdam.* We waited several anxious days in Rotterdam, because the ship's American crew had gone on strike. Only on September 21 could we depart.

Because the channel had been mined, we slept with life jackets at the ready. Luckily, everything remained calm, and soon we were in the open ocean. On September 23, the orchestra began to play "Happy Birthday." I looked around, wondering whose birthday it could be, before I realized it was my own. I had completely forgotten.

2

In America during the War

While still aboard ship, we celebrated Jarmilka's birthday, and three days after we landed in New York, it would be little George's turn. Siegfried Hearst of the National Concert & Artists Corp. greeted us at the pier and conveyed the urgent request that I leave as quickly as possible for San Francisco. Because of the war in Europe, Italian singers had been obliged to return home, and now the San Francisco Opera sought replacements. Mr. Hearst offered me engagements for *Butterfly* and *Traviata,* which I accepted with the greatest pleasure. Teta and the children remained in New York, and George and I left for San Francisco by train on October 10. We found the accommodations surprisingly comfortable, and the three-day trip gave us the opportunity to view much of the country.

Once we arrived in San Francisco, Cleone Pottenger, a representative of NBC Artists Service, took us to our hotel, where newspaper reporters and photographers met us. Lanfranco Rasponi had contacted his friends in the area, so that I found a warm welcome. One friend, Eloise Martin, took me to a shop where I bought two beautiful kimonos because I wanted my Butterfly to look authentically Japanese. (My *Traviata* costumes, especially the Act III gown, were acknowledged still as the most beautiful ever seen, so there was no need to replace them.) And so with *Madame Butterfly* on October 18, 1939, I made my U.S. stage debut, opposite Michael Bartlett as Pinkerton. The next day, the critic of the *San Francisco News Bulletin* wrote: "Another star of great brilliance has been added to the galaxy of sopranos who sing the role of Madame Butterfly. Novotná's voice is light and of beautiful quality, fluent and expressive of the volatile emotions of the drama. Her 'Un bel dì' was a lyric of exultation and buoyant hope. She intoned it in a steady crescendo and arrived at a lovely climax, which brought her a salvo of applause from the audience. She proved a magnificent interpreter of the music." The next morning, NCAC called to ask me to leave immediately for St. Louis, where they needed a replacement for Bidu Sayão, who was to sing Mimì in *La Bohème* that Saturday night, but who had fallen ill. With the Hungarian conductor Laszlo Halasz and the tenor Nino Martini (also a film star and a pupil of

Giovanni Zenatello and his partner, Maria Gay), I would have only one rehearsal, and then be obliged to return immediately to San Francisco for the first day of rehearsal for *Traviata.* Well, when one is young, one does lots of foolish things—so I said yes. Because there was no time to lose, we had to travel both ways by plane, though I had never flown before. By the time we were airborne for St. Louis, night had fallen, and when I looked out the windows, I saw red lights on either side of the plane. "What a wonderful country this America is," I said to George. "They even have traffic lights in the sky!"

How George laughed! "Those lights are on the wings of the plane," he said. I saw that I had quite a lot to learn.

Among the things I had to learn was, of course, English, of which I spoke very little at the time. I had so many laughs as I made my way. Once, after a hard day at rehearsal I wanted to buy some soothing cream for my eyes. At the cosmetic counter at the drugstore, I asked for "eyes cream." The clerk smiled and directed me to the soda fountain—for ice cream.

San Francisco is one of the loveliest cities in the United States, and George and I went on excursions whenever we could, especially impressed with Muir Woods and the enormous sequoias. We also enjoyed the hospitality of the San Franciscans, including Eloise Martin, who invited us to a performance of *Rigoletto* with Lily Pons and Lawrence Tibbett, followed by a dinner for fifty people. The president of the San Francisco Opera, Robert Watt Miller, and his wife threw the most beautiful party at their summer home in Burlingame. Betty Miller became a dear friend.

Traviata was a great success. Nino Martini was my partner once again, now as Alfredo, and Tibbett sang Germont, acting the role so well that even Reinhardt would have approved. The critic of the *San Francisco News* wrote of my performance: "Novotná's Violetta had a distinct individuality that . . . established the Czech soprano as a star of the first magnitude. She was probably the most vivacious and charmingly flirtatious of all Violettas to date. . . . She proved herself an excellent musician as well as singer and actress." We repeated both *Butterfly* and *Traviata* twice; then the whole company traveled to Los Angeles, where both operas were repeated. Bob Ritchie of MGM met us at the station and dropped us off at the Beverly Hills Hotel, which reminded me of a nice old English hotel, pleasant and quiet, along with such Californian touches as a swimming pool and tennis courts, all the appointments for true comfort.

The first day, after lunch, George and I went for a little walk, but we hadn't traveled far from the hotel before a policeman stopped us to ask if we were looking for something. When we explained that we were simply taking a stroll, he didn't want to believe us. We soon learned that nobody walked in Los Angeles; people seem to take a car even to visit the house next door. George and I couldn't stop laughing.

Bob Ritchie took us to dinner that night at the home of Charles K. Feldman, a well-known agent whose clients included Claudette Colbert. Bob's date was Dorothy Lamour, and among the other stars that night were Robert Montgomery and Cesar Romero. A producer from Paramount Pictures suggested that I shoot a screen test for his studio, but I had no time for that.

The next evening, George and I were invited to a late supper at Max Reinhardt's home on Maravilla Drive. High in the hills overlooking all of Hollywood, the house was very cozy, and Reinhardt's wife and son were there, along with Erich Wolfgang Korngold. Reinhardt was planning already: he absolutely wanted me to do Offenbach's *La Belle Hélene* on Broadway, which Korngold considered a very good idea. However, I was under contract to the Metropolitan, so *Helen Goes to Troy* would remain a dream for a while longer. The next day, we dined at Korngold's house, where I met Igor Stravinsky and his lovely wife, Vera; during the trip, we also saw some of our Czech friends, including the director Gustav Machatý, whose film *Ecstasy* created such a sensation because of Hedy Lamarr's nude scene—though today nobody would pay attention.

While we were still in Los Angeles, Bob Ritchie offered to give us a tour of the MGM studios, which were really fantastic. Whole cities were created there on the lot! Just as we were leaving, Louis B. Mayer saw me and invited me to lunch the next day. Of course I accepted, because he was "the little king" in Hollywood, or at least he thought that he was. Several movies were in production, and Mr. Mayer took me from one set to another, introducing me everywhere not as "Madame Novotná" but simply as "Madame *No*," because he found it impossible to forget that I'd refused his offer of a contract. He arranged for me to have my portrait taken by Clarence Bull, one of the finest photographers in Hollywood, and again he asked me for a screen test. This time, I had to refuse because I was expected already at the radio studio, where I was to sing two arias on Bing Crosby's program.

Once again I boarded an airplane, flying from Hollywood to El Paso, Texas. From there, George and I had only to drive across the bridge to Ciudad Juárez, Mexico, for a few formalities before obtaining my official immigration visa. From our hotel in El Paso, we could see the desert surrounding the city, the wild contours of the mountains changing from yellow to red to purple in the sunset. In Europe I had never seen anything like it.

Back in New York, George and I found a nicely furnished duplex apartment at 471 Park Avenue. For the next few years, we would rent a series of apartments, beginning in the fall, and then lease houses in the country during the summer. We did not even think of purchasing a home, for two reasons. First, we hoped and believed that we would return very soon to Czechoslovakia. Second, we could not afford to spend much. The Germans allowed us to take no money out of Czechoslovakia, and as honest citizens, we didn't keep any money in foreign banks. We depended entirely on what I could earn. With two children and Teta, their governess, we were a family of five, and we were used to a certain standard of living, which was costly.

And so I began immediately to make arrangements for more work. Toscanini offered me the soprano solo in Beethoven's Ninth Symphony, which he would perform for NBC on December 2, and I met with Edward Johnson to discuss my repertory at the Metropolitan. He proposed *The Bartered Bride* for my debut, but when I learned that the company performed this opera only in German, I had to refuse. I absolutely could not sing any Czech opera in that language while the Germans occupied my country. Mr. Johnson understood and promised to get an English translation. And so we agreed that I would make my debut as Mimì in *La Bohème,* with Euridice in Gluck's *Orfeo* and Violetta in *Traviata* to follow. I was very pleased with this selection, though I had no costumes for Mimì. Someone suggested Salon Veronica, which specialized in theatrical costumes. I wasn't satisfied with the result, but I had neither time nor money to change them.

Especially given our financial circumstances, we were very happy when Mrs. Murray Crane arranged for our daughter to attend the Dalton School free of charge for the first year. At Dalton, children could study anything they wanted—painting, singing, dancing—apart from the regular curriculum. The headmistress, Helen Parkhurst, was a great progressive educator, and at Christmastime, she presented beautiful pageants with the children taking all the roles. The first year, Jarmilka played an angel in a gold dress, and she looked ravishingly beautiful. The next year, the Dalton School presented its Christmas play at the City Center, under the direction of Leopold Stokowski. This time, Jarmilka played the Virgin Mary, which gave her a little taste of theater. She told us she might like to be a singer or actress.

Our first holidays in New York were bittersweet, however, preoccupied as we were by thoughts of our family in Bohemia. We celebrated our first Christmas Eve with George's cousin, George Reithoffer, and his wife. I tried without success to call my parents and George's mother. On Christmas Day, Mrs. Cornelius Vanderbilt invited us to a large party at her home on Fifth Avenue, introducing us personally to all her guests and making us feel welcome. And David Sarnoff invited us to a New Year's Eve party at his home, with Toscanini and all his family; George and I joined them after praying at St. Patrick's Cathedral for an end to the war and a speedy return to our homeland.

Most evenings, George and I preferred to go by ourselves to the theater, which I found especially helpful once I started my English lessons. Combining all my professional, social, and above all family duties often could be difficult. But George took care of the household, went shopping, and engaged a good cook and an Irish maid. Teta took good care of little Georgie, and Jarmilka was happy in her school and made great progress in English, so we had few problems.

Thanks to Maestro Toscanini's invitation, the soprano solo in Beethoven's Ninth Symphony marked my first concert appearance in New York, on December 2, 1939. At Carnegie Hall that night, Francesco von Mendelsohn said to me, "You must be nervous." I must confess that I was, a little, and yet so long as Toscanini seemed satisfied in rehearsals, I remained confident. Our Beethoven concert went very well, and Maestro extended another invitation, to sing the soprano solo in Debussy's *La Demoiselle élue* on April 13—plenty of advance notice, which I needed, because for the next several weeks my days were filled with rehearsals and performances at the Metropolitan.

I made my debut on January 5, 1940, with Jussi Bjoerling as Rodolfo and Gennaro Papi conducting. I received applause at my entrance, and again after my aria, "Mi chiamano Mimì"; at the conclusion of Act I, we had some ten curtain calls, and the audience chanted, "Novotná! Novotná!" I found my dressing room filled with flowers, beer from the Pilsner Brewery, and tons and tons of telegrams. After the performance, we went to the home of Sam Barlow, a composer (his adaptation of *Babar the Elephant* is still played often), at Gramercy Park. All of New York's musical world was there, including Lucrezia Bori, who had been a great soprano with the Metropolitan and was now a member of the board of directors. She was very pleased with my performance and said that Edward Johnson had told her he felt the same way.

The critics united in praise—excepting one fellow, who said I was too tall to play little Mimì. Well, I couldn't cut off my feet, could I?

My Metropolitan career had begun. Soon, Johnson told me that the *Bartered Bride* translation was being prepared, though he preferred to hold it until the next season. I was glad, since I would have more time to improve my English. For my next performance at the Met, I sang Euridice on January 20, with Erich Leinsdorf conducting and the wonderful Kerstin Thorborg once again my Orfeo. Because I was so familiar with the role, I had no difficulties despite a rapidly worsening cold—but soon the cold was so bad that I had to cancel my first *Traviata.* When finally I did sing Violetta, on February 7, 1940, Giuseppe de Luca sang Germont, making his comeback after an absence of five years. This performance established me firmly at the Metropolitan, with resounding applause and such success that one critic described me as "a singing Duse," and Geraldine Farrar wrote me a note of congratulations. In the *New York Times,* Olin Downes wrote: "Miss Novotná had shown her intelligence, refinement, and sincerity in earlier appearances and other parts. But *Traviata* is thus far and unmistakably her crowning achievement. . . . [S]he conceives the music, from first note to the last, dramatically and portrays the character with an aristocratic sensibility and simplicity which at last bestow upon the role its full meaning and power." As for my scene with de Luca, Downes wrote, "Thus a young singing actress of radiant beauty and interpretive resource and a veteran of many years of mastery gave the whole opera . . . an ordinarily unsuspected measure of meaning." And the critic for *Life* magazine wrote: "When lovely-looking Czech soprano Jarmila Novotná made her debut as Violetta in *Traviata* . . . she stole the show. She sang her liquid melodies with every trick of the diva's trade, set a new standard for operatic acting at the Metropolitan. . . . Critics dusted off ten-dollar adjectives, overlooked nearly a generation of famed Violettas [and] acclaimed Novotná's the greatest in twenty years." I would like to say that I had natural acting talent, but it was Max Reinhardt who helped me to realize it to its fullest. What I learned from him I could apply to every role I had to play. Acting means portraying every moment with such conviction, creating the inner life of a human being so truthfully, that the audience accepts you as the character, and you become the character.

My next assignment at the Met was Cherubino in *The Marriage of Figaro.* The fact is that Mozart had not been the greatest favorite with Metropolitan audiences, and *Figaro,* for instance, had been absent from the stage for twenty-two years. But with a new production and a marvelous cast—most of whom had sung this opera in Salzburg, under Bruno Walter's direction—this opera sparkled, entrancing the audience. From opening night onward, *Figaro* remained in the repertory and was presented almost every year. With Ezio Pinza as the Figaro, John Brownlee as the Count, Elisabeth Rethberg as the Countess, Bidu Sayão as Susanna, and Ettore Panizza conducting, we repeated this opera several times before the end of the season.

Olin Downes's review pleased me: "In the treatment of the melodies, of action and song, Mme. Novotná proved her art and her worthiness as an exemplar of Mozart. . . . [I]f every singing actor or actress on the stage had been of Mme. Novotná's schooling and taste, there would have been nearly an ideal stage presentation of the work at the Metropolitan." But another critic's esteem meant more to me. George took Jarmilka to the opera, and she was enchanted. She surprised us the next day by playing some tunes from *Figaro* on the piano, improvising without sheet music, just as she remembered them.

My managers at NCAC advised me to perform at as many charity concerts as I could, because the more people talked about me, the better. For one concert, benefitting the Musician Emergency Fund, Helen Astor asked me to sing, and on the heels of the success of *Orfeo,* I decided to perform a scene, this time with Risë Stevens as Orfeo, a role in which she would have great success several years later.[1]

New York is home to a large Czechoslovak community, and so I was approached to perform at a memorial concert on President Masaryk's birthday, March 7. Little did I know that the Czechoslovaks in New York had divided into several groups, and by accepting one invitation, I made it impossible to accept another from a competing organization. Such political disunity surprised me, because Masaryk was above all a patriot. I felt that, no matter what our personal beliefs, we all should pay him tribute. (I continued to feel that way, especially after the Communists took over the country and banned his name outright. Without him, the Czechoslovakian state would never have existed.) Later I would sing at many such celebrations and Czechoslovak-American gatherings without any conflict whatsoever.

To prepare *La Demoiselle élue* for Toscanini's April concert, I used to go to his home in Riverdale to rehearse. The Maestro and his wife had moved from the Hotel Astor to a large house, Villa Pauline, in the midst of a beautiful garden, with a terrace from which he could see as far as the Hudson River. "I require peaceful surroundings," he told me, "and I have found them here." Often his wife, Carla, invited me to join them for meals: always a thick soup first, then either chicken or veal, followed by cheese and coffee. During the meal the Maestro liked to take a glass of wine. The Maestro adored Villa Pauline, to which he returned and which he purchased in 1945, and where he lived until his last days. The nearby house, Wave Hill, where the Toscaninis lived from 1942 to 1945, for many years contained the Maestro's archive, with recordings, scores, correspondence, photographs, and other documents; in 1987, the New York Public Library obtained the archive.

One of our private rehearsals took place not at Villa Pauline, under Signora Carla's watchful eye, but in the Maestro's private studio at NBC. There, when we had finished, he suddenly got up from the piano and kissed me. I was stunned. "It was heavenly music," the Maestro explained, "and I could not help myself." Our relationship continued unaffected.

That is to say that he telephoned me often when we were both in New York, and he wrote to me very often, no matter where we were. His letters sometimes took on a self-pitying tone, complaining that I must have forgotten all about him, "old man" that he was; often he was quite gloomy and insisted that he wanted only to be alone. Sometimes, he insisted, he had lost interest even in music. But he seldom failed to ask for photos, and he often asked about my children. I realized that he was much affected by the terrible things that had happened and were happening in Italy, and that he missed his homeland very much. When the Maestro left for America in 1937 and determined not to return to Europe, I thought I would never see him again. But the fates were good to me.

If it were not for Maestro Toscanini, my family and I might never have come to the United States. We arrived at the most crucial political moment, and we began a new life here. I will be forever grateful for Toscanini's understanding and friendship. Whenever I had a problem, I knew that I could discuss it with him, and we always found a solution. I might seem sentimental, but for me friendship is the essence of life. It is a great art to keep friends, especially when you are separated by distance and time. I have attempted to keep my friends, and often letters have helped. I treasure the letters that Maestro Toscanini sent to me.

The Toscaninis invited George and me several times to lunch, and we in turn invited them to our home. On one such occasion, we invited Mr. and Mrs. Robert Watt Miller to join us. Mr. Miller very much wanted Toscanini to come to San Francisco to conduct any opera he liked, but the Maestro replied that for the time being he wanted to conduct only concerts. We also invited the Sarnoffs and Mr. and Mrs. Cornelius Bliss, who became good friends; soon, George and I were constant guests at the Blisses' home in Old Westbury. Several people in the Blisses' circle were very active in the Museum of Modern Art, including Conger Goodyear and Cornelius's sister, Lilly (named for her aunt Lillie, one of the museum's founders); their son Anthony Bliss later became general manager of the Metropolitan Opera.

At another lunch, with our friends Chester and Eleanor Burden, their friend Norbert Bogdan persuaded Maestro Toscanini to bring the NBC Orchestra on a tour of South America—including a stop in Rio de Janeiro, where the Maestro had made his conducting debut fifty-four years before.

Among the musicians with whom we socialized were Lucrezia Bori, Samuel Barber, and Gian Carlo Menotti, who asked for my photo and, upon receiving it, told me that I would inspire every note of music he wrote thereafter. Leopold Stokowski had a farm in Milford, Connecticut, near the country home of Miss Parkhurst, the headmistress of the Dalton School, and so we became acquainted with him, as well as two other neighbors, the actor Fredric March and his wife, Florence Eldridge, whose daughter, Penny, was a classmate of Jarmilka. We also saw many people from the Czech community, including Mario Korbel, the well-known sculptor, and many others. In the short time we had been in the United States, we had already made friendships that were to last for years.

The news from home, however, worried us—when we got it. In April we received a few letters from Czechoslovakia, in which our family complained that they did not hear from us, though George wrote faithfully every week. I was happy to hear that my parents were well, and that George's mother sent them fruit and vegetables, eggs, and sometimes meat from Liteň, since at that time it was very hard to find any food to buy. We also heard the sad story of George's dog, Ignaz, which we called "Nazi" for short. One day the dog was running through the village, and someone called out to him. A German policeman heard this and believed that people were making fun of him by referring to a dog as "Nazi." And so he shot George's dog.

I could not have been happier with my first season at the Metropolitan Opera, which established me with the company. In those days, the Met season lasted only five months, followed by a tour that lasted another month and a half. As a newcomer, I was not asked to join the tour, because plans were made far in advance.[2] However, I did make my debut on the tour that first year after all. When Helen Jepson fell ill, Edward Johnson asked me to replace her in *La Traviata,* and I flew to Dallas to enjoy an overwhelming success.

I had just returned to New York when Marks Levine from NCAC called with an offer from Edwin Lester, general director of the Civic Light Opera of Los Angeles, inviting me to sing Lehár's *The Merry Widow* in June. I accepted and began immediately to learn my role for *Merry Widow* and to prepare for the concert tour that NCAC had arranged for me: twenty-five cities in quick succession after the Los Angeles engagement ended.

George and I decided to leave in May, to spend a little extra time in California. The children were happy to have a change, and George and I considered it important to include them in our activities whenever possible. When children are little, they need the most attention and love. Every morning, George and I had breakfast with them. After Jarmilka left for school, Georgie liked for me to tell him stories—but I had to tell each story the same way each time, which turned out to be excellent training for my memory. The truly masterful storyteller, however, was my husband, who took over when I had to leave for rehearsals. We were grateful to Teta, too. She never took a day off, and told us that she felt so much a part of our family that she never felt she was missing out on anything. She was absolutely happy, she said.

Before leaving for Los Angeles, George and I decided to buy a car, since it was almost impossible to get around without one—and we had learned not to try walking. Though George had been driving for thirty years, he had to pass a driver's test to get his license. When the time came, we loaded the car, a Buick Roadmaster, and thirteen pieces of registered luggage onto the train, taking an additional twenty-five pieces of luggage with us to our compartments. During the three-day trip, the children spent almost every waking minute in the observation car. Stepping out of the air-cooled cars into the Los Angeles heat was like walking into an oven.

After a few nights at the Chateau Marmont, George and I decided that, to be really comfortable, we needed a house. He found a lovely home in Brentwood with a nice, intimate garden. However, it was quite far to the theater in Los Angeles. I used to leave the house at 9:30 a.m. and return after 6:00 p.m.—on those occasions when we did not have dance rehearsals in the evening. It was quite exhausting. The final dress rehearsal began at 11:00 a.m. and lasted until 5:00 p.m., after which I had to go to the hairdresser for a very elaborate coiffure, and at 7:30 I was back in my dressing room for the premiere. This is just to illustrate how hard a singer's profession is.

Everything went well, and the song "Vilja" was such a success that I had to repeat it. Prince Danilo was the handsome Walter Woolf King, who played the opera star in *A Night at the Opera* with the Marx Brothers in 1935. We scored especially with our dancing the famous "Merry Widow Waltz," and one newspaper critic wrote, "Better make a point of seeing this production. Its romantic spell will help you to forget, for a few hours at least, what's going on in the world." Indeed, the morning after our premiere, I received another letter from Maestro Toscanini, grieving for what was happening in Italy. He loved his country very much and had to leave it—just as we had to leave our home.

After a few days in Los Angeles, we took the whole *Merry Widow* production to San Francisco, and on the way home, George and I drove down the Pacific coast. It was very beautiful, except that the road took us over the mountains, with the sea far below us, and so dangerously winding that George got dizzy. Finishing this journey was difficult for him.

Back in Los Angeles, we socialized a great deal with friends from Europe, spending time with Otto Klemperer and Bruno Walter, and dining with the conductor Hans Lert and his wife, Vicki Baum, the author of *Grand Hotel.* She was delightful, very intelligent and amusing, and George enjoyed this evening more than any other during our time in Los Angeles. Erich Wolfgang Korngold introduced us to Igor Stravinsky, whose dismissal of composers such as Puccini, Massenet, and Dvořák amazed me. We also saw Max Reinhardt, who returned to the idea of *La Belle Hélène* on Broadway.

In the course of our stay, we met the composer Emmerich Kálmán and the film directors George Cukor, Ernst Lubitsch, and William Dieterle. On one occasion or another we also met Claudette Colbert, Conrad Veidt, Jimmy Stewart, Olivia de Havilland, Fay Wray, Brian Aherne, and his wife, Joan Fontaine; Fredric March and Florence Eldridge were our neighbors in California, so that we built upon the acquaintance we'd made in Connecticut. We learned that, for movie stars, it was an important occupation (or preoccupation) to be seen everywhere, to be talked about. We invited many of our new acquaintances to dinner, and luckily we had found an excellent Italian cook. She was in heaven, seeing so many famous people.

Universal approached me at this time to play in a film called *Flotsam,* but I declined because I didn't like the role.[3] However, after lunch with Louis B. Mayer at MGM, I relented and made a screen test at last. I did a scene from Molnar's *The Guardsman* with some music interpolated from Kálmán's *Gypsy Princess.* The test met with approval, and Mr. Mayer said he would try to find a suitable role for me. His sister invited me to sing at a gala benefit concert for the Actors Fund, a scintillating affair at the Beverly Wilshire Hotel, where many movie stars also performed.

Near our house was a golf course, so George and I took lessons. In the beginning, we had sore muscles, but we thought it an excellent sport. When the weather permitted, we went swimming every day, and at the suggestion of the Marches, we joined the beach club. The club had excellent facilities, and the children enjoyed playing there. We were not prepared for the strong, high waves in the ocean, though. One picked me up and threw me into the deep with such force that I thought I'd never get out of there.

This was something like a vacation, interrupted only by a trip to Chicago for a concert with Maurice Abravanel, broadcast over the radio, where I sang "Depuis le jour," Liszt's "Ô, quand je dors," and "Vilja." (The *Chicago Daily* wrote, "[O]ver and above her technical excellence, she has a remarkable gift for piercing right to the heart of the piece of music and bringing its true meaning out where an audience can grasp it and be excited by it.") Most of my musical efforts during these weeks, however, were spent preparing for a long recital tour ahead and *The Bartered Bride* in English. I began working with an excellent pianist, Shibley Boyes.

Just before I left on the tour, Ernst Lubitsch threw a farewell party for George and me. Mr. Mayer was there, and he did not move from my side for the entire evening. Over lunch the next day, he asked me to give up opera and move to Hollywood for good. This was flattering, but Mr. Mayer was mistaken. I wouldn't have minded making a picture, but I had no desire to change my life completely.

My tour began on a train to Seattle, and an incident so typical of the United States. I was sleeping in my compartment when a pounding on the door awoke me. "What is it?" I asked, and a voice answered, "Ten to five." I didn't understand, and the man continued, "It's the baseball score. I thought you would be interested." He had been going from door to door with the news.

Though I was embarking on a series of recitals, I started with *La Traviata* in Seattle, where the *Star* described me as "the Czech fireball, not only a marvelous singer, [but] also a swell actress." Someone had to explain to me that "swell" was a compliment, not an insult. There was a large Czech population in Seattle, who welcomed me with a reception in my honor. The state of Washington reminded me strongly of Bohemia, with its forests, hills, and mountains. I became quite nostalgic.

The clean air of Seattle was a great contrast to what awaited me in Pittsburgh. I arrived there at night, and when I awoke the next morning and looked in the mirror, I thought I was sick: my nostrils were black, and I had black rings around my eyes. It took me a while to realize that this was soot, which penetrated everything. In those days Pittsburgh was the center of steel and coal production, though much has changed since 1940.

From Pittsburgh I went on to Spartanburg, then to Dallas, which proved to be a very moving experience. There is a large Czech population in Texas, and many attended the recital—some dressed in folk costumes. Even after many encores, the audience didn't want to leave, and at last I sang our national anthem as everyone stood. The *Dallas Times Herald* found this "quite unforgettable," and I did, too.

Then came Wichita Falls, Abilene, and Harlingen in Texas, Baton Rouge in Louisiana, and Columbus in Georgia, where George waited for me at the station. From there we drove, which I found much more enjoyable than sitting in trains. We drove to Bradford, New York, then to Montreal, with plenty of time to admire Niagara Falls on the way back for recitals in Jamestown and Buffalo, before George had to return to New York City. A few of my engagements differed from the others: in Milwaukee I gave a joint recital with Emanuel Feuermann, the cellist; in Denver I gave a concert with full orchestra, which I find much easier than singing a whole evening alone with a pianist. At the Civic Opera House in Chicago, I sang *La Traviata,* reuniting with Tito Schipa, who sang Alfredo. For me, he was the best bel canto singer, performing with mastery, taste, and charm. It was a luxury to hear him again, and opposite him I sang better than ever. The *Chicago Daily News* said, "Novotná's debut was the highlight of the season so far and is not likely to be eclipsed by subsequent events." During the ovations after the final curtain, a little girl in a Czech costume came up onstage to present me with a bouquet.

But my recital tour was not quite finished, and I went on to Des Moines, Iowa, and Meadville, Pennsylvania. From city to city, it was always the same, except for new faces. A concert artist does not have the time to explore the cities she visits. She arrives, goes to her hotel, and gives a few interviews. There is the concert, a dinner afterward with the concert organizers, and then bed. The next day, the process repeats itself.

And yet I was aware that, by organizing this tour, NCAC had made it possible for me to see more of the country in a few weeks than many Americans saw in a lifetime. Artistically and personally, I was happy with the results of my tour. I was also happy to go home—I mean to New York.

The children and George waited for me at the station for a joyful reunion, after almost two months apart. It seemed to me that both of my children had grown, and I was sorry to have missed spending both their birthdays with them, as well as my own. But that is the life of an artist. George had been lucky to find an apartment on Fifth Avenue at Ninety-Seventh Street, a duplex with a penthouse. From the terrace overlooking Central Park, one could see both the East River and the Hudson River, and at night it was a fairy view, with the illuminated houses and the George Washington Bridge in the background.

I had a few days to relax before beginning my New York season with a radio broadcast for the Metropolitan Opera, where I sang Cherubino's arias. Then it was time for opening night, a good performance of *Un Ballo in Maschera* with Zinka Milanov and Jussi Bjoerling, which George and I attended at the invitation of Mrs. Murray Crane. The spectacle of the opening night itself was like nothing one can see in the whole world. There were dozens of photographers outside the Met, and some women dressed for the occasion so eccentrically, hoping to catch the eye of a photographer and to be mentioned in the newspaper the next day.

My first role of the season was Cherubino, and we began with what was not merely a tour but a tour de force: a performance in Philadelphia, for which we departed at 5:00 p.m. and returned at 2:00 a.m. Our second performance, at the Met on December 13, 1940, was auspicious for another reason: it was the first radio broadcast sponsored by Texaco, and a recording was made of that fabulous cast: Ezio Pinza, Elisabeth Rethberg, Licia Albanese, and John Brownlee, with conductor Ettore Panizza. I thought with pleasure that now people living in places without opera would be able to hear it on the radio every Saturday.[4]

Daily rehearsal began for Massenet's *Manon* and also for *The Bartered Bride.* For *Manon,* I turned to the excellent designer Ladislaus Czettel, who made the beautiful costumes for Reinhardt's *Belle Hélène* in Berlin and who was now living in New York. He designed the most beautiful costumes for my Manon, and everyone remarked on them—even the critics, who mostly ignored dress. I wanted to work with a vocal coach to prepare this role, and Lawrence Tibbett recommended his teacher, Ignaz Zitomirsky. This was a good decision. After the premiere of *Manon,* when I told Edward Johnson I had never sung the role before, he refused to believe me. The *New York Times* called my performance "an emphatic triumph . . . a brilliant portrayal most carefully considered in every detail," and the critic concluded, "A Manon of this caliber has not been visible on the Met stage for a number of seasons."

Such success was beneficial for my soul, and at two concerts after the *Manon* premiere, I sang so much better than before that I astonished myself. Everything seemed easy.

NCAC renewed my contract, though this time I stipulated that the agency would not represent me for film work and that I would engage another agent to field those offers. NCAC had lined up another extensive concert tour for me, however, and I realized I would be unable to take part in Walter Damrosch's new opera, *Cyrano,* which he had asked me especially to perform in a concert with the Philharmonic Orchestra, opposite Ezio Pinza in the title role. I begged Damrosch to let me out of my contract, but he didn't want to hear of it, saying that the opera would stand or fall on my participation. He went so far as to tell the newspapers that I refused to fulfill the contract. I had already begun my tour, so my press agent, Constance Hope, answered for me, telling the press that I asked for the release only because of my artistic integrity, since I could not rehearse properly. I also asked Maestro Toscanini's advice, and he intervened on my behalf with the associate manager of the New York Philharmonic Society, Bruno Zirato, who assured him that the organization would do nothing to harm me. In turn Mr. Zirato arranged for me to be released from my contract, and the whole affair ended peacefully. Still, I felt bad for Damrosch, especially because Pinza fell ill and was unable to sing the concert. But there was nothing I could do, and it was some time before Damrosch and I became friends again.

Constance Hope was the first press agent who represented operatic artists, and I understood that, in America, publicity is important. For artists but also for private people, I learned, one's name must appear in the newspapers as often as possible. My friend Lanfranco Rasponi, who had been writing features for the *New York Times,* soon opened a public relations agency, and because he knew me well enough, I thought I would sign with him for a year—just to try it. I never regretted this move, and he continued to represent me for many years. Soon I appeared in *Harper's Bazaar* in photos by George Hoyningen-Huene, one of the best photographers in the world. He depicted me as Manon, Octavian, Pamina, Euridice, Mélisande, Violetta, and Donna Elvira, as well as in several informal, candid photos. During my career I had to give many interviews—but that is part of our profession.

My concert tour took me through the South, and in Asheville, North Carolina, I shared the stage with the wonderful piano duo Pierre Luboshutz and Genia Nemenoff, for an audience of three thousand. After so many performances and so much travel in the winter of 1941, however, I caught a nasty cold and had to miss a week of rehearsals for *The Bartered Bride.* This delightful opera has never found its rightful place in America, but with Bruno Walter conducting and the Metropolitan Opera audience able to understand the English text and all of the abundant humor in the dialogue, we met with great success, if not as much as this opera truly deserves. The final chorus pleased me very much:

> We rejoice to hear his blessing,
> All our voices love expressing.
> Wedding bells ring far and wide
> To celebrate the Bartered Bride!

I often heard that audiences prefer to hear operas performed in the language in which they were written. This ran counter to my experience in Europe, where artists were engaged for an entire year to sing all the operas in the language of each particular country, no matter the original language of the performer or the libretto. I found this practice very natural, and for some operas, not only *The Bartered Bride* but also such comic works as *The Magic Flute* and *Così Fan Tutte,* I found that English translations helped the Metropolitan audiences to enjoy the performance more.

We had our *Bartered Bride* premiere on February 28, 1941. With the Met on tour, we took the opera to Baltimore, Cleveland, Chicago, and Boston, and with other companies over the years I sang Mařenka in Seattle, St. Louis, San Antonio, Cincinnati, and Michigan City, Indiana. The Seattle production, directed by Felix Brentano (a former assistant to Max Reinhardt), was the most authentic and honest, with the Czech dances beautifully performed.

While performing *The Bartered Bride* in New York, we rehearsed *Don Giovanni.* Before coming to America, I had never sung Donna Elvira, and at first I studied the role with reluctance, only because Bruno Walter wished me to do so. Personally, I could see very little on the surface of either Donna Elvira or Donna Anna. Both ladies walk through Mozart's opera either angry or weeping, it seemed. But Bruno Walter pointed out to me that the key to Elvira's character lies in her music. As I studied, I found that he was right.

I came to the conclusion that Don Giovanni himself can be neither very young nor supremely irresistible, because (despite his 1,003 conquests in Italy alone) during the opera he wins none of the women he pursues. As for Anna, she wants only vengeance on him, and though Zerlina is momentarily fascinated by him, she really loves Masetto. The one woman who persists in loving Giovanni, who shows him tenderness and fidelity, and who would fight like a tigress for him, is Elvira. Tenderness fills the greater portion of Elvira's music. When Leporello, disguised as Giovanni, falls into the hands of

Anna and Ottavio, Elvira believes her beloved's life is threatened, and she practically abases herself in pleading for Giovanni's pardon. Such is the nature of her feelings that, even when the cynical miscreant is dragged off to his everlasting punishment, she remains true to his memory. I suppose that she lives out the rest of her life in some convent.

We had a wonderful cast, with Ezio Pinza as Giovanni, Zinka Milanov as Anna, Bidu Sayão as Zerlina, and Salvatore Baccaloni as Leporello, and with Norman Cordon as the Commendatore and Arthur Kent as Masetto. As for our Don Ottavio, if I admired Tito Schipa before, his performance in *Don Giovanni* completely overwhelmed me and won a tremendous response from the audience. And yet a miracle occurred, and in his review in the *New York Times,* Olin Downes wrote that I was "in a part that is very rarely done justice . . . the most distinguished artist on the stage."

The Met season ended in March 1941, and this year I participated in the national tour: *The Bartered Bride* in Baltimore, *Don Giovanni* in Boston, *Manon* in New Orleans (with the marvelous Raoul Jobin replacing Richard Crooks as Des Grieux), and *The Marriage of Figaro* in Dallas, where a telegram awaited me with sad news. George's mother had died. I was so sorry I could not be at my husband's side at this moment, for he loved his mother deeply. For my part, she was a wonderful, gold-hearted woman, and we understood each other perfectly. Fortunately, George had little Jarmilka with him for comfort. "Don't be sad," she said when he told her that Oma had passed; "she will be happy to be together again with Opapa."

As soon as I had a few days free, I flew to New York to be with George, and while I was in town, the Czech composer Bohuslav Martinů came to see us. He wanted to make money, and George advised him to follow Korngold's example by writing for the movies. "I don't want to be rich," Martinů answered; "I just need $2,000." He did not have to wait long, and he soon began receiving commissions. (In the spring of 1942, he wrote a song cycle inspired by folksongs, *Nový Špalíček,* which he dedicated to Jan Masaryk. For the premiere, in January 1943, I performed the cycle and wore a folk costume, which the audience loved.)

I completed the Met tour with Cherubino in Richmond, Virginia, and finally *Bohème* in Albany, leaving the same night for Ann Arbor, where I sang the Brahms Requiem and scenes from *Eugene Onegin* at the annual May Festival, with the Philadelphia Orchestra and Eugene Ormandy. For *Onegin,* Mack Harrell sang Onegin to my Tatyana, Enid Szantho was Olga, and Charles Kullman sang Lenski. On my free evenings, I attended other concerts, and I discovered that the cellist Gregor Piatigorsky was also listening to music when he wasn't performing. At one intermission, he said to me, "You know, if I were not happily married, I would want to court you. I find you ravishing." Oh, what a compliment!

If only he knew what such a "ravishing" artist must go through in her career. Just think of the travel, and of remembering to bring all the right dresses on a long concert tour. I found that mastery of the art of traveling requires a lot of common sense and a little forethought. First, you must have the proper frame of mind. You cannot rush or leave things to the last minute. Instead, take your time to prepare and pack, because this is the first step to a pleasant journey. It's far better to carry one or two large pieces of luggage rather than many small bags. However, you still need one overnight bag in which to put immediate necessities. In one large case I carried my costumes and concert dresses, and in the other, my everyday clothes. I also found it wise to bring light reading matter and to eat sensibly in order to have a true "bon voyage."

That summer, George and I rented a house in Smithtown, on Long Island, but several times I had to travel or to go to the city. Maestro Toscanini had been writing to me regularly while I toured, but some of his letters had not reached me, and mine had not reached him. Now he seemed very lonely and believed I had neglected him. So, one afternoon when I needed to go to New York to meet with Edward Johnson at the Met, I visited the Maestro in Riverdale. He was preparing to depart for Buenos Aires, and he seemed very happy to see me. "You are always adorable, and it is impossible not to love you," he said.

Also that summer I sang for the first time with André Kostelanetz, who was married to Lily Pons at the time. He was a delightful man, and we became very good friends. For his radio show, sponsored by Coca-Cola ("The Pause that Refreshes"), he prepared fabulous arrangements of "La Paloma" and of two arias from my standard repertory. For the American Sokol Convention in Chicago, I sang for an audience of sixty thousand people at Soldiers' Field; it is quite a sensation to perform for such a crowd, and even more when they joined me in the Czech national anthem.

I sang the Czech anthem, as well as some other songs, for the first program in a series of ten broadcasts, *America Preferred,* part of the Treasury Department's campaign to sell defense savings bonds. Each program featured famous people of foreign descent. The narrator was the Dutch author Pierre van Paassen; and for the first broadcast the speakers included the English actor Claude Rains, the Belgian playwright Maurice Maeterlinck, and the French playwright Henri Bernstein.

Two concerts brought back happy memories of singing under the stars in Verona: one at Lewisohn Stadium (my first) with Charles Kullman in scenes from Tchaikovsky operas, with Efreim Kurtz conducting; and a return to the Hollywood Bowl for *La Traviata.* I was surprised to see reporters and photographers waiting for me at the train station in Los Angeles. Knowing how important the press is, I answered their questions, then invited them to a cocktail reception.

Once again with *Traviata,* it was "veni, vidi, vici" for me, with a capacity audience of twenty thousand. A young bass-baritone named George Burnstein took the role of Dr. Grenvil; he later changed his name to George London. My Alfredo was Jan Peerce, who told me he was making his debut. I was pleased to read his memoir many years later, in which he wrote "Novotná was so good that she made everybody around her look good. And she was a blessing to me, for I lacked experience as a stage lover, and she guided me until I felt secure enough to assert myself."[5] Well, I never forgot my debut as Violetta in Prague, when the tenor upstaged me continuously. That was a hard lesson for me, but I learned from it

Any visit to Los Angeles meant catching up with friends, including Bruno Walter, who wanted me to rehearse—on the spot—for the English-language *Magic Flute* he was preparing for the Met; as well as Franz Werfel and Alma Mahler, Louis B. Mayer, Max Reinhardt, Thomas Mann, William Dieterle, the Korngolds, Italo Montemezzi, and Lily Pons. I made my third appearance on Bing Crosby's radio show, and I suppose he was satisfied, or he wouldn't have asked me back. This time I sang Manon's gavotte, and when I finished, Bing said, "That's the kind of thing that hits me where I live."

"Oh, does that mean you want to go home?" I teased.

"On the contrary, it means I want to stay right where I am and hear some more of it!" Bing replied, so I sang "La Paloma."

For the rest of the summer, we swam and played golf, and I took up horseback riding, which Jarmilka and Georgie enjoyed so much. Toward the end of August, I received another letter from Maestro Toscanini, asking for news of me and yet seemingly aware of everything I had done while he was in Argentina. George and I went to visit him in Riverdale. He was in the best of moods but not alone, as he'd described himself. His son, daughter-in-law, and granddaughter were there, and Toscanini played hide-and-seek with little Sonja, a charming scene.

I wish I could describe Toscanini adequately. He was such a unique man, interested in everything. He went often to the theater, and he saw *Porgy and Bess* at least four times, calling it a musical work of genius. He used to attend other conductors' rehearsals, sitting in a box at the rear of the theater so as not to disturb anyone. Afterward his remarks were seldom flattering, although when he heard Ernest Ansermet conduct Mozart, the Maestro said, "He does it better than I." More typical was his assessment of Serge Koussevitzky: "He is an old man, he sits through all the rehearsal. How can he conduct? *Vecchio, vecchio, vecchio.*" The Maestro slept badly at night, and he called often for long conversations with me. He complained that NBC wanted him to work too much, until at last he recommended that they hire Stokowski, too, to take on some of the burden. (He didn't get credit for recommending Stokowski in the newspapers, he said, though he should have.) Above all, he despaired over the war and over what his poor country must be suffering under Mussolini.

With the fall, new activity started, including several performances in Puerto Rico: *Manon* and *La Bohème* with Jan Kiepura and *Faust* with his brother, Ladis, who was also a tenor. As it was in Vienna so many times, it was a pleasure to sing with Jan. He had such a good voice, and he was very good looking. It was just a pity that he was a little bit conceited. The fourth opera in Puerto Rico was *Carmen,* and since I did not sing in that one, I was able to attend the performance. In Act II, as Carmen is dancing for Don José, Jan suddenly left the stage, then returned a few minutes later. After the performance, I asked Jan why he had left poor Carmen alone, and he explained, "There was not enough light on me. I had to ask the electrician to put more light *on me.*" Jan was notorious, too, for an incident at the Met: in *Bohème,* Jan turned Mimì's chair so that he could sing facing the audience in Act I, but she had to sing her "Mi chiamano Mimì" facing upstage. The next time they sang *Bohème* together, the soprano asked the stagehands to screw the chair to the floor. Jan tried to move it, but it was impossible.

There are many stories like that, and not long after, I sang *Manon* with Jan at the Cincinnati summer opera festival. The conductor, Fausto Cleva, was unhappy with Jan's tempi, but his requests went unheeded. Finally, when Jan held a note too long, Cleva admonished him. Jan shot back, "Who do you think you are—Toscanini?" Cleva quit on the spot. It was a very unpleasant situation. I went to Jan's dressing room, told him that he was at fault, and insisted that he apologize to Cleva. To my surprise, he agreed: I really didn't believe I had a chance of changing his mind. Luckily, Jan was always very polite and nice to me.

Ladis also had a lovely tenor voice, but he cut a less romantic figure because he was short and thick-set. Nicola Moscona and Richard Bonelli also sang with us on this little "mini-season" in Puerto Rico, and Ivy Dale made a charming Sièbel in *Faust.*

At the Metropolitan Opera that fall, we revived *Orfeo ed Euridice,* which was also a revival in the sense that Bruno Walter, taking over as conductor, restored the original overture and several passages that had been cut from the last act. As a result, the role of Euridice was expanded, and one newspaper critic wrote that I "made an Eurydice who looked easily worth going to Hell for."

We also performed *Traviata,* with Jan Peerce making his Met debut as Alfredo. This performance was selected for radio broadcast, but behind the scenes, tragedy took place. A little more than an hour before curtain, Gennaro Papi, who was to have conducted the performance, died. What the audience saw, and all that it knew until after the performance, was that Frank St. Leger conducted the orchestra in the national anthem, then handed the baton over to Ettore Panizza. Panizza had only a few minutes' notice and, of course, no rehearsal, yet he managed to hold his forces together firmly. It was hard for all of us to proceed as if nothing had happened, but that is what theater demands. The show must go on, and it went beautifully. Jan Peerce was excellent, Lawrence Tibbett was also in good voice, and so everything ended with a success.

And yet the news from our home in Czechoslovakia was very depressing. Since my mother-in-law's death, George's sister-in-law had moved to Liteň to take charge of the estate and to confront the many obstacles that the occupying Germans placed before her. For example, the Germans requisitioned most of the grain harvested at Liteň, so that it was almost impossible to feed livestock, or to keep the brewery running. My parents told us that my father had been summoned to German police headquarters in Prague for questioning, not about his own activities but about mine. He told them that I had had a contract with the Metropolitan Opera and had arrived in America just as the war started—I had not intended to go into exile. The Germans seemed to accept this explanation, and after the interrogation they released my father.

George and I felt helpless, unable to intercede on behalf of our families, and soon enough we realized that any hope of returning to Czechoslovakia was lost. We were returning from a luncheon engagement on Sunday, December 7, 1941, when we heard the news of the Japanese attack on Pearl

Harbor. This act of treachery united America behind its president almost instantaneously. The attack meant war—a second world war—and so long as that war continued, we could not go home.

Just days after the attack on Pearl Harbor, on December 13, 1941, I participated in an event, almost overlooked at the time, that commemorated the hundredth anniversary of Antonin Dvořák's birth, at 327 East Seventeenth Street, where the composer lived from 1892 to 1895. Addressing musical and civic notables, Mayor Fiorello La Guardia described Dvořák as a son of Czechoslovakia who belonged to the entire world; the house would be a shrine to his memory. Jan Masaryk, who at this time was Foreign Minister of the Czech government in exile, spoke, as did Harry T. Burleigh, a black singer, composer, and friend who steered Dvořák toward the spirituals that resonate through the "New World" Symphony. With another friend of Dvořák, Fritz Kreisler, I performed several of the *Biblical Songs,* standing by the piano in the very corner where Dvořák's own instrument had stood. Several other of Dvořák's associates attended, and Czechoslovakian and American flags decorated the house.

The Dvořák house may have been a shrine, but it was not designated a landmark. In 1988, Beth Israel Hospital announced plans to buy the property, to demolish the house, and in its place to construct a larger building, a hospice for patients with AIDS. In response, a committee proposed that the house receive landmark status and be converted to a memorial museum and music center. Among the advocates were the Czech-born filmmaker Milos Forman, the arts patron Alice Tully, Rudolf Firkušný, the cellist Yo-Yo Ma, Rafael Kubelík, the conductor Maurice Peress, and myself; President Václav Havel of Czechoslovakia wrote to Mayor David Dinkins for his support. The American Landmark Preservation Commission responded in February 1991 by granting the building landmark status, but the New York City Council overturned that decision a few months later, and Beth Israel proceeded with its plan for the AIDS hospice. The composer was not entirely forgotten, however, and as a result of our efforts, in November 1991, Mayor Dinkins signed a law that recognized the block on which the house had stood as "Dvořák Place."

As the United States entered the war, certain aspects of our lives did not change. I found myself singing several operas, almost simultaneously, at the Metropolitan: Cherubino, *The Magic Flute* in English, *Traviata,* and *The Bartered Bride* for an audience of 2,500 students. In between operas, I raced

1. Novotná as a baby, with her father, Josef; her mother, Josefa; and her sister, Pavla. Prague, probably 1908.

2. Pavla and Jarmila Novotná in childhood. The sisters retained a close bond despite many long separations.

3. The voice student in Italy.

4. Medea Colombara (*left*) and Novotná at the home of Gabriele d'Annunzio.

5. In costume as *Rigoletto*'s Gilda.

6. At the Kroll Opera for Schönberg's *Die glückliche Hand,* with Erik Wirl and Fritz Krenn.

7. Jarmila with George Daubek on their wedding day. Prague, July 16, 1931.

8. "Čechovna," the Daubeks' new home, the baroque house they lived in on the Liteň estate.

9. In Max Ophüls' film of *The Bartered Bride,* with Willi Domgraf-Fassbaender (1932). Novotná disapproved of the director's many changes to Smetana's opera; the movie was not released in Czechoslovakia.

10. With Gustav Fröhlich in *The Night of Great Love* (1933).

11. With Franz Lehár and Richard Tauber (in costume as a German army officer) in a promotional photo for the operetta *Giuditta.* Vienna, 1934.

12. A scene from the film *The Cossack and the Nightingale* (1935), with costar Ivan Petrovich.

13. From rags to riches: Our heroine finds success in a Parisian nightclub. A promotional photo for the film *Frasquita* (1935).

14. Salzburg, 1937: Curtain call for *The Magic Flute,* with Willi Domgraf-Fassbaender (Papageno), Arturo Toscanini, Novotná (Pamina), and Helge Rosvaenge (Tamino).

15. Onstage in *The Magic Flute,* with Domgraf-Fassbaender. Salzburg, 1937.

16. Novotná sang Gluck's Eurydice several times opposite Kerstin Thorborg as Orpheus. This was the first, at the Salzburg Festival, 1937.

17. Relaxing in Salzburg, with (*left to right*) composer Anatol Provaznik, Max Reinhardt, and Arturo Toscanini.

18. The Czechoslovakian 100-crown note, featuring Max Švabinský's portrait of Novotná in the medallion at right.

19. Making her American debut as Madame Butterfly, with Herta Glaz (*left*) as Suzuki. San Francisco, 1939.

20. Newly arrived in America, the Daubeks sit for a family portrait: George, Jarmilka, Georgie, and Jarmila, circa 1941–1942.

21. Making her Metropolitan Opera debut in *La Bohème,* Act III, with John Brownlee as Marcello. New York, 1940.

22. A promotional photo for the Met's production of *The Bartered Bride,* 1941.

23. "We rejoice to hear this blessing / All our voices love expressing": The finale of *The Bartered Bride.* Metropolitan Opera, 1941.

24. "C'est ça l'histoire de Manon Lescaut": Act V of Massenet's *Manon,* with Raoul Jobin as des Grieux. Metropolitan Opera, 1941.

25. Recording *Songs of Lidice*, with Jan Masaryk at the piano and RCA Victor executive Charles O'Connell. New York, 1942.

26. Mutual admiration society: On Long Island with Toscanini and author-actress Cornelia Otis Skinner, 1942.

27. As Debussy's Mélisande. Metropolitan Opera, 1943.

28. On Broadway in *Helen Goes to Troy* (1943).

29. Milada Feilerovà, the beloved "Teta," with Georgie and Jarmilka. Long Island, 1940s.

30. Showing off her gymnastic abilities at Nicholas Kounovsky's studio in the 1940s.

31. Mozart at the Met: Act II of *The Marriage of Figaro,* early 1940s. As Cherubino, Novotná sits in the armchair at center.

32. Mozart at the Met: Promotional photo for *Don Giovanni,* with Salvatore Baccaloni (Leporello), Tito Schipa (Ottavio), Novotná (Elvira), Zinka Milanov (Anna), Ezio Pinza (Giovanni), Bidu Sayão (Zerlina), 1941.

33. At a concert commemorating Czechoslovakian independence, with Bruno Walter (conductor), and the New York Philharmonic. Carnegie Hall, 1944.

34. As Freia in Wagner's *Das Rheingold.* Metropolitan Opera, 1944.

35. As Violetta in *La Traviata,* in the Act III costume designed by Hana Podolská. Metropolitan Opera, 1940s.

36. Workers welcome Novotná on her return to the farm on the Liteň estate, 1946.

37. Acknowledging applause following her homecoming recital. National Theater, Prague, 1946.

38. Onstage with bass Eduard Haken (as Kecal) in *The Bartered Bride.* National Theater, Prague, 1947.

39. As Mrs. Malik in Fred Zinnemann's *The Search* (1948).

40. On location in Germany for *The Search*, with Aline MacMahon, Ivan Jandl, Montgomery Clift, and an unidentified actress in summer, 1947.

41. With Clift to promote *The Search* on Jinx Falkenburg and Tex McCrary's radio program, Easter Sunday, 1948. Having just learned of the death of Jan Masaryk, Novotná wears mourning attire.

42. A tender embrace from Montgomery Clift.

53. On television in *Hans Brinker* (1958). Foreground: Dick Button (Peter), Peggy King (Rychie), Tab Hunter (Hans). Background: Novotná (Dame Brinker).

54. Now a Vienna resident, Novotná goes sightseeing with a friend from New York, Brooke Astor. Schönbrunn Palace, 1959.

55. Frau Daubek at home. Vienna, 1970s.

56. With her friend and longtime publicist, Lanfranco Rasponi, celebrating the publication of his book, *The Last Prima Donnas,* which features a lengthy profile of her. New York, 1982.

57. Six prima donnas celebrate the Met centennial with three of the company's executives. Left to right: Rose Bampton, Bidu Sayâo, William Rockefeller, Risë Stevens, Anthony A. Bliss, Eleanor Steber, Zinka Milanov, Frank Taplin, Novotná. New York, October 22, 1983.

58. At the Met centennial gala with the company's former general manager, Schuyler Chapin (*left*), and Leonard Bernstein.

59. Mutual admiration society: Novotná with Czechoslovak president Václav Havel. Prague, 1990.

60. "Voices of Springtime": Novotná sings for the young visitor who would one day edit her memoir. New York, 1990. Photo by Catherine Karnow, used with permission.

from concert to concert. For example, I went from Cincinnati to Havana, Cuba, where my hostess begged me to stay—but I could not, because I had a joint recital with the pianist Arthur Rubinstein in Savannah the next night. The second half of that program featured Rubinstein performing all my favorites—but I could not stay to listen, because I had to hurry back to New York for *Traviata.* Some of my engagements were tied to local Czech communities: in Toronto, the shoe magnate Tomáš Bata threw a reception for me; in Chicago, I sang an all-Czech program with a Czech choir. When I sang in my own language, I felt like a fish swimming in water.

But the war did change the nature of some events. For example, on January 27, 1942, the Metropolitan Opera gave a gala performance to benefit the Red Cross War Fund, at which (among many other offerings) I sang Cherubino's arias, and Sir Thomas Beecham conducted Bach's *Phoebus and Pan,* a novelty that season. The evening concluded with a thrilling "Salute to the Colors," featuring all of the previous participants, as well as two Red Cross nurses and platoons of soldiers, sailors, and Marines. We packed the stage, then sang "God Bless America" and "The Star-Spangled Banner" with the audience.

The war also prevented my taking part in some ventures. For example, I received offers from the Teatro Colón in Buenos Aires and the Teatro Municipal in Rio de Janeiro for about eighteen performances during the summer of 1942. George and I didn't feel we could take the children with us, and because of the war we couldn't be certain that we would be able to return to New York when the operas had ended. I decided not to accept at this time, and I admit I felt relieved.

Before the Met season ended, there was one more *Don Giovanni,* broadcast on radio on March 7. This was the first time Alexander Kipnis had sung Leporello, which helps to explain why, during the sextet in Act II, he forgot the words. Standing near him, I saw that the prompter gave him no help, and so, quite automatically, I began singing his lines aloud. This helped him, and he picked up his part without further trouble. Other than one friend who had followed along with a score while listening to the radio, probably very few people realized what happened—but this is the only time in my career that I stepped in for a bass!

A few days later, I sang my first Octavian in *Rosenkavalier* with the company. This required a great deal of preparation, including new costumes. Luckily I had photographs of the costumes I had worn in Austria, and the Eaves Costume Company produced copies even more handsome than the Viennese originals. At the premiere on March 13, Emmanuel List sang Baron

Ochs, Marita Farrell sang Sophie, and Erich Leinsdorf conducted. I can't express how much I enjoyed singing opposite the unforgettable Marschallin of Lotte Lehmann. She and I performed this opera innumerable times in Europe, and the warmth and humanity of her singing always impressed me.

The tour followed, including a stop in Boston, where I felt very much at home, somehow. Back in New York, I sang on a radio program conducted by Alfred Wallenstein, who had been first cellist with the Philharmonic until Maestro Toscanini encouraged him to take up the baton. Since Maestro himself had been a cellist, he was very fond of Wallenstein, and I should not have been surprised that he listened to our radio program. Maestro wrote to me immediately, saying that he didn't like my singing—my voice sounded "hard" to him—and urging me to begin working with a new teacher. I trusted his judgment completely. To find a good teacher is never easy, but I saw at once that I would have to try.

My season ended with a guest appearance as Butterfly, in Newark, New Jersey. We had no stage rehearsal, and for our music rehearsal the conductor played through the score at the piano while the singers sat around him. To play Butterfly's son, Trouble, a little girl was cast, which is the usual practice. She was charming, and during the performance she started off very well, kissing me when she was supposed to and behaving as the role requires. But during the Humming Chorus, when Butterfly and Suzuki sit up all night to wait for Pinkerton's return, the little girl began yelling, "Where is my mother?" Standing nearby, I was *supposed* to be her mother—it was very embarrassing. But the audience had a good laugh, and Suzuki quickly escorted the little girl from the stage. I was glad to return to New York.

As soon as we heard that the Czechoslovak government in exile had been established in England, George offered his services to the economic division of the Czech consulate in New York. He knew that, after the war, our country would need to rebuild its agricultural resources, and several times he traveled to Minnesota to learn more about the cultivation of soybeans. At the time, most people knew very little about soy, though it is very nutritious. As always, George was very thorough in his research, and I knew he had found an excellent project to occupy him when I was busy. He also received his first papers from the United States, which permitted him to travel abroad and to be sure of reentry when he returned.

My own war efforts were mostly made at the famous Stage Door Canteen, in hospitals, and on concert stages. At one hospital, I had an unforgettable experience. In an auditorium filled with soldiers, I performed Sigmund Romberg's "When I Grow Too Old to Dream," and I was about to begin my next number when a young soldier stood and asked me to sing the Romberg again. There was a commotion in the hall, but I thought nothing of it, and I was happy to sing for the young man. After the concert, however, I learned that this boy had been one of the most difficult cases in the hospital, and that he had not spoken a word since he arrived—until he asked me to sing again. The song must have awakened memories and restored his speech. Music has such power!

The Metropolitan Opera got involved in war efforts as well. My first appearance in the 1942–1943 season was a gala concert for the March of Bonds, which also commemorated the 450th anniversary of Columbus's discovery of the New World. The Met also dispatched its singers and musicians to army camps, and I participated in the first such program, conducted by Erich Leinsdorf. We set out from New York in heavy rains and mighty winds, with eight singers and a seventy-piece orchestra, but when we got to Fort Dix, New Jersey, the truck carrying the instruments had met with a significant delay. There was no question of canceling the concert, and so the curtain rose to reveal all seventy musicians with their hands in their laps. Leinsdorf led the first two selections from the piano, and when the instruments arrived at last, we proceeded as planned, and we received an enthusiastic response. The following week, I went with another large ensemble to Camp Joyce Kilmer, also in New Jersey, and individual singers also made countless visits to camps and bases during this time. We found these performances immensely rewarding, for the men were so grateful.

Charitable concerts and activities never ceased. We attended an all-Wagner concert by Toscanini to benefit the Red Cross, and the opening of an exhibition of French art at the Parke-Bernet Galleries turned out to be an auction to benefit the war effort. There something funny happened, though it might have been unpleasant for me. As the bid rose to $2,400, I noticed a friend standing nearby, and I greeted her. The auctioneer supposed that I was raising the bid to $2,500—a great deal of money, much more than the average annual wage in the United States at the time. Fortunately our friend Conger Goodyear noticed what had happened and explained it to the auctioneer.

Talk of the war dominated our social engagements, and I recall that George often sought out H. V. Kaltenborn, the CBS radio commentator, for his views. Kaltenborn had visited Russia numerous times and seen the gigantic munitions factories there. He believed that, even if the Germans won at Stalingrad and beyond, Russia could continue the war. George reflected on this information, looking for clues as to when, if ever, we might return to our home.

My most significant artistic contribution during the war years arose during a conversation over dinner at the home of Mr. and Mrs. Chester Burden. Jan Masaryk was also a guest, and as we had done so often before, he accompanied me in a few Czech folksongs. The critic Olin Downes had never heard us before, and now he exclaimed, "This is really a treasure! You must make records, so that all America can hear these beautiful songs!" The RCA Victor Company had asked me to record for them, and when I suggested that Masaryk and I record folk songs, they thought it was an excellent idea. But there were many songs to choose from, and Jan and I discussed our selections at any and every occasion, even sitting out after-dinner movie screenings (which had become the fashionable entertainment at New York dinner parties) so that we could debate which songs were best.

We selected fifteen, and we recorded on May 6 and 7, very warm days. We sweated through two long sessions in the small RCA studio on East Thirty-Eighth Street. Charles O'Connell, the RCA director, brought champagne to revive us when we had finished.

Jan and I decided to call the album *Songs of Lidice,* in memory of the Czech village that had been destroyed by the Nazis in June 1942, ostensibly in retaliation for the assassination of Reichsprotektor Reinhard Heydrich (in Prague on June 4 of that year). After the war, I was able to make a pilgrimage to the village: Nothing, nothing was left. Jan wrote in his liner notes for our recordings:

> A folk song is the purest expression of a people's souls. I used to hear them as a child in the fields and in the mountains of Bohemia and Slovakia, a lovely memory indeed. To bring back these and similar songs to the occupied countries of Europe is one of the fundamental reasons of our struggle. Song has disappeared from the Czech, Polish, and Yugoslav fields and mountains. . . . Let us all resolve to do our best, even more than our best, to shorten this struggle of good against evil. And when we rebuild Lidice, these songs will come back through pure Czech and Slovak air, cleansed once and for all from the destroyers of music.[6]

By coincidence, I was in Chicago when *Songs of Lidice* was released. Due to the large Czech population in the city, the record was much in demand, and

I autographed many copies. I learned that Stern Park, a nearby community in Illinois, had changed its name to Lidice, to perpetuate the name of the village destroyed by the Nazis. So I made a pilgrimage there, and laid a wreath at the foot of a memorial, the work of our good friend, the Czech sculptor Mario Korbel.

In many respects, the war did not seem to make many outward changes in our routines. We continued our practice of summer vacations. Jarmilka won prizes for horseback riding and jumping, and she took up tennis; George asked our friend, the famous Czech tennis player Karel Koželuh, to give lessons to Jar and me. Maestro Toscanini came to visit us in Stony Brook, and knowing that he was a fan of Cornelia Otis Skinner, I invited her and her husband to join us for dinner. I had never seen the Maestro so relaxed. And he was so sweet to my children. Jarmilka played piano for him, while Georgie looked on happily. Wonder of wonders, Maestro allowed us to take a few photos to remember this lovely afternoon together. Lucrezia Bori invited us to visit her at Blue Mountain Lake in the Adirondacks, where she had bought a small island with two guesthouses and a main house. Swimming, boating, and playing golf, I gathered new strength before my next concert tour.

But travel had become more burdensome, because there were so few porters to help with baggage: they had enlisted in the armed forces or were taking part in the war effort in other ways. Having to carry my own luggage now, I invented a zippered clothes bag, made of waterproof, plaid wool. On the train, I could hang the bag, keeping my dresses uncrushed, which was a good thing when trains arrived just an hour before my concerts. I'm very sorry that I didn't patent my design, because very soon such garment bags appeared on the market everywhere. Apart from that, I carried an overnight case with a sweater for every occasion and some blouses, since I usually wore a suit. With less luggage, traveling became much easier.

At the Metropolitan, I sang *Traviata*, *Bohème*, *Bartered Bride*, and *Rosenkavalier*, now with a new Sophie, Eleanor Steber. I also attended a performance of *The Daughter of the Regiment* starring Lily Pons, whom I liked very much. At the end, to an enthusiastic response, they brought on the flag of the Free French, then sang the Marseillaise and "The Star-Spangled Banner," with great enthusiasm. The difficulties of wartime travel, however, cut short our annual tour, with stops only in Chicago, Cleveland, and Rochester. With the Philharmonic Orchestra, I sang Marguerite in *The Damnation of Faust*, with Frederick Jagel and Ezio Pinza, conducted by Artur Rodzinski.

This extraordinary work was rarely heard in those days, though it contains moments of great inspiration and examples of Berlioz's power in both melodic and harmonic lines for orchestra and voices.

I sang very often on radio shows, and one of the jolliest, a real carnival, was presided over by two of the nation's foremost wits, the pianist Oscar Levant and the playwright George S. Kaufman. I sang the *Hoffmann* Barcarolle, the Merry Widow Waltz, and an aria from *Traviata*. When I finished, Oscar Levant remarked, "I have a list here of your repertory: *Traviata, Manon, Rosenkavalier, Figaro, Don Giovanni*. Very imposing!"

I thanked him, then asked for a list of his repertory. Levant replied, "*The Rhapsody in Blue*."

"And what else?" I asked.

"*The Rhapsody in Blue*," he said, and when I pressed him, he snapped, "What's the matter with the *Rhapsody*?"

Kaufman jumped in: "What Mme. Novotná means is that you can't go through life playing just the *Rhapsody*."

"Who says I can't?" Levant replied. "I have!"

In May, I had a call from the composer Kurt Weill, who had just written a musical comedy called *One Touch of Venus* and wanted to know if I would be interested in playing Venus. He and the director, Elia Kazan, came to see me, and Kurt played the score for me. Both were astonished as I hummed the melodies while Kurt played them. The explanation was quite simple. The music was very easy on the ear, and it reminded me of music I had heard before. On the whole, I liked it, but I had other commitments, so there was no way to accept the role. Mary Martin took the part, and had great success with it.

Among the engagements that prevented my playing Venus on Broadway was a South American tour in the summer of 1943. By this time it was a little clearer how the war affected travel in this hemisphere, and the principal difficulty for us was obtaining all the right paperwork. So at last I accepted the offer from the Teatro Colón in Buenos Aires, and I agreed to sing *Traviata, Bohème, Falstaff*, and *Marriage of Figaro*. I also agreed to sing Berlioz's *Damnation of Faust* and Ravel's *Shéhérazade* with the Asociación Wagneriana. Then the paper chase began.

Because of the war, those without priority status had to relinquish their seats on an airplane to anyone with priority. I could have gotten clearance for myself, as an artist, but not for George. It took all the energy and help of many friends to secure priority. However, we weren't in the clear yet, because the Consulate of Panama denied us the visas we needed for a short stopover to change planes. I went to the consul personally, and by some miracle he immediately gave me the visas. But we were still waiting for reentry permits from the U.S. State Department. We postponed our departure for a full week, a good decision, because we received the permits just in time to catch the train to Miami.

When we arrived at Pennsylvania Station on May 19, we were surprised to hear a band playing the Czechoslovakian national anthem. They weren't playing for me, but for President Beneš, who was just arriving from Washington, D.C.

The train trip to Miami is a long affair, and we arrived in the evening. A representative from Pan Am told us that we could begin our journey the next day, and we were in the air at 4:30 the next morning. The plane was very comfortable, and we could even lie down to sleep. But in those days, long before jet travel, nonstop flights over great distances were simply impossible, and overnight flights rare. Our itinerary was very long, but it permitted us to see a great deal of a part of the world that was new to both George and me.

Our first stop was Havana, and then we went on to Balboa, at the Panama Canal, where we changed planes. There we met Norman Cordon, the bass, who was also waiting for transportation to Buenos Aires because he, too, had been engaged by the Teatro Colón. On our way to Colombia, we flew over the Gaucho Valley and saw the most beautiful scenery imaginable. The colors ranged from deepest green to pink and brown. We passed over high mountains, their peaks dotted by little houses with dark-red roofs visible from far away.

We stayed overnight in Cali, which was founded by Pizarro around 1535. Here we were joined by Bruno Landi and his wife, the Argentine soprano Hilde Reggiani. They had waited a whole month in Mexico for permission to fly and had had to make the last leg of their journey by car over the mountains. They were exhausted, and George and I understood how lucky we had been. We continued on our way, stopping at Quito, Guayaquil, Talara, Chiclayo, and Lima, where we spent the night. We received diplomas as souvenirs of our first crossing of the equator, then checked into our hotel. After dinner, we attended a cockfight, which was really repulsive. The poor creatures had blood pouring out of them, while people yelled and bet like crazy.

The next day, we flew from Lima to Arequipa, where we were sorry that we couldn't stay a few days to see Lake Titicaca and the ancient Incan capital,

Cuzco. But we were already overdue, so onward to Arica and Antofagasta, and from there a disagreeable two-hour flight over the mountains. The plane danced in the heavy wind, and sometimes we dropped down suddenly, so that we almost touched the mountaintops. When we arrived in Salto, Argentina, the pilot told us that only four pilots were capable of negotiating this difficult trip, and we could see his relief that it was over.

At the hotel in Salto, I received a call from the Teatro Colón, wanting to know that I had arrived and asking whether I had brought my costumes. It seemed a strange question at this point: I could hardly go back for them. But I had indeed brought my beautiful *Traviata* gowns and Cherubino costumes. This put a burden on George. We were allowed a maximum of 110 pounds of luggage between us, and with all my costumes, George could bring only one suit and his evening wear. The rest he would have to purchase in Buenos Aires.

After another delay, this one due to dense fog, we arrived in Buenos Aires at five o'clock on the evening before my first performance was scheduled. Photographers surrounded us, and I learned that the management of the Colón had decided to postpone the *Traviata* premiere by a few days, to give us time to rehearse. At the Hotel Alvear, a representative from the Czech Embassy and our friend Robert Hadow came to greet us, and we ran into Rudolf Firkušný, who was in Buenos Aires for a series of recitals. Amazingly enough, the next morning, the first people we saw were three friends from Vienna: Prince Ernst Starhemberg, George Schicht, and Count Max Thurn.

That evening was the opening night of the Colón season, and instead of *Traviata,* the company performed *Werther,* with Marcelle Denya and Raoul Jobin. The Argentine president, his entire cabinet, and all the diplomats in Buenos Aires attended in all their uniforms and decorations, and a whole company of soldiers in colorful uniforms marched to the parterre with sabers drawn. It was very imposing. And the opera house is really lovely, with excellent acoustics. Although it looks smaller than the Metropolitan, it seats 3,700.

The premiere of *Traviata* went smoothly on May 28, with Bruno Landi as Alfredo, Leonard Warren as Germont, and Ettore Panizza conducting. The next day, I decided to take it easy, and so George went by himself to explore Buenos Aires. The residential section, with its many parks and statues, reminded him strongly of Paris, he said, and in Florida Street, a shopping center, he discovered many tailors and shoemakers who helped him to augment his meager wardrobe.

Then began the social activities, including dinner with the Hadows and a concert by Firkušný. What really bothered us in the beginning, however, was that everything started so much later than what we were accustomed to. In the evening, one cannot get anything to eat before 8:00 p.m., and dinner typically starts at 10:00 or later. Except in the homes of diplomats, it was the custom to arrive at least half an hour later than the time stated on the invitation. Concerts started at 10:00 p.m., and operas, interrupted with long intermissions, began at 9:00 and lasted until 1:00 a.m.

Rehearsals for *Falstaff*—a complicated opera requiring great preparation—began the day after my second *Traviata.* I arranged for a taxi to wait for me every morning at 10:00. But one morning, I waited in my room for the porter to call. The time passed, and nothing happened. Finally, I called the porter and asked for an explanation. Quite cheerfully, he answered, "Madame, we have a little revolution."

I couldn't believe my ears, but it was true. There had been a coup d'état, and the government had fled by boat. Some fifty people died and two hundred were injured in skirmishes. Nobody knew exactly what was going on, but by noon a junta of four generals, led by General Arturo Rawson, had taken over the government. That night the opera was closed, but the next night I sang *Traviata* again, and social life resumed as if nothing had happened. It seemed that people were used to such sudden changes—"revolutions," as they call them. The governmental crisis continued, General Rawson resigned, and General Pedro Pablo Ramirez took his place. But life went merrily on.

Falstaff, which premiered on June 22, was a triumph for Leonard Warren, who had never before sung the title role. As for me, the role of Alice didn't give me much opportunity either vocally or dramatically, though the press was unanimously very good. Our second performance was even better received: the audience seemed to enjoy it more, laughing and clapping even between scenes. There followed more performances of *Traviata,* one in which I did not sing. The Colón had arranged a special performance at "popular prices," at which a young Argentine soprano would sing Violetta. As she had never done it before, I offered to come to rehearsals and help with her acting. Everybody was enchanted with her work, and she came through with flying colors. Her name was Delia Rigal, and she later became a well-known member of the Metropolitan Opera.

We had another fantastic "parade" of generals and notables for our gala performance of *Bohème* on Argentina's Constitution Day, an important national holiday. I sang Mimì, Bruno Landi was Rodolfo, and Norman Cordon sang Colline, with Victor Damiani and Amanda Cetera as Marcello and Musetta.

When Max Thurn left on a ski vacation, he kindly let us move into his apartment. While I rehearsed *Figaro,* our friend Fritz Mandl took George to visit Mar del Plata, and the home of Carlos Fortabat, a wealthy Argentinian. Fortabat reared prize bulls on a vast *estancia* in San Jacinto, surrounded by lovely, low hills, where the setting sun changed the clouds into a myriad of colors. George fell in love with the place. Fritz Mandl also invited us to spend a day on his motorboat on the River Tigre, and with the Hadows we attended a polo match at the Hurlingham Club, a very exclusive sporting club, where 85 percent of the members must be British—only 15 percent for the rest of the world. George and I also became acquainted with the Czech community in Buenos Aires, and one evening I sang at the Sokol club.

But it seemed that we were very much cut off from the rest of the world. People in Buenos Aires didn't seem to care much about the war, and even English-language newspapers didn't carry much about the situation. We received reports on the children every week from Teta, but since we arrived, I'd had no news from my parents, which was very disconcerting.

Soon it was time for my engagements in Rio de Janeiro. George and I departed by plane on August 19, and after just one stop in Porto Allegre, we landed in Rio. The view of the city from the air was indescribably beautiful. We flew only a few meters away from the statue of Christ the Redeemer on Mount Corcovado, passed the Sugar Loaf, and landed at the airport in the center of the city. The theater was smaller than the Colón, seating only some two thousand, but the acoustics were not very good. Still, we enjoyed performances of *Simon Boccanegra* and Solange Petit-Renaux's Thaïs. As for me, I sang Giulietta and Antonia in *Tales of Hoffmann* with Raoul Jobin, and three *Traviata*s with Charles Kullman as Alfredo, which I enjoyed just as much as I had our partnership at the Met.

In our free time, we went on many excursions, taking the funicular to Corcovado for the breathtaking view, and swimming at the Copacabana when the weather permitted. We socialized, too, and at one party I met the composer Heitor Villa-Lobos. He sent me some of his songs, which I later sang in my concerts. During the intermission for one of my *Hoffmann* performances, the Czech envoy introduced George to Princess Bourbon-Braganza, whose late husband, Pedro de Alcântara, Prince of Grão Palo, had been pretender to the Brazilian throne. She was born Elisabeth Dobřenská, a Bohemian aristocrat, and she and George enjoyed reminiscing about her family, whom he knew quite well. She invited us to her home in Petropolis, and after lunch we visited the former imperial residence, which had become a museum. Before leaving Brazil, Minister of External Relations Osvaldo Aranha presented me with a green tourmaline as a souvenir—I was delighted.

Even before I had completed my engagements at the Colón, the director of the opera in Santiago, Chile, asked me to sing six performances with his company. I accepted, though it meant extending our trip and missing the children a while longer, which George and I both regretted. The companies in Lima and Mexico City offered me engagements, too, hoping that I would sing with them on my way back to New York. This time, I refused. I wanted to see my children.

Arriving at the Rio airport the next morning, we learned that our flight to Santiago had been canceled; the next would not be until October 1, a full week after I was scheduled to begin rehearsals for *Traviata*. Foreign Minister Aranha interceded, securing me a seat on a plane that would take me as far as Mendoza—but poor George had to take a sixteen-hour train ride to get there. The fairly short flight to Santiago the next day took us over the snow-covered Andes, a very beautiful sight, though the high altitude exhausted me. I rehearsed the next day and, with only one day to rest, went on to sing Violetta better than ever. I also sang Gilda and Manon. The *Manon* was such a success that George couldn't get a ticket, and he had to sit in the company director's box. Then, after my last *Traviata* in Santiago, we were winging back to the States the next morning.

From Miami, George and I telephoned the children, whose voices were music to my ears. After the long train ride back to New York, we had just enough time to catch the train to Stonybrook, Long Island. The children and Teta were waiting for us. We had been away almost five months.

We enjoyed a few days of real relaxation. Jan Masaryk came over from London on his way to Atlantic City for a conference on relief efforts. He made a sensation in New York, winning over absolutely everyone with his personal charm, and he invited me to sing at a concert commemorating the twenty-fifth anniversary of Czechoslovak independence at Carnegie Hall on October 28, 1943, with Artur Rodzinski conducting, and Rudolf Firkušný performing as well. Jan accepted our invitation to spend Christmas Eve with our family that year, and said that he would bring along his sister, Alice, who had never married. But two days after the Carnegie Hall concert, we received very sad news: Max Reinhardt died. I admired this great man very much, and I determined that, if his production of *Helen Goes to Troy* went ahead, I would find a way to take part in it.

When word spread that we had returned, George and I were again inundated with invitations. One of the most memorable came from Helen Hull, at whose dinner party we met the Duke and Duchess of Windsor. The Duke adored Viennese music, and after dinner he asked if I knew a song called "Mariandl." I had never heard of it, so he sat down at the piano and picked out the melody with one finger while he taught me the words. "Mariandl" became our theme song, and from that moment on, whenever we met we sang it together.

For a little while I had more time to spend with the children, and so I would take Jarmilka and Georgie to Central Park, most often winding up at the zoo. The children adored animals and made me promise to buy them a dog. Jarmilka's interest in music now extended beyond piano to dance lessons, and one day, after I took her to a rehearsal for a Toscanini concert, Maestro quizzed her and declared himself satisfied with her progress. At Christmas that year, I gave Jarmilka an autograph book, and Maestro was the first to sign, with a few bars of a composition exercise he had written when he was fifteen.

Danger marked my first performances at the Met that season, and an accident during my first *Magic Flute* might have proved fatal to me. During the trials of Tamino and Pamina, the director placed several electric fans offstage to make my gowns flutter in the breeze. On the first night, the veil around my neck got caught in one of the fans, and I might have been strangled if an electrician hadn't hurriedly hit the off switch. For once, I thought, Pamina had endured an *authentic* trial. Then, during a performance of *The Tales of Hoffmann* conducted by Sir Thomas Beecham, Ezio Pinza narrowly avoided a serious injury. As Dr. Miracle, he was supposed to make his entrance through a trapdoor behind the sofa where I, as Antonia, sat. On this evening, however, the stagehands forgot to close the trapdoor, and when Pinza moved across the stage a little after his entrance, he fell straight through the opening. Fortunately the drop wasn't very far, and he wasn't hurt.

At the same time, I began to prepare Debussy's *Pelléas et Mélisande,* an opera I adore. Mélisande was not an easy role to learn. The music is so elusive that I had to know my vocal part independent of the accompaniment. There was nothing to hold onto, so I needed a long time to study. At the behest of George Szell, I also began to delve into the role of Freia in *Das Rheingold.* While I worked on these new roles, I was also rehearsing and performing several familiar ones: Antonia in *Hoffmann,* Octavian in *Rosenkavalier,* Pamina in *Magic Flute,* and Cherubino. This was a heavy schedule, but

I found new strength in the gymnastics classes that I took every morning from Nicholas Kounovsky, whom George had discovered and recommended enthusiastically. It wasn't easy at the beginning, but soon I was able to do handstands, the bridge, and all sorts of difficult exercises. Before, colds used to plague me, but now I noticed that they seldom bothered me.

I accepted the chairmanship of the Czechoslovak chapter of the Red Cross, which required me to attend many meetings and to write many letters to ask for contributions. Luckily, the drive was very successful, but it took up much of my time, so I urged George to accept invitations without me.

One day, I received a call from Helen Hull, the sponsor of the New Opera Company, as well as the Musicians Emergency Fund.[7] The New Opera Company planned to produce *Helen Goes to Troy* in May, she said, asking whether I would be interested in singing Helen. Of course I wanted to participate in this, one of Max Reinhardt's final projects. I asked Edward Johnson to release me from the few Metropolitan Opera performances that conflicted with the *Helen* schedule. At first he opposed the idea vigorously, but finally he agreed, so long as I sang *Bohème* and *Figaro* in Boston on the Met tour that April.

Without Max Reinhardt at the helm, Herbert Graf staged the production; Reinhardt's son, Gottfried, prepared the book to *Helen Goes to Troy* in collaboration with John Meehan Jr.; and Herbert Baker wrote delightfully colloquial lyrics to Offenbach's songs. Léonide Massine choreographed; Robert Edmund Jones designed the sets, and Ladislaus Czettel, the costumes. Erich Wolfgang Korngold conducted and prepared the arrangements, adding the Barcarolle from *Hoffmann* as a solo for me, here called "Love at Last." It always stopped the show. Toscanini attended one of our final rehearsals, and he wrote me a very encouraging letter to wish the entire company success; he wound up seeing the show four times.

Helen Goes to Troy opened on April 24, 1944, at the Alvin Theater. The critic for the *Herald Tribune* described the premiere as "another operetta triumph" for the New Opera Company, and he called me "an ideal choice for the role of Helen . . . a statuesque beauty with a truly fine singing voice. Mme. Novotná stopped the show cold several times last night. The Met's loss is Broadway's gain."

He also described this as my "debut on the legitimate stage," and locally it was. The show gave me the chance to reflect on the differences in performing in different venues: opera houses, concert stages, and theater. In a concert, the audience is quite near you, and you can see their faces: even if you don't look at them, you feel their reactions. It can be terribly disturbing if somebody in the front row talks to a neighbor or plays with a program. You can lose your concentration. In an opera house, the orchestra pit creates a greater distance between the stage and the audience. But playing in a legitimate theater is quite a different thing. The audience becomes a performer in the play. If the people are with you, their reactions inspire you, and you give more of yourself. Every audience varies, and that makes acting a beautiful thing. Playing the same role every day for a long time doesn't become monotonous. In *Helen,* every performance seemed like a premiere.

Something very funny happened one night, and it illustrates the kind of flexibility that opera very seldom permits. In one scene, Helen sits in a bathtub when Calchas, the high priest played wonderfully by Ralph Dumke, comes in and sits gingerly on the edge of the tub, averting his gaze from Helen. Suddenly, Ralph fell into the tub! For a moment, he was quite stunned. Then he tried to get out of the tub, which wasn't easy, because he was quite heavy. As he struggled, the audience laughed, thinking this was part of the show. Meanwhile, Paris, played by William Horne, was supposed to make his entrance, singing "Helena!" Bill was shaking with laughter, so it came out more like "Helen-ah-ha-ha-ha-ha!" That was the last straw. Everybody onstage broke up, and the audience was convulsed with laughter, too. Afterward, Ralph said that, so long as he could be sure he wouldn't break his neck in the process, he'd like to fall into the tub at every performance.

As summer began, we made plans for the children to attend new schools in the fall: Jarmilka would go to Brearley, and Georgie to Collegiate. We rented a little house on a farm owned by the Whitney family, and especially for the children, it was a paradise. Like his sister, Georgie began riding now, and we all went swimming and took long walks in the woods. One afternoon, we came across two kittens abandoned by their mother. One kitten died, but the survivor happily joined our family: if the children couldn't have a dog, at least now they had a cat. Some evenings we dined with Cornelius Vanderbilt Whitney, called Sonny, and his wife, Eleanor. At one such dinner, a beautiful girl, about fifteen years old, sat between Sonny and George. Both men tried to engage her in conversation, but she was so shy that they got only a few words from her. And who was this beauty? Grace Kelly. It seems unbelievable, because she later became such an engaging hostess as the wife of Prince Rainier.

I was still performing in *Helen Goes to Troy* and spending the summer in the country, while a treasured family custom for us, complicated my commute. The heat in New York City that summer was unbearable, and business slowed down at the box office. The cast agreed to a 25 percent reduction in salary, but even this wasn't enough to keep the show alive, and we closed on July 15, 1944. After the final performance, I received a beautiful bouquet from the cast, with a note: "To 'La Belle Novotná,' with deep appreciation for the pleasure of working with so fine an artist. The ensemble." So my Broadway debut ended very nicely, though I couldn't say I was unhappy to say goodbye to the theater. I had started to feel the strain of so many performances each week: I had lost twelve pounds, and I'm not sure I could have continued much longer. This way, the matter was decided for me, and at last I could enjoy a real vacation.

The president of IBM, Thomas J. Watson, invited George to join the Committee on Economic Reconstruction. We had known Mr. Watson for some time, and he also asked me to give a little concert at a committee meeting at IBM headquarters in Endicott, New York—with support from a glee club of women employees. At that meeting, George was asked to give a little speech about Czechoslovakia to the chamber of commerce. Clearly Mr. Watson found George impressive, and he would go on to become an important influence in our lives.

During the summer of 1944, we received good news from Europe. First there was the Normandy invasion, and then Allied armies landed on the French Riviera. After a very long time, toward the end of the summer I received a letter from my parents, saying that they awaited our return. We could not believe that they had accurate news reports in occupied Czechoslovakia, and we wondered whether it was possible they sensed the nearness of the war's end. President Beneš began calling key figures (such as Colonel Oldřich Spaniel, a member of the Czech mission in New York) to London to join the government in exile. George and I began to hope that we, too, might make an early return to our homeland.

Everybody longed to help in some way, and when the Free Europe Committee organized a bond drive, I participated, making a speech:

> It seems strange that a Czech should talk to an American audience about buying bonds; but perhaps it is *because I am a Czech,* perhaps it is because in the few years I have been in this wonderful country, I have learned to love it so, *that I can speak to you* and tell you how important it is *for all of us* to bring victory closer. I think of the people of France, in the areas around Normandy already liberated, and I can easily picture their joy at being *free again.* Yes,

> free—*free* from slavery—*free* from the Nazis—and free to live as men. You see my own Czechoslovakia has been enslaved now for five years. Five years of waiting for the day of liberation to arrive—*the day the armies of the United Nations arrive.* And to bring that day closer for all people—to see peace on Earth—to make sure the evil forces who would destroy Free Men *never rise again*—yes, we can all do one single thing right now to bring that day closer, and that is to buy a bond.

I hope it helped.

On Georgie's birthday, October 1, we moved back to the city. The children began the school year at their new schools, and from the start we were all busy. Within a matter of days, I sang a concert in Toronto with André Kostelanetz for an audience of 7,500, and the next afternoon I sang for the RAF, which I loved to do, because soldiers were such grateful listeners. Then came a concert at Carnegie Hall to commemorate Czechoslovak independence, with Bruno Walter and the Philharmonic Orchestra. The film star Ronald Colman spoke, and Presidents Roosevelt and Beneš sent letters to be read aloud. My schedule at the Metropolitan would not begin until after the New Year, because, Edward Johnson said, he hadn't expected me to be free from my commitments to *Helen Goes to Troy.* But he asked me to participate in a radio concert on December 12, and in return I asked him to a musical dinner at my home. I hoped to interest Mr. Johnson in *Rusalka,* and after dinner Firkušný played through the score and I sang the arias. Everyone seemed to like the opera, but Mr. Johnson said he lacked the funds to mount a new production. I determined to find people who would help to finance the project.

Around this time, Marks Levine, my manager at NCAC, informed me that the great impresario Sol Hurok wanted to represent me. I knew that Hurok had arrived in America quite young, and that his programs found early success, first at the Brooklyn Community Center and then on Sunday nights at the Hippodrome, where he presented such artists as the dancer Anna Pavlova, the singers Ernestine Schumann-Heink and Fyodor Chaliapin, and the violinist Efrem Zimbalist. Pavlova encouraged him to turn his attention to dance, and he introduced Isadora Duncan, Uday Shan-Kar, Escudero, Trudi Schoop, the Ballets Russes, and Mary Wigman to American audiences. I would go so far as to say that he awakened interest in ballet in the United States. As an agent, he represented many of the best musical artists, including the pianist Arthur Rubinstein, and the singers Marian Anderson and

Jan Peerce. After meeting with George and me, Mr. Hurok signed me to a three-year exclusive contract. He wanted to start booking me immediately, and he suggested that a quartet of Metropolitan Opera soloists, performing operatic scenes in costume, would appeal to audiences. I agreed to select the other artists, and it didn't take long: Herta Glaz was our mezzo-soprano, Raoul Jobin our tenor, and Martial Singher our baritone. Lothar Wallerstein would stage-direct, and Felix Wolfes would accompany us on piano. The tour would begin in February 1945, giving us plenty of time to prepare.

Over the next several months, George became more prominent, and he was named to lead the Czechoslovak delegation to the International Business Conference in November 1944, alongside delegates from fifty-two nations around the world, upholding Mr. Watson's motto, "World Peace through World Trade." George's knowledge of the European scene impressed Mr. Watson, who asked him to work for IBM. George replied that he would be very interested, but that he knew nothing about IBM's products. "That's easily fixed," Mr. Watson said, suggesting that George could attend the IBM school at the company's headquarters in Endicott, New York, to learn all about the business.

At a second meeting with Mr. Watson and two other IBM executives, George explained that, until now, he had been his own boss, the head of his family's commercial and agricultural business. He knew how to manage people, and he was interested in learning all about IBM's business. Mr. Watson welcomed him to the IBM family. After ten weeks of schooling in Endicott, George would return to the New York City office and, after the war, take over as general manager of an office in Czechoslovakia, with responsibility for business in other countries as well. George had been terribly unhappy with so little to occupy him in America during the war years. Now a new future opened up for him; and while we still believed that our life in Czechoslovakia would resume its normal course when we returned, he was glad just to be useful.

It certainly wasn't easy for a man of fifty-four, accustomed to being his own master, to sit on a school bench again. And because of the war, when George began his classes in Endicott, he was one of only two men, along with Mr. Lam from China—among fifty young women. "I like women," George said, "but so many is just too much!" However, the work was interesting, and he survived. After ten weeks, when George's class graduated, I asked Mr. Lam to teach me a Chinese song that I could perform at the ceremony. (Afterward, another man from China approached me, believing that I spoke his language, and I had to confess that I had learned the song phonetically.) When George received his diploma, he remarked that this was probably the first time that children had attended their own father's graduation: "Usually, it is just the opposite." I suspect that this is the reason he wanted them to be there. George started in the IBM office on Fifty-Seventh Street, and a salesman took him to the department stores and to the Metropolitan Life Insurance offices, so that he could observe the installation of IBM equipment and how it functioned. He was well prepared for his job. The question was when we would return to Europe.

Our association with Mr. Watson was the luckiest thing that ever happened to George, and it seemed that Providence was looking after us. This proved to be true in 1948, when we lost our home in Czechoslovakia a second time.

I began the new year with a recording for RCA Victor of Offenbach and Johann Strauss, conducted by Frieder Weissmann, and at the Metropolitan I took on several familiar roles—Pamina, Mimì, Donna Elvira, Freia—and with Mélisande at last. Martial Singher sang Pelléas, Lawrence Tibbett sang Golaud, and Emil Cooper conducted. In previous performances, Bidu Sayão had sung Mélisande, and, like me, she had a great deal of preparation. However, I made my role debut on February 14, 1945, without an orchestra rehearsal, and for a role of this magnitude, that was unheard of. It was a miracle that I was able to "Add [Mélisande] to the singer's gallery of appealing portraits," as the critic for the *New York World Telegram* wrote, in a review that was balsam to my soul. "Subtly spun style blended with beauty of person and gesture in Mme. Novotná's version of the woodland mystery woman."

To create such an unusual personality onstage is not easy. You have to begin by analyzing thoroughly the libretto and the character you are to portray. What kind of person is she? What is her relation to the other characters? What are her background and habits? The second step is to create a bridge between understanding the character's emotions and bringing them to life. To gesture or to walk has no value unless it expresses a thought or a feeling, which the audience must understand within the given moment. In other words, our task is not to make motions but to convey emotions.

At the Metropolitan, I always had a very happy relationship with Bidu and with everybody in the theater. Among the singers, there was no jealousy. Although we often alternated in the same roles, we were all good friends. To sing at the Metropolitan was the fulfillment of every artist's dream. But to me it meant so much more. While Czechoslovakia was under occupation, the United States and the Metropolitan Opera became my home. Because of the war, no new artists could come to America, and those already here could not return to Europe. As a result, something very significant happened. Although there was already a large number of American singers on the Met roster, there was now even more room for American artists. Together, both the European residents and the Americans built a true ensemble company. There were no changes when one singer took over a role from another, and the performances were absolutely perfect. We all knew each other well, and the Metropolitan Opera was one big happy family.

Mr. Hurok's "quartet tour" began in Worcester, Massachusetts, the first of eleven concerts in fourteen days. Because of the well-balanced program, we were not overtaxed. But I had my own concerts in the coming days, in Binghamton and Toronto, and they proved to be too much for me. With a bad cold, I had to cancel *Don Giovanni* and rejoined the Met for *Rosenkavalier* just two days before the end of the season. I sang only once on the tour that season, Cherubino in Cleveland, then resumed the quartet tour. When I returned to New York, I found a letter from Mayor Fiorello La Guardia.

Expecting the end of the war in Europe, Mayor La Guardia invited me to participate in ceremonies, open to the public, on the Mall in Central Park. The program was carefully planned to begin at 5:00 p.m., to repeat every hour, and to end around 10:00 p.m. Of course, no one knew what the date would be, because we didn't know for certain when peace would be declared, and the mayor didn't expect that we would have much advance notice.

As the Allied victories in Europe continued, George and I wondered how Czechoslovakia would look after the war. Beneš was in Moscow, and we didn't know how he could resist Stalin. But Jan Masaryk, arriving for the San Francisco Conference, was confident that Czechoslovakia could serve as a bridge between East and West.

On May 6, I sang on a radio broadcast (a duet of "I'm an Old Cowhand" with Buddy Rich, among other songs), and everyone talked excitedly about the end of the war. The next night, we ate dinner at Brooke Marshall's; victory in Europe had been declared already in Britain, and word had leaked that President Truman would make an announcement the next day. The rejoicing was such that George and I didn't go home until the wee hours.

On May 8, after the president's announcement, George and I dined with Mr. and Mrs. Watson, and one of the other guests was H. R. Knickerbocker, a reporter who had the distinction of having spent more time on the battlefronts of Europe, the Middle East, and the Far East than any other war correspondent.[8] Famous for his unerring judgment, he had the reputation of a great journalist, but not everything he told us that evening was pleasant. On May 7, he said, General Patton's armored units had been poised to crush the German forces in Prague but were ordered to fall back to Plzeň. The Russians were still 150 kilometers to the east. Knowing this, the Germans massacred some five hundred Czechs who were trying to protect various monuments from destruction by the retreating Germans. The Czechs rose up in response, and the Soviets did not enter Prague until two days later. "Our armies have come to liberate the valiant people of Czechoslovakia, so close to the Soviet Union," the commanding officer declared, hoping to win the sympathy of the populace.

Despite my misgivings, I sang at the Brooklyn Academy of Music at a benefit for the Russian war effort on May 13. There I again met the Russian consul general, as well as Maxim Litvinov, who recalled our dance together in Geneva so long ago.

George and I rented a summer home from Helen Emmet, on the Pratt estate in Glen Cove, Long Island. George commuted to his IBM office in New York City every day, and one evening he brought home Jan Masaryk, who had returned from San Francisco. Jan was very pessimistic. The only hope for Czechoslovakia, he believed, was free elections, because Molotov had told him that the Soviets did not want to impose any form of government on a nation that knew how to govern itself.[9] But we had bad news from home. Every large property in Czechoslovakia was being nationalized, including George's family properties in Brněnec and Liteň. The Russian army had commandeered our homes, and our hope of returning to Czechoslovakia was vanishing quickly. Jan promised to do everything in his power to restore our property to us.

George suggested to Mr. Watson that he give a luncheon in honor of Jan Masaryk, and Mr. Watson agreed. On July 6 at the Waldorf Astoria, Mayor La Guardia, an irresistible personality, gave the keynote speech. Jan thanked the United States for liberating our country, and Mr. Watson concluded by expressing his hope for freedom everlasting. The writer Marcia Davenport, daughter of the soprano Alma Gluck, was among those who attended, and she became a lifelong friend to George and me. Recently divorced at the time, she captivated Jan, and yet he could speak of nothing but his return to Prague. We saw him a few more times before his departure, and he promised to find out what had happened to our home and to tell us when we could go back.

The rest of the summer continued much as it always did, with a couple of interruptions for my work. I made my first appearance on television, though

I don't remember what I sang.[10] I do remember that it was terrifically hot, because the cameras required the use of so many reflectors in those days. Luckily, my experience in moviemaking meant that I was comfortable on camera. I also traveled to Michigan City to sing *The Bartered Bride* in an open-air theater.

Then, on August 14, 1945, we learned that the Japanese emperor had surrendered, thus ending World War II. Now all our hopes were concentrated on the Peace Conference.

3

After the War

Once the war was over, George and I agreed that he must go to Czechoslovakia as soon as possible. I wrote to President Beneš, asking for his help, and his secretary wrote in reply, saying that nationalization was only a temporary step and that our property would be returned to us as soon as the situation returned to normal. However, others told us that "national committees" were being established in every community, deciding the fate of citizens according to their political views. We also heard that Russian soldiers were everywhere, behaving like barbarians—and using our home at Liteň as a barracks.

The flour mills at Brněnec had been nationalized as well. After our departure for America, George's nephew, Josef Bromovský, managed the mills, while George's sister-in-law, Josef Daubek's widow, continued to live part-time at Brněnec.[1] The war changed everything, and Olga moved with her children to Prague, where she rented an apartment.

Although my thoughts were in Prague, I had to go on with my duties. Another concert tour began in St. Paul, Minnesota, where I sang at the reopening of the Women's Institute with the Minneapolis Symphony Orchestra and my colleague, the excellent baritone Robert Merrill. Taking a quick break, I returned to New York just in time to move the family to a new home for the winter, a lovely house that had belonged to Clarence Day, the author of *Life with Father.*

I was engaged for two television shows right away, and this pleased me. Already I believed that television was helping to popularize opera, to persuade people that the art form was not highbrow but that it was good, exciting theater based on real, significant human values. But soon enough I was back on my concert tour, visiting Memphis, Davenport, Stillwater, St. Louis, Mobile, and St. Petersburg. There, I stayed with Mrs. Natalie Townsend, at whose musicales I had sung in Washington, and though it was early November, she and her husband suggested that we swim in the ocean. Suddenly something large and dark swam toward me. I thought it was a shark, and I yelled for help. Mr. Townsend laughed at me: "It's just a dolphin! They're so playful," he explained. Perhaps so, but it spoiled my swim.

After a quick trip to Chicago and Milwaukee to sing *The Marriage of Figaro* with the Metropolitan Opera, I returned to New York for rehearsals of *Don Giovanni.* Our conductor was George Szell, whose concept of Mozart's score was a little different from Bruno Walter's—I would say more dramatic. I liked to sing for Szell very much.

But now came the news that the Czechoslovak elections promised by President Beneš had been postponed. Monetary reform was announced, and all property would be taxed. Failure to report everything one owned—money, stocks, land, factories, paintings—by a certain deadline would result in severe penalties, even prison. George explained the situation to Mr. Watson, who agreed that George was urgently needed and must leave immediately.

What George found was really alarming. Arriving in Prague, his first concern was to see Liteň and to assess the situation there. Through Jan Masaryk's intervention, George obtained permission from the Russians to visit the estate; Jan had also received approval for my brother-in-law, Antonín Kittler, to administer the property until the government recognized the lawful owner. George went first to the office, where three of his former employees greeted him. Then he went to see our former home.

He wasn't prepared for such destruction. Broken furniture, cushions cut in pieces, the bathrooms absolutely unusable, countless things wantonly destroyed. George noticed that a few pictures remained, including the portrait of me that was used to design the 100-crown bill—but the frame was broken, and the bill that I had framed inside was missing. A signed photo of President Masaryk also stood on a table, but when I returned to Liteň several months later, I didn't find any of these pictures, and nobody knew—or said—who removed them.

George wanted to see the château, which had been his mother's residence during the time we spent at Liteň. When he tried to open the door with his key, three members of what was called the "National Committee" blocked him. "This is national property, you can't go in there," they said, and one of them threatened to shoot George if he so much as tried. Unwilling to argue with such behavior, George left. Immediately he reported to President Beneš and to Jan Masaryk, who told him that the Minister of Agriculture would handle the situation. George went from ministry to ministry, hearing promises but obtaining no results. At last he returned to President Beneš, whom he asked what the future held for Czechoslovakia. But the president spoke mostly of the past, hardly touching on the present and saying nothing at all about the future. George decided right then that I should come to

Czechoslovakia in the summer of 1946, leaving the children in the United States in Teta's care.

George's assignment to head up the Czechoslovak office of IBM was another matter. Because IBM was an American company, it couldn't be nationalized. But all the machines in the Prague office had been stolen, and George had to make great efforts to get replacements from America and to straighten things out, so that business could resume. At the same time, he was responsible for other countries such as Poland, Hungary, and Yugoslavia, where he found similar problems.

I wrote to Jan Masaryk, primarily because a scheduling conflict prevented me from accepting an invitation to appear at the Czech Philharmonic Society's annual festival (which that year was for the first time called the Prague Spring Festival). Yet I found myself pouring out my heart. George's efforts to reclaim our property had been in vain, I told Jan. "Good God, what are we guilty of?" I wrote. And as I thought of the festival in Prague, I couldn't help asking, "Where should I stay? In a hotel?" At last, I wrote, "I beg you, help us. I cannot take the children home, when we have no home. What a lovely dream we had, of walking again in the Czech fields and forests after so many years, and now, when anyone mentions home, my eyes fill with tears."

As busy as he was, Jan wrote back immediately, promising to do everything he could to help us and refusing to let the matter drop before he obtained the results we wanted.

Still in New York, I did what I could for my country. At Lucrezia Bori's home after a performance of *The Tales of Hoffmann* at the Metropolitan, I met Andrés Segovia and Olga Coelho, a delightful singer whom Segovia had taught to accompany herself on guitar. I asked her to join me for a charity concert I was organizing for the benefit of the American Relief for Czechoslovakia organization. Olga and I sang, Joseph Schuster played the cello, and we raised $2,000, which went to purchase food for 1,500 of the neediest children in my country. On another occasion, I had the honor of christening the airplane *Globetrotter,* which had been specially fitted for its first mission, to airlift about 66,000 hatching eggs to Prague. Upon his return, the pilot brought back a children's book in Czech for Georgie, a charming gesture. And at the Met, I participated in a gala to benefit the French, singing the St.-Sulpice scene from *Manon* with Raoul Jobin, on a program that also featured the singer Grace Moore and the actor Charles Boyer.

I also joined with several artists from all over the world who hoped to create an orchestra that would serve as a musical equivalent to the United Nations, with one musician from each country. Because music is the international language, this plan struck me as one of the greatest cultural ideas of the century. By this point I had sung in many world capitals, and Jan Masaryk often had said to me, "Jarmila, you are our greatest ambassador." In a speech before the United Nations, I urged my listeners to participate and to endorse the plan, putting forward musicians without regard to race, color, or creed. My colleagues and I worked very diligently, and we did succeed in creating our orchestra. But in the political climate of the time, it did not last long.

Though I also participated in a concert to benefit the Vienna Staatsoper, which had been badly damaged during the war, many of my activities were "business as usual": singing at the Metropolitan and on the radio, resuming our Quartet tour. At one point I got sick and had to cancel, but luckily there were always three to go on with the performance. In my spare time I posed as Manon for a portrait by the painter Albert Smith, and I attended a recital by Dame Maggie Teyte, still wonderful in her sixties. On another occasion, I met Florence Page Kimball, an excellent singing teacher who soon began working with her most famous pupil, Leontyne Price.

At the Metropolitan Museum of Art, I sang for General Dwight Eisenhower. I was immediately taken by his charm. When we talked, I had the feeling that he really listened, as if there were nothing more important than what I had to say. The general had visited Prague, where his reception overwhelmed him, the streets so crowded that his car almost could not pass. He told me how much he had liked hearing a group of girls who, dressed in folk costumes, sang for him. (A few years later, when Eisenhower became president, I sang at his Inaugural.)

I also frequently received letters from Maestro Toscanini, but one dated March 19, 1946, took me by surprise. He told me that he had dreamed about me; what sort of dream it was I could guess from his rapturous declarations of love for me. A few hours later he wrote to me again, even more passionately—and three days later another such letter arrived! The letters shocked me so much that I didn't know what to do. At last I decided that it would be best not to react at all, and I went on with my work. Maestro continued to write to me, but after a while he regained his composure; his letters, always affectionate, were no longer quite so heated. I did try to write to him whenever I had a free moment.

The Metropolitan Opera tour that year wasn't always smooth sailing. In Chicago, there was a blackout due to a coal strike, and we performed *The Magic Flute* in the dim light provided by generators on two tugboats just for us. The stage was often very dark, however, and in the scene when Papageno is afraid and yells, "Lights here, lights here," he brought the house down. In Atlanta, our luggage was late, and we went onstage in our street clothes. In Columbus, Ohio, I was singing Violetta when I realized that the writing desk I used in Act II hadn't been positioned properly. It was so far to the right of the stage that much of the audience would be unable to see it when I sat there in the little scene before "Amami, Alfredo." So, as discreetly as I could, I tried to move it into place, little by little. I was amused to read the review the next day: "Miss Novotná gave a moving performance." Moving indeed!

Always I tried to learn whatever I could about the situation in Czechoslovakia. Marcia Davenport had just been there; when she returned to New York, she told me that, though matters were still unsettled throughout the country, she believed democracy would prevail. I supposed that this was also Jan Masaryk's opinion, and I took comfort in it. When Sol Hurok invited me to sing at a rally for American-Soviet friendship at Madison Square Garden on May 29, I accepted. The speakers insisted that America and the Soviet Union could live in peace despite their differences, "just as a blonde can fall in love with a brunette," as one speaker put it. Finally I sang, and it was quite a sensation to sing in Madison Square Garden, a huge space, filled to capacity, with my audience seated all around me. Three Soviet writers, honorees at the event, urged me to come to Moscow to give a concert. I promised to speak to Hurok about the idea, but my other commitments did not give me time to consider it.

Now it was time for George and me to prepare for our trip to Czechoslovakia. Meanwhile, George's visa was about to expire; given the situation in Czechoslovakia, he decided to apply for U.S. citizenship. This was a serious decision, but only a U.S. passport would enable him to travel freely in Europe on business for IBM.

We arranged for Georgie and Teta to spend the summer with George's cousins, the Reithoffers, while Jarmilka attended summer camp on Lake Champlain. Worried about what might happen to the children if anything went wrong with our flight, George and I agreed to book separate reservations. But then George's plane ran into technical problems, and he returned to New York the day after he departed. With the help of Jimmy Melton's best friend, the president of American Airlines, George and I flew together after all.[2] From London, we booked seats on a small plane to Czechoslovakia. It was in fact a small German warplane, which the Czechs had kept after the war, and it seated just four people, including the pilot.

For most of the trip, we flew in the clouds, or "soup," as the pilot called it. Suddenly the sky cleared, and below us we could see the river Berounka. Soon we recognized our dear Liteň, and we distinctly saw farm workers bringing the harvest home. In a few minutes more, we were approaching Prague, and I could see the Charles Bridge and Hradčany Castle. I could not help crying. We were home at last—and yet not completely.

Because we could not stay in Liteň, George rented an apartment on Wenceslaus Square. We spent our first evening with my parents in Radotín, a half-hour outside Prague, and I spent all of the next day with them. It had been such a long time since we had been together.

My parents shared vivid memories of the day when the rumor spread that the Germans were about to surrender. Expecting the arrival of the Americans at any moment, the Czechs rose up against the Germans. They began by hoisting Czechoslovak and Allied flags and removing German names from street signs and shop windows. But the Americans were still far away, at least twenty miles outside the city, and the SS men persisted in their gruesome atrocities to the end. During a demonstration at Wenceslaus Square, the Nazis arrested a number of the Czechs, and when the crowd protested, the Germans opened fire. Now the uprising began in earnest. The Czechs threw up barricades and brought out guns they had captured and hidden from the Germans. The Germans responded by attacking from outside the city, deploying a panzer brigade to move in toward the central train station, while other tanks attacked the east bank of the Moldau. For three days, Prague was under constant bombardment as the Germans continuously fired the few guns they had left. The Luftwaffe pounded the city repeatedly from the air, fires burned unchecked in several neighborhoods, and explosions went off frequently. The Czechs had no antitank guns, but eventually they held back the German advance; the Nazis surrendered Prague to the Soviets the day after the fighting ended.

Luckily, my parents were at their home outside of Prague. They were spared the destruction, though not the anxiety.

Now what mattered most to me was seeing Liteň again. I told my brother-in-law, who was still the state administrator for the property, that I wanted to visit, and when I arrived, a crowd of people from the village waited to greet me. Though George had been threatened when he tried to enter the château, I was able to walk right in. There, on the table where it always sat, was our family guest book, more than one hundred years old. To mark my return after seven years, I signed the book with the date: July 3, 1946.

Because Russian officers had been housed in the château, the damage there was less severe than what George had found in our house on the property. Still, I noticed right away that all our silver, linens, and George's collection of antique snuffboxes were gone, and Russians had carved their names into our Steinway piano. I went through all the rooms, noting what was missing. The many beautiful old trees in the garden had been cut down, because that was the space the Russians had chosen to park their tanks. The damage was considerable throughout the property, but I ascertained for myself that it would be possible to live there again—if we ever received permission.

Back in Prague, we went from one ministry to another, and every visit ended with the same promises. George went to the IBM office every day, while I tried to spend my time as normally as possible. But a newspaper reporter spotted us having dinner at the Hotel Ambassador with Jan Masaryk and a few other prominent people. From that moment on, journalists came to me for interview after interview, and in short order, Dr. František Spurný, a concert agent, arrived at my door to propose a concert tour. I was reluctant, but everybody begged me to perform.

My first concert, at the National Opera Theater, sold out within two hours of being announced. A benefit for the Red Cross, hosted by President Beneš's wife, Hana, this was an exceptionally rare occasion, because only plays and operas were performed there. President and Mrs. Beneš and the whole diplomatic corps attended, and the atmosphere was very festive. When I first appeared onstage, the entire audience stood up and cheered and cheered, and I was in tears. I almost could not sing. It was unforgettable.

The Minister of Schools and Culture, Dr. Jaroslav Stránský, kept at least one promise that government officials gave me that summer. Acknowledging my propaganda work on Czechoslovakia's behalf during the war, Dr. Stránský obtained an automobile for me to use on my concert tour. This way, George was able to join me, and he conducted business and arranged a luncheon for the IBM employees in each town we visited. I performed in Brno (twice), Moravská Ostrava, Přerov, and Plzeň, where General Patton's soldiers had behaved so well that everyone spoke of them with love and admiration. The audience in Plzeň went wild when I sang "Goin' Home," which Dvořák used in his "New World" Symphony, and so I sang two more Negro spirituals,

"Nobody Knows the Trouble I've Seen" and "Sometimes I Feel Like a Motherless Child." Then I returned to Prague for two final concerts, one at the large Lucerna Hall, filled to the rafters, and the farewell at Smetana Hall.

I also had the pleasure of showing the beauties of Prague to RCA's David Sarnoff, who had come to town on a special assignment. But before it was time for me to return to New York, I paid a visit to President Beneš himself to discuss the unresolved questions of our family properties. He promised me that he would look into the matter personally, and he assured me that everything would be settled when I returned to Prague the next year.

I arrived back in New York just in time for Jarmilka's birthday, and my hectic schedule resumed immediately. I began my season in San Francisco, first with *Der Rosenkavalier* opposite my beloved Lotte Lehmann as the Marschallin. Gaetano Merola, the founder of San Francisco Opera, amused me very much when he declared that my Octavian was "too ardent." How else should a seventeen-year-old boy behave but ardently? I also sang Cherubino with the company, and traveled with them to Los Angeles for more performances of *Rosenkavalier* and *Marriage of Figaro.* I also sang recitals in Santa Ana, Ventura, Bakersfield, and Eugene, Oregon.

Los Angeles meant seeing many friends and acquaintances again. Louis B. Mayer invited me to dinner at his new house, which had previously belonged to William Randolph Hearst. Still hoping to interest me in a movie career, Mr. Mayer introduced me to a prospective agent, and he asked Oscar Levant to play for us after dinner—ending, quite naturally, with the *Rhapsody in Blue*. But a reunion with Otto Klemperer proved troubling. He invited me to accompany him to church one Sunday morning, and I saw that, in the aftermath of brain surgery, he had difficulty walking. He seemed well enough, however, until we returned to the hotel and sat down by the pool. Suddenly, he suggested that we go swimming, and I had a hard time restraining him from jumping fully dressed into the water. I also saw Italo Montemezzi again, and I met for the first time the composer Olive Dungan, who was visiting from her home in Miami, Florida. She gave me a few songs, which I tried out on the next stops on my recital tour, in Phoenix and Tempe. I was sorry that she could not attend the performances, which were very well received.

With the encouragement of Olin Downes, I had begun to include a set of Czech and Slovak folk songs at the end of most of my recital programs, for which I changed into a folk costume. The audience just loved it, and I made my way onward, with several stops in Texas: Longview, Dallas, Corpus Christi, and Laredo, always accompanied by Alexander Alexay.

By now I had seen a great deal of the United States, and I was very much aware that circumstances in Czechoslovakia might remain unsettled for a very long time. At last I decided that, like my husband, I should apply for my final citizenship papers. Even Jan Masaryk told me that he understood my decision and that I was doing the right thing; and on December 2, 1946, Cornelius Bliss served as my witness at the naturalization ceremony. A few days later, George returned from Prague with the good news that we could live again in Liteň. It was a moment of great rejoicing.

We had hoped to see Jan Masaryk at Christmas that year, but he wrote to say that he had just returned from Chicago, and that he was very tired. People constantly asked him questions about Czechoslovakia and the Soviet Union, as if they didn't understand how hard his situation was. "It will take a long time before Europe and Czechoslovakia normalize again, and we all have to help," Jan wrote. Though he continued to see a great deal of Marcia Davenport, he added, "If you hear that I am getting married, you may deny it. I am intensely married to my country, and that will suffice for the few years that are left to me."

George preferred to travel to Europe by boat, and he departed for Prague on the *Queen Elizabeth* on January 18, 1947. Our children and many people from IBM came to see him off; our chief hope was that we would be reunited in the summer. Meanwhile, I had a number of performances on my calendar, including *Rosenkavalier, Figaro,* and *Manon* at the Metropolitan; a pops concert in Toronto; and another concert in St. Augustine, Florida, where I received a visit from the author Marjorie Kinnan Rawlings. She presented me with some songs she had written. With Mr. Alexay, I learned the songs quickly and sang them that night. Mrs. Rawlings was very pleased.

Our quartet—still consisting of myself, Herta Glaz, Raoul Jobin, and Martial Singher—prepared to embark on another tour. These artists were so congenial and pleasant to work with. By now we understood one another perfectly; we played games and exchanged jokes whenever we were not focused on our music. For this tour, we performed our usual program for fifteen concerts in several cities across the south, including locations in Texas and Oklahoma. In Oklahoma City, I met the composer Sigmund Romberg, who was very enthusiastic and invited me to join two other artists on a concert tour with his orchestra, which he would conduct. I promised to think it over, but it was more than two years before I found time to do it. In San

Antonio, we visited several of the old Spanish missions, including Mission San Jose, "the queen of missions," with its beautiful rose window; and of course the Alamo. Visiting the missions was for us a very agreeable and interesting break.

I want to emphasize that, while these concert tours may look like nothing on paper, in reality they often involved changing trains in the middle of the night, arriving late, sometimes having to make up time by taking a bus or hiring a car. In addition to keeping to a hectic schedule, we traveled with a lot of luggage, containing all of the elaborate costumes we brought with us. This was the last tour for our little quartet, although we were invited several times to perform selections from our program on the radio.

Back in New York, Maestro Toscanini advised me to stop studying with Zitomirsky, and Shibley Boyes, whose judgment I respected, recommended Robert Weer to me. After such a long tour, I wanted to work with somebody, and Weer's lessons did me a lot of good. I was quite happy with my first performance, which was *Traviata* at the Metropolitan, on February 28, 1947.

As the children and I planned to leave for Czechoslovakia in May, I began securing the necessary visas. I had heard that we would need special permission to pass through Germany, which was divided into French, British, American, and Russian zones. Luckily, the Russian zone was on the other side of Germany, so that we didn't need a permit from the Soviets. But there was so much paperwork that I had almost no idea how to go about obtaining it all.

Luckily, the columnist Elsa Maxwell invited me to sing at a ball at the French embassy, to benefit the rebuilding of St. Lo. As Elsa explained it, the organizers had sold 1,500 tickets for the ball at the Statler Hotel, but they had no stars to perform; to "bribe" me (as she put it), she promised to seat me next to General Eisenhower. Elsa herself played for me, and just as we were about to make our entrance onstage, Eisenhower took her aside and said, "You must black out the ballroom, leaving just a light on Mme. Novotná, and people will be quiet." In fact, Eisenhower himself took charge of the lights, and the effect was just what he wanted. It was a marvelous evening, Elsa and I were invited to spend the night at the embassy, and—luckiest of all—I met Senator J. William Fulbright, who offered to procure all of my permits for me. He did just that, and we had no trouble crossing through Germany.

Before we could depart, I still had a few concerts to sing, including a gala at Carnegie Hall to present Mayor La Guardia, Maestro Toscanini, and Fredric March with One World Awards for their distinguished achievements. Also, Edward Johnson, my managers at NCAC, and Sol Hurok all wanted to meet with me to plan my future engagements. At the moment, however, I didn't know what my future would look like. I didn't expect to be able to remain in Czechoslovakia forever: I still had various contracts to fulfill, and George and I wanted to keep the children in their schools in America.

Meanwhile, I went shopping for all the things I knew we would need at Liteň: the house had been stripped of linens, towels, and silver. So much had been stolen that I filled fifty trunks with provisions, and also with some of the belongings we had acquired in New York, because I did not want to leave much in storage at the Gramercy Park Hotel, our home at the time. In the midst of these preparations, I received a letter from Jan Masaryk with the good news that he, too, planned to be in Prague for a short time during the summer, so we would be able to see him soon. He suggested that I let him know how he could help us, and he tried to give me an idea of what to expect in Czechoslovakia: "Some things you will not like, some yes. But it is home." He did not try to hide the strain to which his work subjected him; he had just left Moscow, was about to leave for another conference in Paris, and was suffering from the flu. "I will rest when I break my leg," he wrote with a weary humor. "In the meantime, I must do the important work that is often difficult and painful."

Joseph Califano of IBM, the father of the future Secretary of Health, Education, and Welfare, helped us to board the SS *America* with all our luggage. Our cabins were filled with flowers, and I received hundreds of telegrams wishing us well.

Apart from a few days in the middle of the trip, when the *America* seemed to dance in the rough weather, we had good weather for our crossing. We landed in Cherbourg, then took a train to Paris, where we waited for George to join us. The director of the Paris Opera, Georges Hirsch, invited me to perform, but for the moment I could think only of Czechoslovakia; still, Jarmilka and I attended a very good performance of *Faust,* starring Raoul Jobin.

Our plan was to send Teta and the children to Prague by train, while George and I would drive; and, with that in mind, I had gotten my first driver's license before I left New York. However, a railroad strike changed our plans, so the entire family had to drive for three very long days. George obtained tickets from the American Consulate for gasoline, which was rationed. But we discovered along the way that the easiest way to get gasoline in Germany was to offer either cigarettes or chocolate to the attendant, who in return would provide whatever you needed.

We arrived at Liteň on Friday, June 13, and although it's said that this is an unlucky number and day, for us it was a paradise. I marveled at the way George had managed, in such a short amount of time, to make the house ready for us, and once we had unpacked all our trunks, Liteň was more than livable. I had never felt so happy to be home.

I had promised to sing at the National Theater, and they wasted no time. Just a few days after we returned to Liteň, the conductor Rudolf Vašata and the tenor Jaroslav Gleich came to me for a preliminary rehearsal for *The Bartered Bride,* and the following day the full cast rehearsed at the opera house. We performed on June 23 and July 1, and on July 3 I gave a recital at Smetana Hall in Prague, with Alfred Holeček my excellent accompanist. The summer heat was terrible, and even the newspapers marveled that all these performances sold out while other events played to empty halls. The same thing happened when we performed in Brno and Olomouc. It was a joy to sing for people who showed their enthusiasm so openly.

On July 19, 1947, true to his word, Jan Masaryk came to visit us at Liteň. He had just returned from Moscow, and he was completely crushed. The United States had offered the Marshall Plan to all of Europe, including Czechoslovakia, Jan explained. As foreign minister, Jan recommended that the Czechoslovak cabinet accept the plan, and the cabinet agreed unanimously. Thereupon Stalin summoned him to Moscow. He informed Jan that acceptance of the Marshall Plan by Czechoslovakia would be interpreted as an unfriendly act toward the Soviet Union. There was nothing Jan could do but call Prague and urge the cabinet to rescind its vote. Now, reflecting on Stalin's promises to allow Czechoslovakia to remain a free country, Jan observed, "My greatest mistake was that I refused to believe that Stalin was lying to me all the time." I had never seen him so depressed.

Jan Masaryk, Marcia Davenport, and our friend Karel Steinbach stayed at Liteň overnight. By coincidence, we had asked the American ambassador, Laurence Steinhardt, to lunch the next day. Naturally he wanted to discuss Czechoslovakia's situation, but Jan told him, "There is nothing I can do at the moment." I could not know that I would never see Jan again.

Around this time, I had a call from Zurich with a very interesting proposition. The director Fred Zinnemann wanted me for a movie he was making in Switzerland and Germany, the story of a Czech mother and her little boy, who are torn apart in a concentration camp. The child, terrified by the brutality and suffering around him, loses his memory and his ability to speak. After she is liberated, the mother spends months trying to find the boy. They finally reunite.

Zinnemann had already found a nine-year-old boy, Ivan Jandl, whom he had heard singing on a Prague radio station. Because Ivan didn't speak English, Zinnemann hired a woman in Zurich to tutor Ivan while he continued to audition actresses to play the mother. Still he was not satisfied, and then the tutor said to him, "Why don't you take Novotná?" Zinnemann answered, "Novotná? Novotná is in America, and I have to start filming next week." The tutor answered, "No, Novotná is in Prague. I just heard her singing *The Bartered Bride* there." So Zinnemann called immediately and asked to see me at Liteň. He arrived on July 20, just as we finished our lunch with Jan Masaryk, Ambassador Steinhardt, and our other friends.

Zinnemann told us the gripping story, which I found very touching. "Such a film could help to prevent further wars," Jan Masaryk said, and he urged me to take the part. I had hoped to enjoy a quiet summer at home, but George also believed I should make the film. We discussed the idea a little while, and then I told Fred Zinnemann I would accept his offer. He begged me to come as soon as possible to Zurich, and eight days later, I arrived. The following day, I had to go to the studio for tests and makeup.

As I was sitting with the hairdresser, Zinnemann came to introduce me to Montgomery Clift. At the time, Monty had worked in New York theater, but he was not widely known, and as a matter of fact our picture, *The Search,* was only his second movie. (The first, *Red River,* would not be released until a few months after *The Search* came out.) This was our first encounter, and we became friends on the spot. He was so natural, and I never laughed as much with anybody else, because he had such a hilarious way of describing people and situations. And yet he was very sensitive and unsure of himself. Once, he watched me take and retake a scene several times. I had to cry each time, and finally he asked, "How can you have these feelings at your disposal, despite all these interruptions and repetitions? I couldn't do something like that more than once."

He liked children very much, and he got along well with the Zinnemanns' little son, Tim. The two of them had a grand time on some national holiday, when there was a big celebration in Zurich. Monty bought the largest fireworks he could find. To fire them off, they had to dig a deep pit in the ground. Finally they found a spot in the park, and when they set off the fireworks, they made such a noise that a policeman came running and almost arrested Monty.

I don't think Monty was drinking at the time. Frank Sinatra had a great influence on Monty, and I believe he started to drink in 1953, when they made the film *From Here to Eternity* together. Sinatra was just the opposite of Monty, and that seemed to make Monty want to be more like Sinatra. He even wanted to start singing, and so he took some lessons. However, he simply didn't have the ease that Sinatra had, and that made Monty even more insecure. He began to drink more heavily and had an automobile accident that disfigured his face during the filming of *Raintree County* in 1956. He was really in love with his costar in that picture, Elizabeth Taylor; he carried her picture and even pictures of her sons. "Isn't she beautiful?" he would say to me when he showed me the photos. When he wrote to me, he signed his letters Le Singe ("the monkey" in French). The friendship that I developed with the Zinnemanns during the filming of *The Search* has continued the rest of our lives, and I know the same would have been true of my friendship with Monty, if he had not died so young.

While I was in Zurich, Franz Lehár saw my name in the newspaper and called me up. Nothing could have given me greater pleasure than seeing him again, for the first time since our last *Giuditta* ten years before. He told me that he had come to Switzerland because the Austrians treated him badly after the war, reproaching him for what they believed was friendliness toward Hitler, who adored *The Merry Widow* and played it repeatedly. The Austrians confiscated his lovely home, which he called his *Schlössl,* or "little castle," so he and his wife moved to Zurich. (Later, after she died, he moved back to Austria, and died in his beautiful villa in Ischl.) Lehár was the most unassuming, natural, delightful man, and we spent a delightful evening together. The dinner started with Wiener Würstchen and champagne, duck à l'orange, and Salzbürger Nockerl for dessert.

We shot all the interiors for *The Search* in Zurich, and the rest was filmed in the American zone in Germany. The bombed-out cities were grim reminders of the war. Our first stop was Munich, where we were put up at the press camp, because the American army had taken most of the hotels. However, we found the camp quite comfortable, we even had a swimming pool at our disposal, and one evening I met the author Anne Morrow Lindbergh, whose beautiful book *Gift from the Sea* I have reread many times.

Driving in the dark through Munich in a jeep was a nightmare, but by day I saw tremendous destruction. One day I remember passing six entire blocks with nothing but sand where the houses had stood, and only one building left standing in the middle. In front, a woman was scrubbing the sidewalk. To my great astonishment, the Bavarian State Opera was performing in spite of the devastation. I made a point of going to hear Janáček's *Káťa Kabanová,* an excellent performance.

Before we started shooting, I asked Fred Zinnemann whether it would be possible for me to visit some of the camps where displaced children were kept. This was easily arranged, and I spent four days in one of the largest centers for displaced persons in Chiemsee. The children had survived German concentration camps, and I could see the numbers tattooed on their arms and the marks of Nazi torture, if not always on their bodies, then always in their eyes. Some children were starved for affection, but others were afraid even to speak because they trusted no one any more. I saw some happy reunions, but most were heartbreaking. Often the children didn't even recognize the parents who had come for them, and they refused to go.

Yet the human spirit is such that I saw moments that made us laugh. The children were housed according to their ages, and one day I visited the house for the smallest children. This was just after lunchtime, and most of the children were sitting on little potties. As I was talking with one of the nurses, an older man came in and asked to see his granddaughter, Sonia. Before anyone had a chance to ask for more details, he cried out, "Sonia! My Sonia!" He ran to one of the children, lifted it off the potty, and held it high in the air—only to see that the child was a boy. Luckily, he found his Sonia a little while later.

I wanted to cheer up the children, and I often sang for them. They took pots and pans from the kitchen, and we made an orchestra. The children enjoyed this immensely, and when it was time for me to leave the camp, they serenaded me, singing while they "played" their pots and pans. Many of the children were in tears. I must confess that at that moment, I could think of no greater orchestra on earth.

This wonderful experience helped me to project the character of the mother when I returned to Munich. I did not play her distress, I felt it. We had a wonderful cast, including Aline MacMahon as a Red Cross worker, and Monty as an American soldier. I still believe *The Search* is his best film. Ivan Jandl played so perfectly that he was given an honorary Oscar for his role. Working under Fred Zinnemann's direction was a joy. We rehearsed each scene before shooting, and he told me there was just one thing that worried him: Could I carry myself less elegantly? That was easy enough, but he wasn't satisfied yet. He thought of something clever to "help" me. I had to carry a little suitcase as my character went from camp to camp, and once, when I lifted it, I realized that it was very heavy. Zinnemann had put a few stones inside so that it would be harder for me to walk. Well, that wasn't necessary, and I showed him I could play it the way he wanted—without stones. We both laughed about it.

It took three more months to finish the movie. With only one exception, every scene that has rubble in the background was shot on location in Ingolstadt and Nuremberg, which had suffered terribly. On one location shoot, a German said to me, "Germany is ahead of the rest of Europe again." I asked what he meant, and I was impressed—or should I say angry—when he replied, "Everything was destroyed. Now we must rebuild, and we'll do it with the most modern means. This way, we will have better capabilities." In a way, I suppose he was right.

Zinnemann's chief worry was for the children. We worked with about forty, all of them actual war victims who had been picked out of a group of six hundred, with the assistance of workers from the United Nations Relief and Rehabilitation Administration. Zinnemann worried that it wasn't right to shave these children's heads again, to make them wear concentration camp clothing, and in general to force them to remember horrors that were much better forgotten. The children's anxiety was enormous, and it took time for them to respond to the film crew without fear or suspicion.

For one scene, the crew explained to the children that they would be transported from one camp to another in Red Cross ambulances. This way, the children knew what to expect, and the scene went fairly well until they saw the ambulances coming toward them. They became withdrawn, and we could see the strain in their faces. When the adult actors ordered the children into the ambulances, some broke away and ran, and others got inside but began yelling and banging on the sides, desperate to be let out. Despite all the precautions, nobody had realized the terror that ambulances represented to the children. Many had seen their loved ones taken away in such vehicles, and they knew that the Nazis had disguised mobile gas chambers as Red Cross ambulances.[3] Later, Zinnemann told me that the children performed most eloquently what they knew and remembered.

I had to interrupt the filming because I had to return to Liteň for the children and take them back to New York for the start of the new school year. I was terribly sorry to have spent so little of the summer with them. They had fallen in love with the country. Georgie was busy playing the farmer, and I was told that he had been helping in the brewery, earning his first paycheck when he was nine years old. I don't know what his duties were in the brewery, but to him it was very important work. My husband was doing everything he could to improve conditions on the estate. He installed a new central heating system in our house, and gradually we were able to live there quite normally.

I had three weeks to spend in Liteň before I had to return to Munich for filming, and I must say that I never felt as happy as I did in those days. We were home again, and somehow we foolishly thought it would last. The political situation at that moment looked rather promising, and everyone hoped that elections would take place in May as planned. We expected to make Liteň our home base. George would conduct his IBM business with Prague as his headquarters, and he had even managed to transfer earnings to New York, a wonderful accomplishment given the political situation. We also expected that I would continue my performing career, taking airplanes when needed, so that I could continue to live in Czechoslovakia.

Around this time, *Life* magazine sent a photographer to Liteň to take some pictures. I kept several copies of the magazine; they were all that would remain of our lovely dream.

After completing the few remaining important scenes for *The Search* in Munich and Zurich, I returned home; and, four days later, I performed a recital in Beroun, a town near Liteň. I invited all of our employees, and they overfilled the hall. After I finished singing, they did not want to let me leave. I gave many encores, and it was a very moving experience. Then I returned to Prague to sing Tatyana in two performances of *Eugene Onegin* with the National Opera, the last of these attended by President and Mrs. Beneš. This would be in effect a farewell performance.

The new year of 1948 began in New York with the American premiere of Arthur Honegger's *Jeanne d'Arc au Bûcher*, with Charles Munch conducting the New York Philharmonic at Carnegie Hall. The dancer Vera Zorina took the speaking role of Jeanne, and Raymond Gerome took the speaking role of Frère Dominique. Nadine Connor sang the Virgin, I was Marguerite, and the cast also included Enid Szantho, Joseph Laderoute, Lorenzo Alvary, and the Westminster Choir. We had very bad weather in the last days of December leading up to the premiere, and the snow did not melt. Then on the day of the concert, more snow fell, and there were no taxis to be had. So I went to Carnegie Hall in my evening gown—by subway.

Around this time I had a chance to star in a world premiere. The writer Bella Spewack called me to ask me to attend a meeting with her and a few Broadway producers to discuss a new project: a musical adaptation of Shakespeare's *The Taming of the Shrew*, with a libretto by Bella and her husband, and with a score by Cole Porter. The Spewacks had seen me as Manon and thought I would be perfect for Katherine. In due course we went to see Mr. Porter in his apartment in the Waldorf Towers. Bella told him that her idea was to make a play-within-a-play, and because of my accent, the characters would be Austrian.[4] Porter was quite enthusiastic, and he asked Bella to prepare a scenario so that he could begin to determine what kind of music would be suitable. Viennese waltzes seemed a natural fit, and so for our next meeting, I asked our friend Merton Powell, who also knew Cole Porter very well, to play all of the best waltzes he knew. As he finished, I exclaimed, "Wunderbar! Wunderbar!" This was sufficient inspiration for Cole, and at our next meeting, he presented a lovely song: "Wunderbar." When the show—*Kiss Me, Kate,* of course—opened, this was one of the most popular numbers in the score.

The first preview of *The Search* screened on January 8, 1948. The hard-boiled movie executives reacted in incredible ways, and a few of them cried unabashedly. Prince Baudoin of Belgium (who later became king) attended another preview screening, and he insisted that the movie must be shown in Belgium as soon as possible.

On March 10, three days after that year's concert in honor of President Masaryk's birthday, came the terrible news that Jan Masaryk had been found dead in the courtyard of Czernin Palace. It was reported that he had committed suicide by jumping out a window. I found it hard to believe he had killed himself. Everybody knew how much he loved and enjoyed life. I am afraid we will never know the truth of what happened.

In Jan's memory, Jinx Falkenburg and Tex McCrary invited me to appear on their radio show on Palm Sunday.[5] Because the advance word on *The Search* was so good, they invited Monty Clift, as well. He knew how difficult it was for me to talk about Jan, and he did his utmost to be helpful and considerate. No jokes this time. I really appreciated that.

The Search had its premiere at the Victoria Theater on Broadway on March 24, 1948, and it was a terrific success. The critics agreed unanimously; Alton Cook of the *World Telegram* declared it "among the most genuine and profoundly stirring pictures ever made." The critic of the *Sun* observed that I "kept [my] emotions in restraint, leaving tears for the audience to shed. It is the unusual spectator who can keep from crying at this film, especially in the last quick movement." And so on. It seemed there was not one radio or television program that did not want to interview me about the poor refugee children. I was glad that I wasn't busy at the Metropolitan, because I don't know how I would have managed.

When it came time to present Ivan Jandl with his honorary Oscar, he could not attend the ceremony in Hollywood, and so Fred Zinnemann accepted it for him. Then representatives from the American Academy of Motion Picture Arts and Sciences took the award to Ivan in Prague, along with offers galore for more film work. However, representatives of the Czechoslovak government's film office insisted that the boy's first duty was to movies of his own country, and they sent the gentlemen back to Hollywood empty-handed. Unfortunately, Cold War politics had come into play: for the rest of Ivan's life, the Communists blamed him for accepting an Oscar from the Americans. He played small roles in just two more films, after which no director cast him again. After graduating high school, he tried to study theater, but the administrators refused even to discuss the matter with him. He studied law for a while but gave up after a few semesters. Later he tried his hand at many occupations. When I went to visit my sister in 1985, I saw Ivan several times. By then a man of fifty, he had changed very much, and I have some lovely photos to remember that reunion. We promised to see each other again the following year, but I never saw him again. He died of diabetes in 1987.

Only a few days after the release of *The Search*, the Czechoslovakian regime confiscated our property. George was ordered to leave Liteň, and the government immediately dismissed our brother-in-law from his post as the estate's administrator. Land reform of all larger properties had been pushed forward aggressively. Those who worked the land with their own hands were allowed to keep only fifty hectares, but that allowance was reduced to one hectare if the landowner had an occupation other than farming. We had not foreseen these developments when our family planned to return to Liteň after the war, and all the clothes and belongings we had brought to Czechoslovakia only a year before were now beyond our reach: George told me that, when he tried to retrieve at least a few suits and shirts, the National Committee refused to let him enter the house. All the large landowners were being treated this way. George wrote to say that I should come to Prague to try to take some sort of action, but because of the political situation, he felt it was wisest to leave Jarmilka and Georgie in the United States.

I had to honor a few commitments before I could depart, however. I joined the Metropolitan Opera on tour for *Rosenkavalier* in Atlanta and Memphis, and I had to fly to Washington for the first showing of *The Search*, which was a gala to benefit the National Symphony Sustaining Fund. General and Mrs. Eisenhower, many members of the government, and the whole diplomatic corps attended, and Perle Mesta gave a sumptuous luncheon for the filmmakers at the Sulgrave Club. Before leaving, I also had to see Cole Porter, to tell him that I couldn't take part in *Kiss Me, Kate* because I didn't know when I would return from Europe. Cole had been writing songs diligently, and he was very disappointed. "I wrote with you in mind," he said, "and you have been such a great inspiration to me." I regretted the situation, too, but such is life.

After crossing on the *Queen Mary*, I arrived in Cherbourg and took a train to Paris, where George waited for me with exciting news. IBM had invited us to a meeting of its "Hundred Percent Club." Intended as a reward for every employee with a strong sales record, each year's three-day meeting took place in a different country, offering banquets, sightseeing excursions, and theater performances. One year, when the meeting was in Rome, IBM arranged for an audience with the pope for the entire club. That year's meeting was in Madrid, and it was the occasion for such diversions as a trip to the historic Escorial Palace and its wonderful art collection; a flamenco performance by Jose Greco and Pilar Lopez, and my second bullfight. After the meeting, George and I drove to Portugal for a few days, where we were struck by the contrast between somber Spain and the white houses and smiling faces of the Portuguese. We drove back through Seville, Zaragoza, Barcelona, and Montpellier, stopping at Beaulieu on the French Riviera, where we spent a few balmy days.

As refreshing as this little vacation had been, we were anxious to attend to our affairs in Prague. We arrived on June 1, 1948, and immediately George and I went to see several ministers to persuade them of our rightful claims. At last we obtained permission to retrieve a few pieces of our furniture, and also the clothes that we had brought with us from America just a year before. A commission went to Liteň to make an inventory, and I went several times with my sister to make certain everything was in order. Once the commission had evaluated our belongings, I hired a van to transport them to Prague, for storage. But when we arrived at Liteň with the van, the same fellow who was head of the People's Committee suddenly appeared and once again tried to prevent our entering our home. This time, however, he did not succeed, as I had the official permission in hand.

Unfortunately, I wasn't allowed to take any paintings, and one in particular upset me very much, a portrait titled *Josefina* by the Czech painter Josef Manés. The Daubek family had presented me this painting as a wedding gift. During the war, as the armies moved on Czechoslovakia, our former butler, Jelínek, made arrangements with the National Gallery in Prague to keep safe our most important artwork. After the war, I went to the Gallery to retake possession of *Josefina,* but the director at the time asked me to lend the painting temporarily, for a special exhibition. I agreed, with certain provisos. In 1948, I asked for the return of the painting, and we discovered that the government had confiscated *Josefina* as payment for a property debt on Liteň. This was absolutely illegal, because the painting belonged to me personally. But there *Josefina* remained until 1988 when I visited my sister and received a gold medal for my artistic achievements in promoting Czech music. Now the National Gallery showed interest in buying the painting, and as I wouldn't be allowed to take it out of the country anyway, I gave it to them.[6]

We lost many other precious possessions, including books personally dedicated to me by Gabriele d'Annunzio, and letters from Richard Strauss asking me to sing *Arabella* and assuring me that he would orchestrate the score so that my voice would "soar" over the instruments. The family guest book, which contained so many historic and interesting signatures, disappeared as well. All my inquiries went unanswered. Will there be justice some day?

With only a few days remaining in our stay, I went to see my parents and sister, who had invited Ivan Jandl to join us. This was a nice reunion. On June 19, 1948, George and I returned to Paris for a few days, and then set sail for New York. We shipped the belongings we'd salvaged from Liteň—and we had to pay duty fees on them.

For the summer we rented a cottage in Hancock, New Hampshire, from Ambassador Cecil Lyon and his wife, Elsie. She and I had become good friends, because she loved music and played piano very well, sometimes accompanying me. The Lyons' older daughter was the same age as Jarmilka, and it was wonderful for the children to have playmates. But of course I had to interrupt this idyll for a few singing engagements. Thomas Watson invited me and George to a convention at Endicott, which General Eisenhower would also attend. It was clear that I would sing, and the general took me aside and said, "I am looking forward to hearing you again—but I hope that you won't sing 'My Hero.' Others have done so, and it embarrasses me no end."

"Oh, no, I don't even know 'My Hero,'" I said. "Tell me, General, what is your favorite song?"

"'I Dream of Jeannie with the Light Brown Hair,'" he replied. And so I sang it for him, and he was delighted.

During the summer, I also made my first appearances with Sigmund Romberg, first at Philadelphia's Robin Hood Dell and then, before a crowd of twenty thousand people (and Peter II, the exiled king of Yugoslavia, and his wife, Queen Alexandra, who became my good friend), at Lewisohn Stadium. I sang "Depuis le jour," a group of Czech folk songs, and duets from two of Romberg's operettas, *Blossom Time* and *The New Moon,* with the baritone Donald Johnston; Romberg himself conducted. Our next concert, a month later, was at the Hollywood Bowl, also very well received by a capacity audience. Romberg was a very amusing person, full of charm and anecdotes, and we had a wonderful time at a party at his home. Cole Porter threw a party for me and invited many of Hollywood's glamour boys—Errol Flynn, Clark Gable, Gary Cooper, Douglas Fairbanks Jr., and Rock Hudson—as well as Bette Davis and Madeleine Carroll. Arthur Rubinstein was there, and he invited me to a party at his home the next evening, to which Monty Clift escorted me. Rubinstein loved to entertain, and his beautiful wife, Nela, enthusiastically helped to make the party an enchantment. He seemed to savor every day of his life, and how he loved to talk! His smallest anecdote was as rich as a whole book. And of course he was unsurpassed as a pianist.

At a few events in New York around this time, I encountered even more notable people. At a benefit for retired singers, hosted by the Bagby Music Lovers Foundation, I sang alongside Maggie Teyte, Blanche Thebom, Giuseppe di Stefano, Mack Harrell, and Ruben Varga, a young, blind virtuoso violinist. At an anniversary gathering for *Child's World* radio, I met the novelists Fannie Hurst and John Hersey, whose *A Bell for Adano* and *Hiroshima* I admired, as well as William Saroyan, whose plays *The Time of Your Life* and *The Human Comedy* I had enjoyed, as well as his short-story collection, *My Name Is Aram.* What fun we had with these brainy people! At the invitation of the Watsons, I attended the opening night of the Metropolitan Opera, where I met Margaret Truman, the president's daughter, an aspiring singer herself. And at the opening of an exhibit at the Metropolitan Museum of Art, I met the Secretary of the Navy, John L. Sullivan, who presented me with a painting. When I tried to take it out of the museum at the end of the evening, however, three guards closed in on me. The museum officials had to do quite a lot of explaining before the guards would let me go, but we had a good laugh.

Another amusing evening was the "Bal de Tête" benefit for the Musicians' Emergency Fund, to which Countess Rasponi invited me.[7] "What do you plan to wear on your head?" Lanfranco asked me the day before the ball. I hadn't known I was expected to wear anything on my head, I replied, so he called on the gifted designer Valerian Rybar. The next day, Valerian brought me the most fantastic headdress made of iridescent blue twigs and butterflies. For this I won first prize: a pair of diamond earrings from Van Cleef & Arpels, presented to me by Walter Pidgeon and Douglas Fairbanks Jr. Elizabeth Arden was so impressed that she called Valerian the next day and offered him a job; he would go on to a brilliant career, the darling of the international set, who decorated many beautiful homes.

George spent the autumn in Europe, but he returned in time for Christmas. He brought the news that Arthur K. Watson (Thomas's son, whom we called Dick) had proposed moving George's base of operations to Paris, though he would retain the apartment in Prague for business in Czechoslovakia. To celebrate the holiday, we threw a large cocktail party, to which Elsa Maxwell brought Ali Khan. Therese and Nathan Milstein attended, too, and invited us to a dinner at their home, where Maestro Toscanini and another great conductor, Ernest Ansermet, encountered each other. Maestro was in a very good mood and declared that Ansermet conducted Mozart even better than he himself did—what a compliment!

I had signed for my ninth season with the Metropolitan, beginning on January 18, 1949, singing several performances of *Figaro* in New York, Philadelphia, and Los Angeles—and for a concert tour with Romberg—so I had to decline when the producers Sherman and Marjorie Ewing called me. They wanted me to sing Lucretia in the American premiere of Benjamin Britten's *The Rape of Lucretia,* but there was no way that I could accept, and Kitty Carlisle went on to sing the role.

The public seldom realizes how much time and work are involved in preparing a concert tour like Romberg's. We had a company manager to oversee every detail for a company that included three vocal soloists and an orchestra of sixty players. We performed a total of sixty-four concerts, averaging six concerts a week, for the better part of two and a half months. Sometimes we played twice in one city, but usually each night found us in a different city. For longer distances, we traveled by air, but for shorter distances, Romberg hired a bus for the orchestra and a car for us. He sat in front with the driver, constantly telling him how to drive.

Yet there were never any difficulties in performance, because Romberg's marvelous coordination with the musicians made every concert thoroughly agreeable. The program consisted of popular music by Rodgers, Strauss, Sousa, Lehár, Herbert, Kálmán, and of course Romberg; in addition, I sang Czech folk songs, Sandoval's "Eres tu," and an aria from Massenet's *Hérodiade.* The other singers were Victoria Sherry and Gene Marvey, both very attractive.

Someone once asked Romberg how he selected his artists, and he replied, "I know a good voice when I see it."

Finally I returned to New York and began preparing for the summer in Europe. I had agreed to return to the Salzburg Festival in two roles that I loved, Euridice and Octavian; but before leaving America, I had a few engagements, including Ed Sullivan's TV show and a big rally for Russian-American friendship at Madison Square Garden, at the invitation of New York's Mayor William O'Dwyer. Most important was Jarmilka's graduation from the Masters School in Dobbs Ferry. When it was time to board the RMS *Caronia,* I discovered that the great success of *The Search* had made me newsworthy: photographers waited for us at the dock, and my departure was even televised. I was highly amused.

George was waiting for us in Le Havre, and we drove the children and Teta to Blonville-sur-Mer for a short stay, because we didn't want them to suffer in the summer heat of Paris. Soon enough we were on our way to Salzburg, where George had made reservations for us at the Schloss Hotel Fuschl, on a lake where the children could swim and go boating while I attended rehearsals.

For *Orfeo,* Elisabeth Höngen sang Orfeo and Josef Krips conducted. During the first orchestra rehearsal, something funny and touching happened. We had just gotten to the scene in which Orpheus awakens Eurydice, and my first words are, "Is it you, do I see you, Orfeo? Is it not a dream?" But instead the orchestra suddenly began to play "Meine Lippen, sie küssen so heiß," my aria from *Giuditta.* I was so shocked that I turned, wide eyed, to Krips, but he just went on conducting and smiling. This was the way he and the Philharmonic Orchestra chose to welcome my return to Salzburg after a twelve-year absence.

We performed *Orfeo* at the Felsenreitschule, an outdoor theater. The day of the second performance, we had rain that stopped only just before we were to begin. We almost froze, and as the days went on with even more rain, I developed a nasty cold. I wanted to cancel the *Rosenkavalier* premiere, but the conductor, George Szell, begged me not to. I had no idea that the performance was being broadcast, and no way at all to know that Angel Records would release that broadcast on disc. I was quite angry, because I really had not been in my best voice. Years later, how would listeners know why I sounded the way I did? Yet with a cast that featured Maria Reining as the Marschallin and Hilde Gueden as Sophie, we met with approval from the press. Max Graf wrote in *Weltpresse,* "The high point of this performance is

Jarmila Novotná's Octavian. Everything is supremely poetic. Her slender figure, delicate face, her smile, aristocratic bearing, her sensitivity, and above all her voice. She is simply perfect."

We repeated *Rosenkavalier* and *Orpheus* each four times during the 1949 festival. Luckily the rain stopped, and the children and I had a wonderful time sightseeing. We went on excursions to Bad Reichenhall and to Hitler's "Eagle's Nest," Berchtesgaden. At the time, Salzburg was still in the American Zone of occupation, and at a party at Schloss Klesheim, George and I met the senior commission officer for Austria, General R. J. Dervan. He was planning a trip to Czechoslovakia, and when I mentioned that my parents still lived there, he suggested that Jarmilka and I make the trip with him. This was a wonderful opportunity, because in order to travel through the different occupied zones, such as the Russian Zone around Linz, one required special permission. But General Dervan took care of all those matters for us. Yet even with the general's help, we were surprised by the thoroughness of the luggage searches as we crossed into different zones. Officers inspected every bag, every dress, and went into every pocket. This was disagreeable, even though we had nothing to hide. Our visit with my parents was short, but I was very grateful to General Dervan for making it possible.

We returned to Paris, where George asked me to let Jarmilka stay with him for a while. He would have preferred for all of us to move to Paris, but I still had many engagements to fulfill in America. Before we left, I arranged for Jarmilka to take singing lessons with Bernadette Delprat, a member of the Opéra, whom Mary Garden recommended to me. Jarmilka had a nice voice and wanted to cultivate it, so I thought her stay in Paris offered a good opportunity for her to do so. I also visited Marcelle Chaumont, one of France's best dressmakers, and ordered a beautiful gown, the top embroidered with flowers, the leaves gold and the petals pink. What happened to that gown? I would find out soon enough!

Having spent the summer together as a family, we found it hard to part ways. Georgie, Teta, and I bade a tearful good-bye to George and Jarmilka as we returned to New York.

My 1949–1950 season began in San Francisco. I sang Donna Elvira opposite Ezio Pinza in *Don Giovanni* twice, and twice sang Giulietta in *Tales of Hoffmann* opposite Raoul Jobin. Then the company traveled to Los Angeles to reprise both operas, but this time I sang Antonia in *Hoffmann*. Robert and Lindsay Hadow invited me to stay with them while I was in town, and nothing could have pleased me more. Robert was now the British consul in Los Angeles, and I saw many nice people at his house: Sir Charles Mendl, Darryl Zanuck, Louis Jourdan, Clifton Webb, Joseph Cotten, Joan Fontaine, Jean Negulesco, Sophie Tucker, Ethel Barrymore, Nigel Bruce, and many more. I also went to the opera to hear Kirsten Flagstad sing an unforgettable Isolde. She also gave a recital with the wonderful accompanist Edwin McArthur, who later wrote a very good book about her. This was Flagstad's first U.S. performance since the war, and many people protested outside the theater because she was reputed to be a Nazi sympathizer. But this was not true: she returned to Norway not because she liked the Germans, but because she wanted to be with her husband. After the concert, I went to see her backstage, and she appreciated my support.

Back in New York, Georgie's interest in music continued to grow, and he made great progress in his piano playing. I took him and Teta to one of Toscanini's concerts and to meet Maestro backstage. At the Metropolitan, I sang Octavian and Cherubino several times, and when the penthouse in the apartment where we lived became available, I signed the lease immediately, not even waiting for George's approval. We would have the upper floor entirely to ourselves, and a terrace surrounded the apartment, so that we could plant trees and flowers. I knew George would like it. But George had important meetings to attend and could not join us at Christmas; Jarmila spent the holiday in France with Count Jean d'Aramon. The count had three children and spent part of each year in a château near Nevers, where Jarmila, a great horsewoman, could join in a variety of sports and improve her French. This meant that Georgie, Teta, and I were alone for Christmas, but Georgie played the piano, and we sang carols and had a wonderful time.

George arrived on December 29, 1949, and we spent New Year's Eve with Peggy Phipps Douglas (soon to marry the French diplomat Etienne Boegner) and the Bliss family. During the month that George was in America, I had only a few performances at the Metropolitan and concerts in Dayton, Atlantic City, and Denver; otherwise, my time belonged to my husband. When it came time for him to return to Europe, his farewell party turned out to be one of my most glamorous moments as a hostess, at the instigation of the newspaper columnist Louella Parsons. Knowing how eager she would be to write about celebrities in her column, I invited Salvador Dalí, Serge Obolensky, Elsa Maxwell, Cecil Beaton, Wanda Horowitz, Monty Clift, Lanfranco Rasponi—well, about one hundred people came.

George's work for IBM had expanded to include Turkey, Greece, India, and the Far East, so he was constantly traveling. He enjoyed this, though it meant we were far apart, each of us pursuing a very busy life. He and I wrote to each other almost daily, and when I reread the letters, I see how we managed to remain close. I told him that I wanted to resume voice lessons with Robert Weer, but that he had moved to Los Angeles. George agreed that we should spend the summer in California, after the Met season ended, and Lindsay Hadow found us a house not far from the Hadows' own, on Mansfield Avenue.

Before leaving for Los Angeles, we marked a great change at the Metropolitan: Edward Johnson was leaving; and on February 28, 1950, I joined in a gala concert in his honor. We loved Mr. Johnson dearly, and everyone was in tears. My first meetings with his successor, Rudolf Bing, were very friendly, and we signed a new contract to begin in mid-December. My contract with Sol Hurok had expired, and Harry Squires persuaded me to sign him as my new manager. He immediately came back with a proposal for a radio broadcast from Los Angeles on March 22, which I accepted—though it meant missing out on Maestro Toscanini's birthday celebration. Wanda Horowitz had come up with the idea that that a few of us perform a kick line, like the Rockettes, for her father, and Therese Milstein, Cia Toscanini, Pauline Heifetz Chotzinoff (the sister of the violinist Jascha Heifetz), and I agreed. Before signing with Squires, I had already attended several rehearsals, and though we had a professional coach and the example of Cia, a trained dancer, before us, I discovered that it's not easy to kick one's legs so high.

Squires arranged for photographers to greet us at the train station in Los Angeles, and the resulting publicity meant that invitations began to pour in almost immediately. The first day I lunched with the Hadows and Italo Montemezzi and his wife. At a dinner at the home of Charles Brackett, I saw Ethel Barrymore, Joseph Cotten, Sophie Tucker, Clark Gable, Zsa Zsa Gabor, the producer Peter Rathvon, the journalist Harry Crocker, and Paul Reynaud, who had been president of the French Council of Ministers but resigned rather than sign an armistice with the Germans in 1940. The columnist Cobina Wright invited me to Ciro's, Elsa Maxwell to Romanoff's, and so on.

Once again, Louis B. Mayer urged me to make a movie, especially since I was already planning to be in Los Angeles for a little while. He advised me to sign with the agent Fefe Ferry, which I did soon afterward. But I didn't care for the script MGM sent to me, and so I sent it back.

I did not forget my main purpose for being in Los Angeles, and I started my lessons with Mr. Weer immediately. We worked every day, and I was greatly satisfied with the results. With Shibley Boyes, I sang a concert in

Pasadena, and we performed several times in veterans' hospitals. The soldiers were always such wonderful audiences. Meanwhile, I enrolled Georgie in the Cathedral Chapel School, which he found very pleasant. I also sang a concert with Romberg at the Hollywood Bowl. Maestro Toscanini was in town for two concerts with the NBC Orchestra, part of a coast-to-coast tour. Age eighty-three by this time, he was touched by the admiration people showed him wherever he went; and on this evening in Los Angeles, he really was enjoying himself, drinking two glasses of champagne.

I had to fly back to New York for two Viennese concerts, with Julius Rudel conducting, one at Lewisohn Stadium and one at the Robin Hood Dell. The timing could not have been better, because Jarmilka returned to New York on the *Caronia,* bringing with her a little dog, Flip. I wore my beautiful Marcelle Chaumont gown for the concerts, but I didn't want to wear it to dinner afterward, and so I left it on the bed in my room. When Jarmilka and I returned home, Flip greeted us, barking and jumping for joy. He looked so funny, with shiny whiskers. I laughed, but not for long, when I realized that he had chewed up my gown. I almost died. But what could I do? It was my fault.

The next morning we left for California. Jarmilka took to Hollywood like a fish to water, making great friends with the Hadows' daughter, who was about the same age. Jarmilka was a beautiful girl, and everybody admired her. She took voice lessons with Mr. Weer and attended a drama school; when Mr. Mayer saw her, he suggested that she make a screen test. Jarmilka prepared a short scene, and everybody liked it, but nothing ever came of it. Later, however, when we returned to New York, she took acting lessons from one of the MGM coaches, and soon she enrolled in the American Academy of Dramatic Arts.

With Weer, I worked on vocal health. Generally we began with an exercise for correct breathing, really working the diaphragm and exhaling as slowly, gently, and evenly as possible, without any movement in my shoulders. Only the action of the breath on the vocal cords produces sound. I also benefited greatly from practicing the open-throat "Ah," thinking of that "Ah" sound as the foundation of all vowels. I practiced for some time, simply phonating "Ah" with my throat wide open, my jaw free, and my tongue relaxed and flat in my mouth, the lip barely touching the lower teeth. After several repetitions without pitch, I would sing the "Ah," then move on to other vowels: long strings of "Ah" and "Ooh," for example, without changing the "Ah" in the slightest degree.

A concert at the Music Academy of the West gave me the chance to work again with Hans Lert, who told me that he and Vicki Baum had moved to the

United States for good. At the orchestra rehearsal, I met Ganna Walska, a retired opera singer famed for her beauty, who invited me to stay at her house. We spent an enchanted evening discussing her career, and she showed me an entire room filled with costumes for roles she had sung—and for roles she had hoped for but never sung.

When I returned to Los Angeles, Mr. Mayer asked me to make a test, because they were planning to produce a musical film in which he thought there might be a part for me. This turned out to be *The Great Caruso* starring Mario Lanza, and I found myself in a cast that also included Ann Blyth and Dorothy Kirsten, directed by Richard Thorpe and produced by Joe Pasternak. The preparations, dress fittings, and hair and makeup tests took up the rest of July. Lanza was extremely pleasant to work with, and he had an exceptionally beautiful voice. Once, when my children visited the studio, he insisted on taking a picture with them, which was very sweet of him.

All the singing for the movie was prerecorded, then dubbed into the film later. At one recording session, I was supposed to sing the duet from *Rigoletto* with Lanza. However, just before this, he had recorded "La donna è mobile," and, as is typical in recording sessions, he had to repeat the aria several times. We finished one take of our duet, but then he announced that he was exhausted, and he refused to sing any longer. This created great consternation, because recording sessions with a full orchestra are very costly. Pasternak sent Lanza's secretary to try to reason with him, but to no avail. We were left to idle about until, after two hours, Lanza suddenly reappeared, completely refreshed, so that we finished the recording without any further delay.

Lanza performed often in concert, and his tragedy is that he overtaxed himself, then started to drink heavily. That brought on his early death. What a curse drinking is! We have known so many victims.

Life in Hollywood was an unending stream of parties. This was fine with me, as long as I didn't have to work. It also amused me to make the acquaintance of stars whom I'd known only from the screen. I became a fixture at Jack Warner's parties, where I saw Danny Kaye, Mary Pickford, Ginger Rogers, Jimmy Stewart, Myrna Loy, and Greer Garson. Newlywed Elizabeth Taylor came with her husband, the young Nicky Hilton; when Mr. Warner tried to seat them separately, she told him she'd leave if they couldn't sit together. Such parties usually ended with a screening of the latest film. At the home of Walter Reisch, an Austrian who became a movie producer, I socialized with an entirely different crowd: Otto Preminger, Louis Jourdan, Joan Fontaine, Rouben Mamoulian, Danielle Darrieux. I also made a point of visiting Max

Reinhardt's widow, Helene Thimig, and at her home I sometimes found Gottfried Reinhardt and Erich Wolfgang Korngold, a nice reunion.

Perhaps the most meaningful invitation, however, came from the Hollywood Bowl Association. Lotte Lehmann, Artur Rodzinski, Gregor Piatigorsky, Vladimir Horowitz, Arthur Rubinstein, and many others of us who performed there often were asked to dedicate a little bit of soil from our homelands, which would be enshrined under the pit at the Bowl. Because I could not get any soil from Czechoslovakia in time for the ceremony, I gave the association a few of the violets that Jan Masaryk had given me from the night table in the room where his father had died; I carried them with me almost like a talisman, because they were so very precious to me. The ceremony took place on August 1, and the Hollywood Bowl Orchestra played the Czechoslovak national anthem.

Another new season began with performances of *Rosenkavalier* with the opera company in New Orleans, a city I loved to explore. I used to walk from the French Quarter to the Garden District, admiring the graceful houses, the endless gardens thick with azalea bushes, magnolia trees, gardenias so white they dazzled the eye, camellias of all colors, oleanders, jasmine, and other flowers in profusion. It seems that something is blooming all year 'round.

After the first rehearsal for *Rosenkavalier,* the New Orleans opera company posted an advertisement for extras to play the lackeys in the Presentation Scene in Act II. The newspaper carried the ad with the headline "Bodyguards for a Beauty," and continued: "Tall men wanted, minimum 5 feet, 10 inches, as bodyguards for Jarmila Novotná. Moderate compensation." The next day, at least twenty men showed up, hoping to escort me to Antoine's for a good dinner. They were terribly disappointed to be handed rococo costumes and sent out onstage! But after the performance, they all said they'd happily do it again.

When I returned to New York, who should greet me at the airport but Jarmilka and Monty Clift. What a surprise! I asked Monty to lunch, and he told me that he had movie offers from all sides; he didn't know which to accept.

The next morning, rehearsals started for *Das Rheingold* at the Metropolitan, in which I was to sing Freia, with George Szell conducting; shortly afterward, we began rehearsals for *Die Fledermaus,* in which I was to sing Orlofsky. I wound up making front-page news because, on January 25, 1951, I sang Freia at the Saturday matinée, which was broadcast, and then the same evening I sang Orlofsky. The *Herald Tribune* ran pictures of me, both as Freia and as Orlofsky, and the accompanying article explained that, while it's rare for one singer to take leading roles in two different operas on the same day, this was the *only* time anyone remembered a singer playing a woman in one opera and a man in the other! As I explained to the paper, the biggest challenges about Orlofsky were the props: I had to carry a fifteen-inch cigarette holder, though I never smoked before; and I had to wear a monocle that wouldn't stay put when I hit my high notes. My Orlofsky costume provided a little extra entertainment when several Met artists performed for the crew of the USS *Independence*—and in costume, I danced with Lucrezia Bori.

We had marvelous casts for both operas, with Hans Hotter our excellent Wotan in *Rheingold,* and Maria Jeritza making her comeback as Rosalinda in *Fledermaus.* Patrice Munsel as Adele and Jack Gilford as Frosch were especially popular with the *Fledermaus* audience. Performed in an English translation by Garson Kanin and Howard Dietz, *Fledermaus* was a big hit, and we repeated it twelve times in New York before taking it on the spring tour. Our first stop was Baltimore, and about halfway through my aria, "Chacun à son goût," the entire audience at the Lyric Theater began to roar with laughter—I thought I was losing my pants. But no, a big bat—a *Fledermaus,* in German—was flying over my head. This was the first time that a real bat starred in this opera. He seemed friendly enough, so I waved my cigarette holder at him, and he flew off into the audience. The incident made news, and even *Time* magazine reported it, so it was good publicity. We continued on to eight other cities, and by the time I got home, George joked that he had seen so little of me, it was almost as if he were still abroad.

There had been other engagements that season, including my first appearance on the Arthur Murray television show. He and his wife put together programs that were quite varied, and I had great fun with them each time I appeared. I usually sang an aria, and for my debut it was the Habañera from *Carmen,* and also "Love Has Found My Heart" from Kálmán's *Countess Maritza.* Later in the program I usually sang something the audience wouldn't expect from an opera singer, such as a pop song—Bill Haley's "Crazy, Man, Crazy," for instance. This had great appeal, and the Murrays asked me to sing on their show many times. I also had the fun of working with Abbott and Costello on *The Colgate Hour,* spoofing *Rigoletto* and *Carmen* with them. And I interrupted our summer vacation—in Oyster Bay that year—to fly to Los Angeles to appear again on Bing Crosby's show. Working with him was always such a joy that I didn't want to cancel.

Monty Clift came to visit us on Long Island that summer. He liked the children and went swimming with them, having a good time. I was greatly surprised a short time later to receive a letter from him, telling me that he loved me and that, if circumstances were different, he would have asked me to marry him. This I really didn't expect. He got along so well with my husband, and he never showed me any improper affection. I didn't know how to react, so I showed the letter to George. He only smiled and said that I should act as if nothing had happened. I followed his advice, Monty never said another word about the letter, and he and I remained the best of friends.[8]

That summer we made friends with Archibald and Grace Roosevelt, who took us to see Sagamore Hill, the house Archie's father, President Theodore Roosevelt, had built. Both Archie and George had a tremendous knowledge of history, and whenever they got together it was great fun to listen to their conversations.

Just to show how much times have changed: on the first night at the house in Oyster Bay, I asked George whether he had locked up before going to bed. He told me that the owner of the house, Mrs. Harold H. Weekes, had told him that they never locked the doors, and she hadn't even given him the keys. We asked her again, and she did send over a set, but I wonder what would happen today if we left the doors unlocked!

In the fall, Georgie returned to the Collegiate School, and Jarmilka began her studies at the American Academy of Dramatic Arts. Alexander Alexay and I prepared a new concert program, trying it out on a highly critical audience, the singing teachers at the annual meeting of the Tennessee Education Association. And with nine other women (including the journalist Dorothy Kilgallen, the television star Imogene Coca, Dorothy Sarnoff, and Mrs. Douglas MacArthur), I was named one of the "Sweetest Women in New York," part of a campaign to promote participation in American Red Cross blood drives and gift programs for hospitalized veterans, orphans, shut-ins, and other needy people. The response was enormous. My activity for the remainder of 1951 consisted largely of television appearances, the annual concert to commemorate Czechoslovak independence, and the Voice of America Christmas program.

Not long after that Christmas program in 1951, the U.S. State Department asked me to make some recordings with Bruno Walter for Voice of America, and I immediately accepted. Walter came to our apartment with the recording crew, and he accompanied me on the piano while I sang songs by Schubert, Brahms, Smetana, and Dvořák. Singing to Walter's accompaniment was a joy, affording me the greatest musical satisfaction; we created an absolute unity of spirit. I felt this much more strongly when he accompanied me than when I sang under his baton. It was sublime.

Time seemed to pass much faster when George was with us. Maybe this was because we had more social engagements. One of these was most interesting: a dinner given by Thomas J. Watson in honor of King Faisal II, the seventeen-year-old ruler of Iraq. More than 150 people attended the dinner, and I was asked to sing. I was shocked when Faisal was assassinated the next year, and Iraq was proclaimed a republic.

I had the pleasure of singing *The Bartered Bride* again in 1952, first with the local company in San Antonio, where members of the large Czech-American community greeted me in folk costumes and assured a tremendous success for our performance. Dr. Victor Alessandro led the orchestra, and though he was Italian-American, he conducted in a thoroughly authentic manner. Shortly thereafter, I sang the opera again, this time with the local company in St. Louis, to great acclaim. We had an excellent cast, including Ralph Herbert and William Hess, and Edwin McArthur conducted with sparkling good humor. We sold out all seven performances, and it was during this visit that I met Kurt von Schuschnigg, the former Austrian chancellor, who was by this time a professor at Saint Louis University.

Back in New York, I had the opportunity to think more seriously about acting when Florence Kimball Smith asked me to coach one of her students, Mariquita Moll, who was preparing to sing the Marschallin in *Der Rosenkavalier* with the New York City Opera. I never sang the Marschallin, but knowing how badly singers without guidance sometimes move and act onstage, I agreed. I see the Marschallin as a woman of mature charm, wisdom, and grace. In the eighteenth century, women aged quickly, but to me this character is youthful, gay, capricious, and not at all a martyr to her marriage. Once in a while she thinks about growing older (who doesn't?) and it brings a tear to her eye, but she is basically a happy woman. Her husband, whom we never see onstage, is absent so often that she is able to enjoy her life as she chooses. I worked with Mariquita, achieving very encouraging results, and the critics especially praised her acting, which pleased me.

This experience and my friendship with Monty Clift led me to the Actors Studio. I did not become a member, but I was allowed to be an onlooker, watching short scenes. Best known as the domain of the teacher Lee Strasberg and the director Elia Kazan (one of the Studio's founders), the Studio has produced some of the most important American actors, including Marlon Brando and Monty himself. The teachers put emphasis on remembering things from one's past that could apply to the character and situation one was playing. This approach would make the performance true to life.

I found this very interesting, and yet it was nothing new to me. I even think that "sense memory" is unnecessary. You must familiarize yourself with the character and give it a life of its own. For instance, if you have to kill somebody onstage, would you have to experience the act of murder in order to play the scene? I think that is going too far. We must use our imaginations, not reality.

Our family was growing up. George and I had decided that this would be Georgie's last year at Collegiate, and that we would send him to Le Rosey, a prestigious boarding school in Switzerland. We wanted him to learn French, and Le Rosey is known for the quality of its education and the academic discipline of its students; for the winter session, the school moved to Gstaad, so that the children could ski. At the time, the school had children from thirty-six countries, each of whom had to pass an entrance exam, and all of whom were treated equally—no matter that one was the son of the King of Belgium (simply Baudoin), one the son of the Aga Khan (Karim), one the son of the Duke of Kent (just Kent).

George had to interrupt our summer vacation on Long Island that year when IBM sent him to Asia on important business. The trip lasted three months and took him to India, Burma, Indochina, Singapore, and Pakistan. While he was away, Thomas Watson thoughtfully invited me to dinner, where he told me how pleased he was with reports of George's trip. George had done a great deal in a short amount of time, and he had made many new friends for IBM, Mr. Watson said. This made me very happy, though it didn't surprise me: George was born under the sign of Leo, and he was always very positive and confident, able to analyze any situation and to find a solution. When George returned from Asia, I enjoyed his descriptions of the cities and people he had encountered, and George told me that his greatest regret was that I had not gone with him. But that was the curse: each of us had duties to perform.

Meanwhile, Jarmilka's friend from AADA, Elizabeth Montgomery, the daughter of the actor Robert, invited her to play summer stock at the John Drew Theater in East Hampton.[9] Jarmilka acted in several plays at the theater while staying with the Montgomerys. I visited several times, and the Montgomerys asked me to appear at a benefit concert for the Guild Hall. I did so gladly, but my concert coincided with a full day of rain. The next morning, we were surprised by a hurricane, which uprooted many trees and kept me in East Hampton longer than I had planned.

George returned from India a few weeks before the 1952 election, and sure enough, I was asked to sing at a rally for Eisenhower at Madison Square Garden on October 30. The event lasted five and a half hours, and it featured singers, dancers, and comedians. So many stars that I can't recall all the names: Helen Hayes, Irene Dunne, Jack Haley, Robert Montgomery, Fred Waring, Irving Berlin, and many more. Thomas E. Dewey introduced General Eisenhower, who made a spectacular entrance down the center aisle, with the Women for Eisenhower seated on either side. When he gave his speech, everyone was certain he would win the election—which of course he did, on November 4. A few days later, I received a request to perform in the Inauguration Concert in Washington on January 19, 1953.

As Eisenhower's inaugural approached, George felt unwell, and his doctor advised him not to try to make the trip to Washington with me. What a pity he had to miss the festive atmosphere, where George Murphy, the Hollywood actor, had assembled the talent. Esther Williams, Walter Pidgeon, Adolph Menjou, Irene Dunne, Lee Bowman, John Wayne, Ed Sullivan, and William Gaxton acted as cohosts, and Fred Waring and his orchestra played. The crowd in the packed Uline Arena cheered and whistled for the many favorites from the entertainment world: Allan Jones, Ethel Merman, Sid Caesar and Imogene Coca, Tony Martin, Abbott and Costello, and Hoagy Carmichael, to name just a few. Six stars from the New York City Ballet performed Balanchine's brand-new piece, *Valse-Fantaisie*, and I sang an aria from *La Traviata* and a duet with Jan Peerce. It was a long evening, but those who stuck it out left happy.

The next day, we were blessed by beautiful weather, and we were able to watch the inauguration from special stands. To crown it all, there was a ball in the evening, with men in black tie and ladies in glittering formal finery, and everybody danced until morning.

I had returned to the Met and *Fledermaus* on New Year's Eve, and on February 1, 1953, we performed it again on the television program *Omnibus,* with Eugene Ormandy conducting. I admired his approach to the score, and the show was a great success. Ormandy worked with us several times on *Fledermaus* at the Met, and Tibor Kozma conducted many other *Fledermaus* performances there. Also that season I sang Octavian again, this time with Fritz Reiner conducting and my dear Hilde Gueden as Sophie. It seemed as if Mr. Bing believed I was destined to play only boys' roles.

Anita Loos, the author of *Gentlemen Prefer Blondes,* called on me with a proposition. She was writing a musical called *Caresse,* with music by Jule Styne and lyrics by Mack Gordon, and she wanted me to appear in it. She gave me a section of the script and an outline of the entire story, but when I read it, I didn't care for it. In fact, it's never been produced. But Broadway beckoned once again when Basil Rathbone wrote to me, telling me that his wife, Ouida, had adapted a Sherlock Holmes story for the stage. Rathbone himself would play Holmes, as he had done so often in movies, and they wanted me to play Irene Adler. We met to discuss the project further, and I promised to do it. They planned to open in the fall, so—apart from the usual concerts with Charles Kullman, conducted by Julius Rudel, at Lewisohn Stadium and Robin Hood Dell—I was free as a bird to enjoy my summer vacation in Oyster Bay.

Georgie had returned from school in Switzerland, and he had been accepted for the fall semester at the St. Paul's School in Concord, New Hampshire. He and Jarmilka had many friends in Oyster Bay, which made their time so much fun. One friend brought his roommate from Yale, an ardent polo player named Peter Packard. Peter kept a ten-meter yacht moored off our dock and often took the children and their friends sailing. Did I sense already that a spark had lit between Peter and Jarmilka?

When I returned to New York at the end of the summer, I had first to obtain permission from Mr. Bing to perform *Sherlock Holmes,* since rehearsals were to begin in September 1953. Luckily, he had no objection. Because Irene Adler is a singer, I was given two numbers, Grieg's "Ich liebe dich" and a setting of a Browning poem by Alexander Steinert prepared especially for this production.

We had two weeks of rehearsal before leaving for out-of-town tryouts, and even my long rehearsals with Max Reinhardt could not prepare me for what awaited me in Boston. Our final dress rehearsal began at 8:00 in the evening and ended at 8:00 the next morning; our first preview was that night. Even on the day of the premiere, we rehearsed at 2:00, with only a short interval before the performance, at 8:00. All's well that ends well, and we received excellent reviews the next morning. The *Boston Globe* called our play "a full-bodied spoof" and declared that "*Sherlock Holmes* deserves a long and profitable run." I liked the description of my work from the critic for the *Boston Herald:* "The Metropolitan Opera's gorgeous Jarmila Novotná is a superb Irene Adler and she plays her so enticingly it is incredible Holmes can resist her."

We gave fourteen performances in Boston before coming to New York. Because the Century Theater was larger than the Majestic in Boston, we needed more rehearsal. We played just one preview and then opened on Friday, October 30, 1953. The next day we played a matinée, and then—to the surprise of everyone—our final performance was that night. I don't know what the reason was, although the New York critics did not like our show as much as their colleagues did in Boston, and Brooks Atkinson in the *New York Times* described Ouida Rathbone's script as "sprawling" as well as "cumbersome and uneven." He asked, "Is Mrs. Rathbone affectionately satirizing the genre of superman detective fiction, or the stuffy manners of Victorian society, or is she taking Holmes' exploits at face value? . . . There is a confusion of styles that dissipates the story." Atkinson described me as one of "a number of very able actors," "a highly vocal Irene Adler, international concert singer and crook."

Thus ended this episode. It was an interesting experience, and Rudolf Bing was glad to welcome me back to the Met. Immediately he cast me in several performances, including the inevitable *Fledermaus.* Around this time I also made my first appearance on a color television program, *The Armstrong Circle Theater.* The drama was called "Evening Star," and I played an opera singer who had been in retirement for twenty years, now making her television debut. The *Herald Tribune* said that I was "not only a fine singer, but also an extremely competent actress" That made me happy.

Jarmilka had better luck in the New York theater than I had in *Sherlock Holmes* when she made her stage debut a few days later, as one of six nuns in *Cyrano de Bergerac,* starring José Ferrer, at City Center. The delightful Anita Loos, with whom I had remained in close contact, accompanied George and me, and she thought Jarmilka had real talent. Our daughter was beautiful, twenty-one years old, and had many suitors. Who knew what the future would bring?

On January 23, 1954, after a broadcast performance of *Fledermaus* at the Met, Mrs. O'Donnell Hoover of the Metropolitan Opera Guild came to me with, as she put it, a very big request. She collected manuscripts and memorabilia to display at the opera house, and now she asked me to obtain a baton from Maestro Toscanini. Well, that was not an easy task! But I called Maestro and asked to come and visit him. We discussed the request, and a few days later, not one but two batons arrived in the mail: one for the Guild, and one to make someone else happy. I gave Mrs. Hoover the first baton, and it is still on display at the Met—but I kept the other for myself, and this pleased Maestro very much.

We seldom missed any of Toscanini's concerts in New York. That year, however, he decided that his concert on April 4 would be his last. He sent George and me a pair of tickets with a little note, and so we went to Carnegie Hall, where Maestro and the NBC Orchestra performed an all-Wagner program. Suddenly, during the Bacchanale from *Tannhäuser,* Toscanini stopped conducting and put his hands over his eyes. We all sensed that something was wrong; although a little confused, the orchestra went on playing. Maestro regained his self-control and began to conduct again. The concert ended with the *Meistersinger* prelude, and as the last chords played, Toscanini dropped his baton, stepped slowly from the podium, and made his way to the exit. Thunderous applause followed him, but Maestro did not acknowledge it. He was eighty-seven years old, and there was nobody like him.

About two weeks later, Maestro called me and asked me to visit him in Riverdale. He had recovered from whatever had overcome him during the concert, and now he was full of plans. He thought constantly of Italy, and he reminisced about the reopening of La Scala in August 1946. When he returned to conduct at the theater on that occasion, the reception overwhelmed him. The theater was jammed, and thousands gathered in the Piazza del Duomo to hear the concert on loudspeakers; the concert was also broadcast on radio throughout Italy. After the performance, the Scala orchestra presented Toscanini with a gold medallion carrying the inscription: "To the Maestro—who was with us always." The memory made him smile as we spoke.

He told me that, ever since the Scala reopening, he had been constantly on the go: concerts with the Scala orchestra, the NBC Orchestra, radio broadcasts, television broadcasts. His energy seemed inexhaustible. In 1950, when he was eighty-three, he had set out on a six-week tour of the United States, from coast to coast; I had been lucky to hear his concert in Los Angeles.

I last saw Maestro on October 26, 1956, when he invited me and George to Riverdale. I had never seen him so talkative. He was very happy to report that his granddaughter was expecting a baby, and he teased me, asking when I would be a grandmother. This was a wonderful evening, but for us it would be the last. Maestro died on January 16, 1957.

The world lost a great man and a great artist. He spent all his life learning and relearning, striving to attain perfection. He was never satisfied with himself, and that was the reason he demanded the utmost from everyone else. He used to say, "Man is a slave to habit, and who wants to be a slave? Get rid of the habits—only then you will progress." Artistically and as a friend, he was precious to me, and I will treasure his memory forever in my heart.

Our summer of 1954 in Oyster Bay started with a frightening incident. George had just come home from work, and he and I decided to go for a swim. While we were in the water, we heard the wail of a siren, which sounded very urgent. George said that it must be a fire alarm of some kind. We had just returned to the house when we heard the telephone. It was the Glen Cove hospital, telling us that Georgie and Peter Packard had been in an accident. They had been motor boating when the boat exploded; both boys had sustained burns. We rushed to the hospital, where we found that Peter's hair, eyebrows, and upper body had been very badly burned. Georgie's burns were only on his legs, because he had been thrown out of the boat by the explosion. Swimming underwater, he had been spared the worst, because flames covered the surface. Georgie remained in the hospital for eight days, but poor Peter had to stay almost three weeks. Luckily they both recovered, and soon sailing and polo were once again the main attraction.

The rest of the summer passed in the usual way, with interruptions for a few concerts and for *The Bartered Bride* in Cincinnati, at the zoo. Sometimes the animals made noises during the operas, or the birds sang along, which was quite a riot. At one performance, the temperature at night was still 96 degrees! But the audience was most enthusiastic, and one critic wrote that I was "deservedly the most famous Marie." We also drove to Rhinebeck to visit Brooke and Vincent Astor; Vincent liked to play croquet, but only when he won. (He usually did.)

George spent most of the fall of 1954 in Europe for IBM, and my schedule was somewhat lighter than usual, concluding yet again with *Fledermaus* at the Met to end the year. This opera was becoming so popular that, in the new year, I sang it not only at the Metropolitan but also with the local troupe in San Antonio, Texas—and then the entire company flew to Brownsville, Texas, to sing it there.

My performance in the TV drama "Evening Star" paved the way for another television appearance, this time a straight dramatic role in a drama called "The Bridge" for *The Elgin Hour.* Kim Stanley played my daughter, whose boyfriend (John Ireland) jumps off a bridge; my role was to console her. This was sad but very interesting to play, and so well received that I immediately received another offer to appear in an episode of *Justice,* "Thunder on Troy Street," starring Gary Merrill.

George and I attended a concert by the Berlin Philharmonic, conducted by Herbert von Karajan, at Carnegie Hall, with picketers outside. Reminders of Karajan's relationship with the Nazis did not affect the enthusiastic reception he found inside the hall, and afterward George and I attended a party in Karajan's honor, thrown by Walter Damrosch's daughter. I had not met Karajan yet, so I welcomed the opportunity. We had many mutual acquaintances, and conversation was very easy. He urged me to look him up at the Staatsoper the next time I came to Vienna.

In May we accepted an invitation from our friend George Bagby to spend a few days with him at his estate in Versailles, Kentucky. The central event was the running of the Kentucky Derby, and it is difficult to describe the thrill of the Derby to people who have not been to one. The next morning Bagby asked me to drive with him to hear some auditions in Lexington; there was a young baritone who seemed to have great promise. The young man was good looking and had a remarkable voice, but it seemed to me that the quality was more that of a tenor than of a baritone, and I told him so. I forgot all about it until a few years later I went to hear *Fidelio* at the Vienna State Opera. I went backstage afterward and met the excellent singer who had sung Florestan. "You don't remember me, do you?" he said. "You heard me sing in Lexington. I took your advice seriously and never regretted it. I'm very grateful to you." His name was James King, and he became the most sought-after heldentenor at Bayreuth and around the world.

Peter Packard had been courting Jarmila quite intensely, and in the summer of 1955, he asked George and me for permission to marry her. Peter's own parents were divorced, and he introduced us to them. His mother was very musical, and she and Jarmila used to play piano duets for four hands; right from the beginning, we liked her very much. We threw the children an engagement party on August 6, just before George left on a long trip to Asia for IBM. He returned to America on November 6, just two weeks before the wedding. As soon as he arrived, however, he began bleeding internally, and the doctors at New York Hospital diagnosed him with diverticulitis. He required immediate surgery. I proposed that we postpone Jarmila's wedding, but he would not hear of it.

So the wedding took place as planned on November 19, 1955, in the church of St. Ignatius Loyola on Park Avenue. It was snowing heavily, but the church was full, and our son George stood in for his father to give the bride away. We held the reception at the Lotus Club, and it was a very happy gathering of good friends, including the Packards, the Astors, the Whitneys, and

Monty Clift, whom I had asked to escort Elsa Maxwell. She was thrilled and raved about him in her next newspaper column. Immediately following the reception, I went to see George in the hospital, where Jarmila and Peter met me shortly afterward. George was recovering satisfactorily and permitted to go home ten days later, but he required two more operations, the last one just after New Year's. I was glad that I wasn't too busy during this time; my daily visits with George made his long hospital stays less tedious.

At the Metropolitan, we were rehearsing a new production of *Tales of Hoffmann,* directed by Cyril Ritchard, with Richard Tucker as Hoffmann, Martial Singher as the villains, and Pierre Monteux conducting; this time, I sang Giulietta, but for only one performance, on Christmas Eve, 1955. At the invitation of Dag Hammarskjöld, the Secretary-General of the United Nations, I sang in a Sibelius concert at Carnegie Hall and attended a luncheon at his home a few days later, where I had the pleasure of meeting the actor Michael Redgrave and Oona O'Neill, the widow of the playwright Eugene. And for Hanukkah, I sang once again at Madison Square Garden in a celebration of the modern-day Maccabees of Israel; the performers also included Edward G. Robinson, Betty Field, Louis Calhern, Jan Peerce, Mischa Elman, and Morton Gould conducting the Symphony of the Air.

We ended the year with *Fledermaus,* and for the performance, Rudolf Bing's right-hand man wrote special lyrics for my aria:

> Another year comes to the end, a thousand bells will ring,
> And since it is much too late to mend, let's dance and shout and sing.
> But though the greatest bells may chime for Nineteen-Fifty-Six,
> You know quite well from time to time we may be in a fix.
> But if you feel that life will be tough for dear old Foster Dulles,
> Just think that Bing has Milanov, Tebaldi, and La Callas!
> The poor man will have Milanov, Tebaldi, and La Callas!
> He will deserve your pity, for through this blessed year,
> They'll shout into his ear.
> This is the way I sing it: Chacun à son goût.
> If you think you can Bing it, then I have news for you!

After his last surgery, George came home for good on January 15, 1956. The same evening, I had to sing *Fledermaus.* I was sorry that I couldn't devote myself to him fully. The doctors had told him to take things easy for a while, and I wanted to have more time for him. I decided to ask Rudolf Bing to let me out of my contract. He fully understood my situation, and so that *Fledermaus* on January 15 became my final performance at the Metropolitan Opera.

Before George returned to work, we decided to join another couple on a trip to Havana, Cuba. Our friends took a vacation there every year, and they showed us all the sights and managed to book us rooms at the country club, so that we could play golf and go swimming every day. At the time, Havana was an El Dorado, and we loved watching Cuban dance performances, an entertainment unsurpassed. After three weeks, we returned to snowy New York, a real contrast after balmy Cuba.

With George fully recovered, I felt free to accept an invitation from my friend Robert Tobin to attend the glorious Coronation Ball in San Antonio. All the ladies dressed in costumes inspired by the court of Emperor Franz Joseph, and I was asked to sing Johann Strauss waltzes and other Viennese songs. Robert was my escort, and we danced until morning. It was really lovely.

There were signs, both joyous and sad, that life was marching onward. Our son George's graduation from St. Paul's was a happy occasion, and he had decided to attend Columbia University in the fall. Then in June, we lost both Thomas J. Watson and my dear father. I learned of Father's death by telegram, and it pained me to know I would not see him any more.

The more we knew Mr. Watson, the more we admired him. He referred to all of his employees as the IBM family, and he saw the potential for international business very early. While George worked there, IBM grew and spread all over the world; by the early 1960s it would develop to unheard-of heights.

I had thought that my last performance at the Metropolitan would be my farewell to opera, but the Cincinnati Opera, where I had sung so many times, begged me to return for two performances of *Figaro.* I loved Cherubino very much—and for Cherubino's sake I accepted. Those performances, in July 1956, would be my last in opera.

4

The Happiest Times

Even in retirement, I was not completely idle. In June 1956, a man named Colston Leigh wrote to me with a contract for a series of lectures that also would feature vocal selections. I wasn't sure I could do it, but I found the idea intriguing. Over the summer, I prepared my program with Gibner King, my new accompanist; and Mr. Leigh began booking engagements to start in October. With the rest of my summer free, I accepted George's offer to join him on a business trip to Vienna and Budapest. In Vienna we stayed at the Hotel Sacher, and soon it seemed that the entire city knew we had come.

Countess Christl Schönfeldt, who organized the fabulous Opera Ball every year until 1980, invited me to inspect the newly rebuilt Staatsoper. As we walked, she recalled the terrible day, March 12, 1945, when the opera house had been bombed. The stage and auditorium were obliterated, with only the outer walls remaining. The ensuing fire consumed everything and brought the roof crashing down. She said that for days afterward crowds of people stood in the street to see the damage, and many of them wept openly. With the help not only of the nation but of the entire world, funds were raised. In America, too, artists including myself participated in several benefits, and now the opera house had been rebuilt in all its glory.

We climbed a marble staircase and walked through spacious promenades, the walls covered with exquisite tapestries. The new stage was equipped for every kind of effect, and backstage I saw more than forty luxuriously furnished dressing rooms for soloists, chorus, ballet, and supernumeraries. A speaker system connected them all, making late entrances all but impossible. At last the countess took me into the empty auditorium. It looked much as I remembered it, with its lovely, intimate proportions and its four tiers of boxes decorated in red, ivory, and gold. I was most grateful for this tour.

As a matter of fact, the director of the Staatsoper had invited me to the reopening, but on that same night—November 5, 1955—I was contracted to appear in *The Great Waltz,* a television production produced by Max Liebman, starring Patrice Munsel, Keith Andes, and Bert Lahr. Nothing would have made me happier than to attend the Staatsoper's reopening, but

Bob Sarnoff of NBC (David Sarnoff's oldest son, who later married the soprano Anna Moffo) understood the sacrifice I was making. On the evening of the telecast of *The Great Waltz,* he sent me a telegram, expressly thanking me for having missed the celebration in Vienna. Now, just a year later, I was able to attend opening night. George couldn't join us, because he had to continue his business trip in Budapest, but our good friends Count Carl Des-Fours and Count Richard Coudenhove-Kalergi, the founding president of the Pan-European Union, escorted me to a lovely *Rosenkavalier,* with Christa Ludwig as Octavian.

At the theater, I ran into Dr. Marcel Prawy, an advisor to the Volksoper at the time, who introduced many musicals to Vienna, including *Kiss Me, Kate* and *West Side Story.* Now he told me that I would be perfect for the Volksoper's beautiful production of Leo Fall's *Madame Pompadour,* and he hoped I would agree to sing at least a few performances. I told him that it was hard to say yes to something I wasn't familiar with, so he sent me the score and a pianist to play it for me. I don't know why I can't resist trying something new—so I said yes and signed a contract for ten performances in January and February 1957. I knew it was crazy, as I had so many other things to do.

As soon as George returned from Budapest, we left for New York. He did not like the situation in Hungary at all and was anxious to report back to IBM headquarters. The Cold War truly had begun, and the Hungarian government had imprisoned the company's general manager in Budapest. George felt strongly that the company must do everything possible to get him released. Only a few months later, however, during the popular uprising against the Communists, the general manager was released, and he managed to leave the country with his wife and children before the Soviet tanks rolled into Budapest on November 4, 1956, crushing every hope of change.

We arrived home the day before my birthday. I found waiting for me a letter from Colston Leigh, setting out an itinerary for an eighteen-city lecture tour, beginning October 3 and ending December 28, 1956. I enjoyed the tour, and Gibner King proved an excellent pianist and agreeable companion. According to one newspaper critic, my program was "more like an informal at-home than a concert or lecture (although it partook of both)." I shared anecdotes about some of the people I have met, including Emmy Destinn, Toscanini, Eisenhower, the Masaryks, and so on; I also told many of the backstage stories that I have included in this book. Among the memories I interspersed songs by Mozart, Rodgers, Romberg, and others. "Quite as eloquent in anecdote as in song, the beautiful diva overlaid the whole with a sense of humor and a gracious, unselfconscious charm," the same critic wrote.

As a Christmas surprise, George told us that IBM had named him chairman of the board of IBM Austria, and that he and I would be moving to Vienna. We agreed that he would depart in March 1957, and Teta and I would follow as soon as I finished my next lecture tour. Peter and Jarmila would take over the penthouse apartment, which pleased them both, because they had been living with Peter's mother in Hackensack, New Jersey.

Even before George began his new job, I flew to Vienna to keep my promise to sing *Madame Pompadour* and to keep my promise to Marcel Prawy. He awaited me at the airport with a television crew and many reporters. Because I had last sung in Vienna in 1938—almost twenty years before—my return was considered big news. I took a room in the Hotel Sacher, and rehearsals began the next day, a Sunday. This was necessary because the premiere was scheduled for the next Saturday, which meant I had only six days to familiarize myself with a completely new play. Of course I had already learned the music, but bringing a piece to life onstage is always different. The director, Alexander Pichler, was very helpful, and so was the excellent cast, which included the baritone Karl Dönch, remembered by Metropolitan audiences for his highly praised Beckmesser in *Die Meistersinger.*

When I appeared onstage, the welcoming applause stopped the show. The Viennese audience is so faithful. The *Wiener Volksblatt* wrote that, when one character describes Pompadour as "a great lady," he's making fun of her. "But this time, he is correct, because it is Jarmila Novotná who plays her. And she is in every aspect, every movement just that great lady, whom no mockery or ridicule can touch. . . . We admit that this beautiful woman is no Pompadour, but she does not play the role, she plays *with* it, she makes fun of it, just to show how Pompadour could have been." For me, *Madame Pompadour* was a glass of champagne, with nothing but bubbles.

It was carnival time in Vienna, so I went to the Philharmonic Society ball, where I danced with the General Intendant of state theaters, Dr. Ernst Marboe. He wanted me to sing a few performances at the Staatsoper, but I had commitments back in the United States. I also saw Herbert von Karajan—but he did not dance.

Those commitments were, of course, more lectures, from February 13 to April 11, 1957, interrupted only by a few days so that I could see George before he left for Vienna. In Dallas, the demand for tickets was so great that the club that sponsored me scheduled the same program for three consecutive days. Then in October, I was scheduled for another round of fourteen lectures. If it weren't for the constant, tiresome traveling, I must confess that I enjoyed this type of entertainment. It brought me much closer to the audience, and it awakened greater interest in music and art. And sometimes, funny things happened. At one stop, just as I was about to go onstage, a workman appeared, waving a screwdriver and beckoning to the chairwoman of the club. They spoke hastily, and then the chairwoman said to the audience, "I am sorry, there will be a slight delay. I've just been given word that our speaker has a screw loose."

While I was on my lecture tour, Teta began all the preparations and packing for our move to Vienna. As our children grew older and had less need of her, she had learned to cook very well; now it was decided that she would come to Vienna with George and me to run our household. When I returned from my tour, I had only a few finishing touches to take care of, and then Georgie, Jarmilka, and Peter accompanied us to the *Flanders,* on which we were to sail. The voyage was extremely pleasant, and I recall that the painter Max Ernst was on board. The captain asked me to sing at a benefit one night, and I gladly accepted. Since I had no music with me, I asked the orchestra if they knew any Lehár songs. Naturally they did, and so even on the crossing I was kept busy.

From Le Havre we left for Vienna, where George had found for us a garden apartment belonging to an elderly, cultured lady, Frau Gerngross, who kept the upper floor of the house for herself. This was so much pleasanter than staying in a hotel. We hired a maid to help Teta around the house, and within two nights, George and I were at the Staatsoper for *Die Walküre,* with Birgit Nilsson, Hans Hotter, and Karajan conducting. A few nights later, we heard *Otello* with Mario del Monaco and Leonie Rysanek, again with Karajan. What a treat! In every way, Vienna was as pleasant as I remembered it.

Vienna has the advantage of being almost in the center of Europe, so it was easy to travel everywhere. George and I did just that, and when we were in town, we went almost every other day to one of the excellent theaters, the opera, and symphony concerts. We were pleased to welcome many friends and business associates, too, when they came to Austria, and I enjoyed giving sightseeing tours of Schönbrunn Castle; the Vienna Woods; the grand Abbey of Leopoldsberg; the town of Cobenzl, with its excellent restaurant; and the

Kahlenberg, site of the Battle of Vienna in 1683, from which one can clearly see the distant Alps.

We had hardly arrived when the next Hundred Percenters meeting began, and this year it was held in Vienna. George and I arranged for our guests to attend a performance of *La Bohème* at the Staatsoper, to hear the Vienna Boys Choir at the Hofburg Chapel, and to attend a private ball hosted by the Count and Countess Schönborn. We also went to see the Lipizzaner horses at the Spanish Riding School. During World War II, the Nazi authorities removed the horses from Vienna and from the stud farm to locations in Bohemia and Upper Austria. If not for the intervention of General George S. Patton, himself a keen horseman, the Lipizzaners would have been scattered, possibly ending up hitched to farmers' carts—or worse. It was a delight to watch the supple horses go through their paces to the music of Mozart, Haydn, Boccherini, and the military marches of the Austro-Hungarian Empire. The riders wore costumes from the Napoleonic Era, completing the lovely picture.

The Hundred Percenters meeting was the first occasion for what would become a ritual whenever we entertained out-of-town guests: taking them to a Heuriger. This is the Austrian name for a young wine, and it is served in taverns and inns that are also called Heuriger. If you see a bunch of pine branches hanging from the entrance, then you know that the owner is selling new wine from his own land. In summer, people sit under the chestnut trees to listen to Heuriger music, and soon everybody is "happy." It's all very informal, and if you cannot find a free table, you just sit down with strangers. That is what happened to our party the first time. We sat down with a young couple and went about with our conversation. At one point, Dick Watson called me by name, and the young man sitting at our table exclaimed, "Jarmila? There is only one Jarmila! Jarmila Novotná!" We all laughed, and I confessed that I was she. I had to promise to send him a photo.

Not long after the Hundred Percenters meeting concluded, very sad news reached me: on June 12, 1958, my dearest mother died. For me, this was the greatest possible loss. She took such wonderful care of my sister and me, especially when Father was at the front, and she awakened in me my interest in and love for music. I tried to obtain visas for me and George so that we could attend the funeral, but the consulate refused. We were just over two hundred miles from Prague—and yet so very far.

Among the first trips George and I took beyond Vienna were Paris, for an IBM conference, where the first person I met in the lobby of the Ritz was Elsa

Maxwell; and Bad Gastein, where we went for the cure, since both George and I suffered from rheumatism. We rented a room in a little old hotel that had been founded by the Archduke Johann, who lost his title when he married a postmaster's daughter. From that point onward, the head of the family took the title Count Meran. The hotel had been the archduke's hunting lodge, comfortably decorated with the original furniture, and one could take the baths there in the house. In Bad Gastein we ran into several friends from New York, including Chester and Eleanor Burden, and Florence Page Kimball. From then on we had pleasant company for our walking excursions in the mountains. George and I inaugurated what would become an annual treat: the Salzburg Festival. That first season, we attended a concert conducted by Rafael Kubelík, with Rudolf Firkušný as soloist, and it was a pleasure to hear these Czech musicians together. We also heard *Falstaff,* with Tito Gobbi, Elisabeth Schwarzkopf, and Giulietta Simionato, conducted by Karajan; and *Elektra,* with Inge Borkh in the title role. She had an outstanding voice and was also young and good-looking, making this an unforgettable performance. In later seasons, we also heard *Don Carlo,* with Karajan conducting Sena Jurinac, Giulietta Simionato, Cesare Siepi, and Ettore Bastianini, directed by Gustaf Gründgens; and most memorably of all, the opening of the Festspielhaus, in 1960, with Karajan conducting *Rosenkavalier.*

Our son arrived in Vienna soon after. He had interrupted his studies at Columbia for a year, so that he could stay with us and learn German. We enrolled him in the World Trade University, and he soon made astonishingly good progress and many friends. The son of our friends the Count and Countess Schönborn was one, and Prince Alfred Liechtenstein invited him to shoot roebuck. Georgie shot one, but when he saw the beautiful animal lying dead, he vowed never to go shooting again.

I had only a little time to enjoy my son's stay, since my next lecture tour began. Between October 2 and December 20, 1958, I gave twenty-five lectures, returning to New York just a day before my husband, who had come to spend the holidays with Jarmila, Peter, and me. Then, after the New Year, I went to work on a *Hallmark Hall of Fame* adaptation of *Hans Brinker,* a favorite story of children everywhere, in which I played Hans's mother. Tab Hunter, an immensely popular actor and singer, played the title role, and it emerged that he was an expert skater. Under the direction of Sidney Lumet, Peggy King played Hans's girlfriend, and Hugh Martin fashioned a delightfully sentimental musical score, with lovely songs for Tab, Peggy, and me. The former world and Olympic champion Dick Button also appeared, and Basil Rathbone played a surgeon. The television show was lovely and a huge success. But once it was over, I told Colston Leigh not to book any more lectures for the rest of the year, and I returned to Vienna.

Because we were now based full-time in Vienna, George felt we should buy a house, and he had found one in Hietzing, near Schönbrunn. I was enchanted. It was an old house with a large garden, fruit trees, and lots of privacy. It needed renovation, however, and the architect told us we wouldn't be able to move in before September. That gave George and me time to look for furniture, because we had left as much as possible in New York for Jarmila and Peter. Every week I went to the auctions at the Dorotheum, and George and I combed every antiques store. We had great fun.

We also began traveling not for business but simply for pleasure: no hurry, no social obligations, just enjoying each other's company and the things we liked best. Our first such trip was to Italy. Venice would become a favorite destination for us in the next few years, and we even went shopping there, finding a pair of Murano candlesticks and a chandelier for our home.

In May, we were off to Milan for another Hundred Percenters meeting, and then to an IBM conference in Brussels, timed to the World's Fair. I found the fair most interesting, and as I wandered from one pavilion to another, I sensed the values, contributions, pride and peculiarities of each nation. Most of the visitors I talked to agreed that the United States pavilion was the most beautiful by far, by day or night. The "Circorama," an eighteen-minute color film depicting a trip across the United States, made a great impression, but the biggest hit was the American drugstore. Every European had heard of that famous institution, and for those who had never visited one, it could be as much fun as an English pub or a Venetian gondola ride.

Russia, on the other hand, filled its pavilion with heavy machinery and heavier propaganda. Everything was done on a colossal scale, and a replica of Sputnik hung in the center. To entertain the public, the Russians brought the Bolshoi Ballet, a full symphony orchestra, and a troupe of Ukrainian singers and dancers. It was undeniably impressive. The shiny Russian cars drew crowds, too, and I was witness to an amusing scene. Two Americans were standing near, pointing to one of the Russian cars. "It looks like a Ford Mercury," said one, and his friend replied, "No, no, more like a Chevrolet." At last, one tried to purchase a car. The fellow in charge tried to ignore him, but at last, in exasperation, the Russian said stiffly, "We are not here to sell cars." You should have heard the laughter from the crowd.

On October 24, 1958—a month later than the renovators had predicted—George and I slept for the first time in the house in Hietzing. We soon realized that we could not have chosen a better house. Our bedroom windows faced the garden, and in the morning it was a delight to be awakened by the songbirds. In the garden was enough room for a croquet ground, and usually when George came home from work, we played a game or two. We found an excellent cook, maid, and butler, and we were able to entertain our friends. Many of them told us we had the best-kept house in Vienna.

Jarmila and Peter came to visit just after Christmas, and Fritz Mandl invited us to his New Year's Eve party. He always had many guests, and this year he hired a magician. The magician asked each of us to give him a mystery to solve. I thought of my gold powder box, which had been missing for some time. The magician closed his eyes, and after appearing to fall into a trance for a few moments he said, "Go to the sitting room, lift up the pillow on the right side of the sofa. You will find the box, which has fallen in the crack between the cushion and the back of the sofa." Sure enough, I found it there.

Only a few days after the start of 1959, Colston Leigh began bombarding me with letters asking when I would return to the United States. The demand for my lectures was enormous, and even cities I had visited already were requesting that I return. This time, I gave a firm answer: "No more."

For me, this marked the beginning of our normal life in Vienna. We had many friends there, and we also had constant visitors from abroad. Brooke Astor's visit was especially memorable. She was always a joy to be with, and we visited Melk on the Danube, the earliest residence of the Austrian rulers, which is now a splendid Benedictine abbey, founded in 1089. From there, we drove to Dürnstein, a ruined fortress where the Duke of Austria had held Richard the Lionheart hostage. A year or so later, my sister, Pavla, and her husband, Antonín Kittler, finally received permission to visit us. Unfortunately, it was a very short visit, because the Czechoslovakian government would allow citizens to remain outside the country for no longer than one week. Still, Antonín, whom we called Tonous, an amateur painter, had time to make some lovely sketches of our house and garden.

Our annual trip to Venice was especially memorable that year, because Count Giovanni Volpi di Misurata invited us to a ball at his magnificent palazzo on the Grand Canal. The men and women dressed in beautiful, festive attire, and everyone arrived in gondolas, like a scene from *The Tales of*

Hoffmann. As we passed from room to room, I recognized our friend Prince Alfons Clary, who had moved his family from Bohemia to Venice. He invited us to watch the regatta from his palazzo, and it was indeed a unique spectacle.

Near Venice lies Abano Terme, reputed for the excellence of its cure, and later that year George and I went. At the time Abano was an ugly village (though it has grown rapidly since) in the most beautiful surroundings. Petrarch lived in the charming hills, called the Colli Euganei, and he wrote in his poems of his love for their deep green valleys. In the nearby villages are Palladian villas with superb gardens, and our repeated excursions helped George and me to overlook the cure, which is quite boring, yet, I must admit, very effective.

George traveled often to Yugoslavia, Hungary, and Germany, as well as to the Austrian offices of IBM in Linz, Graz, Klagenfurt, and Salzburg. But he found free time, too, and took advantage of the good shooting in Austria. In October, George was invited to shoot wild geese on the Neusiedlersee, but he had no decoys, which were not available in Austria. By this time, Georgie had completed his studies in Vienna and returned to New York, so George asked him to send some decoys. They turned out to be the wrong kind, and the Austrian geese found these American strangers terrifying; they flew away as soon as they saw them. George's shooting was spoiled for the moment, until he could remove the decoys and wait for the geese to return.

For Hundred Percenters meetings and other IBM conferences, George and I traveled to such places as Rome, where we had an audience with Pope John XXIII, whose simplicity, compassion, and wit made him just the right man for the times; to Cannes, where we enjoyed the Film Festival, and Tom Watson Jr., asked me to sing "Meine Lippen" at an IBM reception; and to London, where we saw Margot Fonteyn and Rudolf Nureyev in *Swan Lake* and met them after the performance. A conference in Madrid gave us the opportunity to visit Toledo, Malaga, and Granada. Entering the walled precincts of the Alhambra palace, it seemed as if we were passing into another world. In our free time, we spent more and more time on the French Riviera, often as guests of Fritz Mandl. At the bullfights in Vallauris, I met Pablo Picasso, and the famous bullfighter El Cordobes was almost gored by the bull. In Menton, we attended a concert by Arthur Rubinstein, who enjoyed chatting with me at intermission so much that they had to call him twice to go onstage for the second half. One year, Carl Des-Fours invited us to visit his property in Cagliari, Sardinia, but as the years passed, George and I devoted much of our travel time to family.

In Vienna, our social lives were very active. During our twenty-three years there, we got to know all the ambassadors, and an especially good friend was the wife of the Swiss ambassador, Mary Escher, a former actress who was the soul of every party. I call myself especially fortunate that the American ambassador, John P. Humes, and his wife, Jean, who came to Vienna in 1969, remained our friends. At some point, I mentioned how much I enjoyed pancakes with maple syrup when I was in the United States, and how difficult it was to find maple syrup in Austria. When John retired, in 1975, he and Jean invited us to lunch to say good-bye. To my surprise, John himself cooked for us the most delicious pancakes with maple syrup that he had sent from America. This shows what a nice person he was. We had many good friends in Vienna, and whenever our son came to visit, he was so busy reuniting with his own friends that we seldom saw him!

In 1960, Teta had to return to the United States. Naturalized American citizens like her were permitted to live abroad, but only for three years at a time, or else they forfeited citizenship. Because George worked for an American company, he and I could remain in Austria indefinitely, but Teta's return to New York proved very well timed. Jarmilka was expecting a child, and now Teta would be able to help her care for it. Our family was on the brink of many changes.

On January 9, 1961, our first grandchild was born. She was christened Jarmila Theresa Maria Juliana Georgette Packard, and I was not only a proud and happy grandmother, but also her godmother. Soon we began to call her "Jaji," because with three Jarmilas in the family, all of us would answer whenever anyone called out the name. We began a pattern of Christmas visits: one year, George and I would fly to New York; and the next, Jarmila and Peter would fly to Vienna.

A few months after Jaji's birth, our son George graduated from Columbia with excellent grades. He continued his studies at the European Institute of Business Administration (INSEAD) in Fontainebleau, during 1961–1962, and then went to work for IBM.

In 1965, Jarmila wrote to me to say that she had been appointed to a committee to arrange the upcoming Metropolitan Opera Guild luncheon, that year marking the twenty-fifth anniversary of Texaco's sponsorship of the Saturday afternoon radio broadcasts. Because I had appeared in the first of those broadcasts, *The Marriage of Figaro,* Jarmila invited me to join other cast members on the dais, twenty-five years later to the day, December 7. Jarmila also asked me to find a silver rose to present to the luncheon's special honoree, Geraldine Souvaine, who with her late husband, Henry, produced the intermission features for the Met radio broadcasts.

Before George and I returned to Vienna, Jarmila told us that she and Peter were expecting another child. Their son, George William Warren, was born in June, but George and I did not see him until he was four months old. What a contented baby he was! Our visit was marred by recurring pains that George had in his stomach. His doctor diagnosed gastritis combined with a duodenal ulcer. He prescribed a special diet, a quiet lifestyle, and long walks, which we enjoyed with two new family members, our two pugs Šašek (which means "clown" in Czech) and Panena (which means "doll").

Even George's new regimen did not help, and he had to undergo surgery. During the operation, the doctor found that George's aorta was enlarged and required urgent attention. Because this kind of operation was unusual in Vienna, George's doctors advised us to fly to New York. It wasn't an easy operation, but George's recuperative powers were miraculous, and he was released from the hospital in only two weeks.

While we were in New York, Lauder Greenway, chairman of the Metropolitan Opera Association, inquired about a portrait of me to hang in Founder's Hall in the new opera house at Lincoln Center. I decided to give them my Manon portrait, which at the moment hung in Jarmila and Peter's apartment. On January 30, 1967, the Met hosted a special hanging ceremony, attended by Mrs. August Belmont, Anthony Bliss, Kurt Waldheim, Archibald and Gracie Roosevelt, and many other friends. (A few years later, we exchanged the Manon portrait for my portrait as Violetta, which still hangs there.[1])

George and I had only two weeks left before returning to Vienna, but on the way to the airport, George's heartbeat became irregular. He felt dizzy and hot, and I thought it might be wiser to cancel our flight and remain in New York. But George decided that we should press on, and we were happy when we finally reached home. The heart irregularities continued, and in fact it was almost two years before George's extra systolic heartbeat disappeared and a normal heartbeat resumed. Nevertheless, he was able to lead a completely normal life, and at the next IBM conference, in Nice, he found our long walks along the Promenade des Anglais very beneficial.

I was nearing my sixtieth birthday, and around this time our son George wrote to say that he had met "a terrific girl named Carol Jackson." As their relationship developed, they announced plans to marry in St. Louis in May

1968. George and I left for New York on April 23, to be able to participate in all the wedding festivities and to spend more time with our grandchildren.

The wedding was beautifully arranged, and we met Carol's relatives at a dinner the night before the ceremony. During the following years we saw Georgie and Carol often, and they were blessed with two beautiful daughters, first Francesca and, later, Antonia. We were very sorry that the marriage did not work out, and in the end George and Carol divorced, with Carol taking custody of the children, as is customary in the United States.

That summer, Jarmila came to visit with her children and Teta. We had a marvelous time, and I took them to Salzburg, where we heard Karajan in a concert, and to Heilbrunn, where the Marionette Theater gave an exquisite performance of Mozart's *Magic Flute.* Then we returned to Vienna, and Teta went to visit her brother in Prague.

She had been there only one day when the Soviet Army invaded Czechoslovakia on August 20, 1968. We were frantic for word from her, but all telephone service had been suspended. When we were finally able to talk to her, she told us she was afraid to leave her brother's house, that Soviet tanks and armored trucks were all over town. Soldiers pointed their rifles at any and all, and sometimes they fired. We advised her to contact the American Embassy, where the U.S. government was transporting its citizens out of the country by bus. Unfortunately, every bus was filled beyond capacity, and most were traveling to France or Germany, not to Austria; there were no trains. Finally, Teta got word of a bus sponsored by the Danish Embassy bound for Vienna. Completely exhausted, Teta arrived safely on August 24, to our relief.

In 1970, the whole family reunited to celebrate George's eightieth birthday. Jarmila and Peter brought their children and Teta, and Georgie and Carol brought little Cesca, who was growing up to be a real beauty. Our sister-in-law, Olga Daubek, came with her three children, and Jozi and Brigid Bromovský and Jozi's brother Jirka came as well. We threw a surprise party, which George enjoyed immensely.

Two years later, I returned to Czechoslovakia for the first time since 1949. George had returned once before, in 1966, when Dick Watson asked him to accompany him on a tour of IBM offices. Now George and I both obtained visas, and I was fascinated by the beauty of Prague, though I was dismayed to see how many buildings were damaged or torn down, without any sign of rebuilding.

We drove immediately to Liteň, which was now a boarding school for apprentices in house painting and masonry. At least this meant that our house had been freshly painted. All our furniture and paintings were gone, with one exception: a sketch of the design for the curtain at the National Theater by the well-known painter František Ženíšek. The curtain itself had burned, along with the rest of the theater, in 1881, and this sketch was all that remained of it. Ženíšek had painted the sketch in the dining room, and it was very large, 5½ yards by 4½ yards, which probably explains why the authorities hadn't removed it: they would have had to open up an entire wall to get it out. Now the boarding school used the dining room as a sort of dormitory, with the beds pushed up against the painting, so that the glass had broken.

We also visited the Daubek family mausoleum, built in 1888 by the architect Antonín Wiehl and decorated by several other artists. The mausoleum contains a marble altar with a statue of St. Joseph by Josef Václav Myslbek, and over the altar hangs a triptych painted by Max Pirner; passages from the Scriptures are carved into the marble walls. We found the beautiful mausoleum in a sorry state, and one of the paintings from the triptych was lying on the damp floor.

Ostensibly, the mausoleum was under the protection of the National Monuments authority, but we contacted Dr. Jiří Kotalík, the director of the National Gallery, and asked him to take charge of the triptych, which he did. My sister Pavla's son, Jirka, promised to visit Liteň as often as possible to keep the mausoleum clean, at least, and we began a long campaign to obtain permission to make repairs, simply to save the place from falling into ruin. We engaged a lawyer in Prague, but even his efforts were of no avail. It is hard to describe our feelings for our country and for our home, which we lost and loved so much.

Several years later, Jarmila brought the children and Teta to Vienna, and together we went to Liteň. Already Jaji was an enthusiastic photographer, and on our way from Prague to Liteň, we passed the historic Castle Karlstein. Jaji took a picture of the castle, which I treasure. This was the children's first visit to Liteň, and I showed them our own castle—meaning the château—as well as the baroque house in which their mother lived as a little girl. By now the house had been converted into a museum in honor of the Czech poet Svatopluk Čech, who had lived there with his father, for a while the supervisor of the estate, in the 1850s. I showed them the family mausoleum, and we also visited my sister and her family in Radotín.

On the way back to Vienna, we stopped at Hluboká Castle, where the Prague National Gallery sometimes exhibits representative pieces from its rich collection. By coincidence we found an exhibition dedicated to Josef Manés and there among the paintings hung my *Josefina*. We passed several other estates, including Krumlov, with its baroque theater and wonderful collection of Gobelin tapestries; and Romberg Castle, also from the thirteenth century. All of these sites are now popular tourist attractions, but once they all belonged to family friends of the Daubeks.

My thoughts naturally turned to George's father, who died in 1922, before I joined the family. I knew Josef Sebastian Daubek had been an extraordinary man, whose achievements in politics and business earned him a hereditary title, and he was a great lover of art. Ženíšek was only one of the painters whom he encouraged, and Ženíšek returned the favor by using his likeness in a painting that depicts the meeting of Prince Oldřich and his love, the beautiful maiden Božena, which now hangs in the National Gallery in Prague. Josef's father counted Antonin Dvořák among his friends, and the composer once visited the Daubeks at Brněnec. On that visit, Dvořák enjoyed fishing in the river that passed through the estate; he always kept worms in his pockets—mixed in with the candies that he kept to give to little children. George was only seven at the time, but he remembered Dvořák vividly as a result.

Back in Vienna, George continued to go to the office every day, even if only for a few hours, though he was now past eighty. He wanted to be informed about everything that went on, and his associates sought out his advice in every difficult situation. At one point in 1972, he underwent cataract surgery, after which his doctor suggested that he begin wearing a contact lens in the affected eye. Now it was my duty to put in the lens every morning and, what is worse, to take it out again in the evening. This wasn't easy, and I was afraid of scratching his eye. My responsibilities went further, too. One day at lunch with friends in a restaurant, George told us that the lens had fallen out. We couldn't find it, and so George went to the eye doctor to get a new prescription. I wanted to go back to the restaurant to look again, but the doctor said that, after several hours, I wouldn't have much luck. Nevertheless, I went back, and there under the table, just opposite George's seat, was the lens. Unbelievable but true.

One Christmas, when George and I flew to New York to spend the holiday with all four of our grandchildren, I realized, more than ever before, that the key to happiness is a happy family life. So George and I were very happy when, at the end of 1975, our son told us he had met a young woman whom he wanted to marry. Like George, Cathy was divorced; she had a little boy. We were in New York at the time, so we arranged to meet in Bedford, in Westchester County. We liked Cathy instantly. Highly intelligent, she had studied to be a landscape architect, and in the countryside she had every opportunity to indulge her gifts. Nothing could have made us happier than to give our son and his intended our blessing, and they married on April 17 on Shelter Island. They now have a lovely daughter named Tatiana.[2]

I was reaching that time of life when I began to receive invitations to help to commemorate people I had worked with and events in which I had participated. The Metropolitan Opera Guild luncheon for the cast of *Figaro* and the unveiling of my portrait were just the beginning. Granted, I was not present for Beethoven's birth, but when that event reached its two hundredth anniversary, in 1970, a Czech journalist asked me to write an essay about the composer for the Prague newspaper *Lidové Noviny.* I wrote about Beethoven's passion for freedom and revolt against oppression, but they published it anyway.

For my own sixtieth birthday, in 1967, a Prague radio station requested an interview with me, in quite an unusual process: the writer and journalist Dr. Jan Wenig made an audiotape, asking his questions and leaving plenty of space for me to answer. With the help of a radio station in Vienna, I was able to record my replies in between his questions, and we also included several songs and arias.

In April 1973, a trip to New York coincided with a celebration of the fiftieth anniversary of Bruno Walter's American debut. Leonard Bernstein conducted a commemorative concert with the Philharmonic, and Nathan Milstein was soloist in a Brahms violin concerto. Many artists were asked to remember Walter, who had died in 1962, and I paid tribute to "the inestimable service that artists such as Bruno Walter render through their profound devotion to the masters, whose greatness they make part of our experience. . . . Only a great conductor of surpassing insight and consummate art can reveal the truth. To Bruno Walter we owe an eternal debt of gratitude for the wonderful interpretations of great music from Mozart to Sibelius." Many years had passed since I had sung with Walter, not only in New York but also Salzburg, Florence, Vienna, and Berlin, and I remained proud and happy to have had the privilege of working with him.

The same year, I was invited to attend the celebration of Max Reinhardt's centennial at Schloss Arenberg in Salzburg. His widow, Helene Thimig, and many artists associated with him also attended, and his son, Gottfried, interviewed many of us for a television program. A special exhibition featured stage designs and photos of his productions; local officials and the directors of the Salzburg Festival hosted a luncheon; and the celebration ended with a reception at Schloss Leopoldskron, Reinhardt's former residence. The anniversary brought back many wonderful memories. I owe Reinhardt so much.

One other centennial is especially noteworthy: Richard Tauber's, which was commemorated with a gala concert at Carnegie Hall. Francis Heilbut produced this event, through his American Landmark Festivals, a nonprofit group; I first met Francis in Vienna in 1969, when he gave a piano recital. At the Tauber gala, in 1991, I had the pleasure of appearing with the tenor Alfredo Kraus. But by then I was no longer living in Vienna, and a great deal had changed for my family and for me.

As George approached his ninetieth birthday, his health was reasonably good, but he was growing weaker, and so we stopped traveling. In Vienna I seldom went out, since George was happy only when I was near him. However, we still had many friends who visited us, and the children came to us every year. We celebrated his birthday on August 7 with a small family gathering, and our nephew Jirka Kittler and his wife, Jana, managed to get permission from the Czechoslovakian government so that they could join us.

Then, on February 1, 1981, the great sorrow came. It was a beautiful day, and George and I sat in the garden before lunch. There was no sign that he was unwell. After lunch, he went to take a nap. Around five o'clock, the hour when we used to take tea, he told me he didn't want any. Then, about ninety minutes later, he asked for tea, and he went to sit in an armchair to drink it. Suddenly, his head fell back and his breathing became heavy. Our family doctor lived around the corner, so I called him to help me get George back to bed. A priest came, and George died peacefully.

We had been married almost fifty years. He was everything to me, probably because I was seventeen years younger: he was husband, friend, teacher, lover. He made me very happy.

To manage a private life and a profession with equal success is a twenty-four-hour job, and marriage requires constant give-and-take. Both sides must contribute equally to what we call happiness. I was lucky to have had such a wonderful, understanding husband, and I owed him the happiness I had found at home and in my work.

I telephoned the children, and they flew as soon as possible for the funeral; then Jarmila stayed behind while Peter, George, and Cathy returned to New York. George wished to be cremated and to have his ashes taken to the mausoleum in Liteň. It took a little time to arrange this, but Jirka Kittler was very helpful. The authorities insisted that nobody in the village, apart from the priest, be told about the service, but on March 9, when Jarmila and I drove to Liteň, we found the little grove around the mausoleum filled with people old and young. When I spoke with them, many of them wept and said, "If our dear master were only here, everything would be different." It was a touching moment.

Then the priest performed the mass, with four local women singing. They sounded so beautiful. I was very happy that I could fulfill this part of George's last wish, and I am sure the rest of that wish will be fulfilled, too: that when my time comes, I be near him.

George and I had often discussed what would be best for me, should he die. We both were of the opinion that I should move back to the United States, to be near my children. With this in mind, I left for New York, and by a miracle I found an apartment in the building where my daughter lives. I sold the house in Vienna, and in October 1981, I became a New Yorker once again.

I must confess that I was a little afraid that I would be uncomfortable in New York. I had not lived there in twenty-three years, and lately I had fallen out of the habit of socializing. During the last years in Vienna, I spent all my time with my husband, and I got used to the tranquility. "The best place for me would be a convent," I said to my daughter. She laughed and answered, "I'd like to see how long it made you happy!" She was right. Living in New York was a wise decision. I reconnected with many friends, and soon it was as if I had left only the day before. I am happy here.

Numerous activities opened up for me. I became a member of the advisory committee of the Metropolitan Opera Archive, and I was eager to assist the archivist, Robert Tuggle, in any way possible. Bob was looking for costumes to display in a special exhibit at the Lincoln Center Library, in advance of the Metropolitan Opera's centennial. My first assignment was to contact Ezio Pinza's widow, Doris, to ask her to lend her husband's costume from *Boris Godunov,* and she agreed In the exhibit, that costume joined thirty-five others belonging to many of the greatest artists in the Met's history, including Marcella Sembrich, Adelina Patti, Jean de Reszke, Enrico Caruso, Geraldine Farrar, Kirsten Flagstad, and Lauritz Melchior. I gave the Met several of my costumes: the lovely black gown from *Traviata,* the white-satin costume from *Rosenkavalier,* another for Cherubino, and another for *The Bartered Bride.* At this time we replaced my Manon portrait in Founder's Hall with John Winslow's portrait of me as Violetta, wearing that same black gown.

On Christmas Day 1981, producer Richard Mohr invited me to participate in a "singers roundtable" with Dorothy Kirsten and Risë Stevens during a performance of *Hansel and Gretel,* which was not only broadcast but also televised. I enjoyed this very much, as some of the questions were hilarious. At one point, the moderator asked whether there was ever an accident during a performance that caused the audience to burst out laughing. I remembered one *Traviata* in a provincial theater, where for some reason there was no sofa for the last act. The stagehands improvised by taking an empty crate and throwing a rug over it. In the last scene, Germont sat down—and promptly disappeared inside the crate with his feet high in the air. The stagehands had placed the crate with the open side up before throwing the rug over it, and the poor baritone never suspected. He couldn't get out, and the more he struggled, the more the audience roared with laughter.

Not long after, my friend George Volckening, a great music lover, brought an interesting project to me. He represented the record company Qualiton Imports, and an English producer, Charles Haynes of Pavilion Records, wanted him to put together some of my old recordings for a two-disc album. The result was released in September 1983, on the Pearl label. The first disc contains the "Songs of Lidice" with Jan Masaryk, as well as songs and arias by Smetana, Dvořák, and Fibich; the second contains excerpts from radio broadcasts from Salzburg of *Magic Flute* with Toscanini, and *Marriage of Figaro* with Bruno Walter; and, from the Met, *Hoffmann* with Beecham and *Traviata* with Panizza. I was not entirely happy with the selections, as some of my favorites had been omitted: the lullaby from Smetana's *The Kiss,* and Dvořák's "Songs My Mother Taught Me," for example. But the album was well received by both the public and the press.

In September 1983, I visited my sister in Czechoslovakia. A widow, she was still in Radotín, near her son, Jirka, his wife, and their daughters. I had hoped for a quiet time with my family, but as things turned out, I was busier than ever. The record company Supraphon sponsors a theater in Prague that presents stage performances, as well as "Medaillons," lectures about singers and musicians. Some years earlier, Emanuel Kopecký, who once sang Germont to my Violetta in Bratislava, had written to request permission, biographical material, and recordings for just such a "Medaillon" about me, and that was just the first of several.

As soon as Dr. Kopecký heard that I was coming to Prague, he posted announcements in the newspapers and immediately sold out two "Medaillons," with me as the featured subject. He invited me to attend one of these lectures. I sat in the front row, and at the end, I got up to thank Dr. Kopecký. Suddenly I remembered part of a poem by Jaroslav Seifert, the Nobel Prize–winning Czech poet, and I turned to face the audience as I recited: "I cannot look enough at this beautiful country of mine, and everything in me starts singing, singing and weeping. My dearest mother, you know how lovely it is to be home." By the time I finished, everyone, including me, was in tears. I wasn't prepared for the ovation I received. I was truly moved, and grateful that people had not forgotten me.

The next day the newspapers carried long articles about me, my career, and the "Medaillon," with the result that television and radio stations requested interviews. I really didn't have a free moment.

But the main purpose of my trip was to go to Liteň to have a mass read for my husband. The church was overflowing, with many people having to stand outside. They said beautiful things about George, and some wept.

I would have stayed longer, but I had promised to take part in the celebration of the Metropolitan Opera's hundredth anniversary in the fall of 1983. By coincidence, the National Theater in Prague was also celebrating its centennial, and I would have loved to have been present at that occasion, too. But one cannot be on both sides of the ocean at once.

The Met Centennial began with a Golden Horseshoe Dinner at the department store B. Altman & Co., with costumes from Met artists displayed on the first floor, my *Traviata* gown among them. The dinner was on an upper floor, with enough space cleared for dancing. I had the pleasure of opening the dance with Frank Taplin, president of the Met. What a dancer! Although I hadn't danced in a long time, with him it was easy. Another day, Mayor Ed Koch hosted a reception at Gracie Mansion and declared October 16–22 Metropolitan Opera Week in New York City; not to be outdone, Governor Mario Cuomo declared all of October Metropolitan Opera Month in New York State, and the state assembly and senate passed legislation recognizing the Met's contributions. President Ronald Reagan proclaimed October 22 Metropolitan Opera Day across the United States and praised the company in his weekly radio broadcast.

The crowning event was a spectacular gala on October 22, an event unsurpassed. More than eighty of the most famous singers and conductors, along with the orchestra, chorus, and ballet, performed arias, duets, and ensembles for eight hours, a true marathon. Before the music began, the company's general manager, Anthony Bliss, the son of our dear friends, stepped before the curtain to usher in the next hundred years. Then James Levine led the orchestra in a dazzling rendition of the overture to *The Bartered Bride.* Retired singers were invited as guests of honor, and for the final third of the performance we were asked to sit onstage, where the audience greeted us warmly.

It was wonderful to meet again with colleagues from so many years before. What memories that evening awakened! There was Erna Berger, so often my Sophie; and there were two of my Donna Annas, Zinka Milanov and Rose Bampton, along with Bidu Sayão, who often sang Zerlina. Eleanor Steber had been a lovely Countess and Licia Albanese a lively Susanna to my Cherubino in *The Marriage of Figaro,* and there, too, were a Marschallin, Irene Jessner; and the delightful Adele from *Fledermaus,* Patrice Munsel. Unfortunately, many of the men with whom I had sung were not present: Ezio Pinza, Jussi Bjoerling, Charles Kullman, Tito Schipa, John Brownlee, Lawrence Tibbett, Leonard Warren, Salvatore Baccaloni, Martial Singher, Raul Jobin. I had hoped to see Jan Peerce, but he could not come. Still, I enjoyed seeing Ferrucio Tagliavini, Lorenzo Alvary, Kurt Baum, Italo Tajo, George Cehanovsky, Jerome Hines, and others. The performance was broadcast on radio and television, so that it was possible for people in many countries to share this exciting, unforgettable evening.

Seven years later, the Metropolitan Opera marked the fiftieth anniversary of my debut with an exhibition of many photos beautifully displayed by Bob Tuggle in Founder's Hall, and John W. Freeman wrote a lovely article about me in *Opera News.* To crown it all, President George H. W. Bush wrote me a letter of congratulation.

Especially for one who was born in another country, recognition from the American president is wonderful, transcending politics. Living in New York again, I was reminded that untold millions have come from all over the world to live in this country. Each brought some new talent, some new contribution. Many of them remained in New York, and nowhere on earth can you find so many people from so many different places. Over the years, these people blend. Almost all share English in their daily exchanges, but at home many speak their native languages. These combined talents have made New York the incredible cosmopolis that it is, and so you can imagine my surprise and joy when, in 1986, Mayor Koch selected me among eighty-six foreign-born citizens to honor for our contributions with the city's Medal of Freedom, on the occasion of the centennial of the Statue of Liberty.

We are lucky in America to be free to go about our lives without interference, and the experience of my homeland illustrates just how lucky we are. That is why, for me, the greatest event of 1989 was the liberation of Czechoslovakia from Communism. Communism can never truly break the people's collective spirit and yearning for freedom; if you live in a free country, you must not accept any form of oppression anywhere. I always believed that one day my homeland would be free again, but I did not think I would live to see it.

Now it was my dream to set foot in a free Czechoslovakia, and in May 1990, and again in October 1991, I did.

The second visit coincided with the publication of my memoir and the reissue on Supraphon of an album of my old recordings. On October 28, 1991, the anniversary of the date on which Tomáš Garrigue Masaryk proclaimed the Republic of Czechoslovakia, President Václav Havel presented me with the Order of T. G. Masaryk, and the mayor of Prague named me an honorary citizen. The Jarmila Novotná Society was established, and for several years our house in Liteň was the Jarmila Novotná Museum.[3]

Each of these honors means a great deal to me. But in many ways, that first visit was the most memorable. President Havel welcomed me at Hradčany Castle, and I attended a concert at the annual Spring Festival, with Rafael Kubelík conducting the Prague Philharmonic and Rudolf Firkušný playing. For both Kubelík and Firkušný, this was the first time they had performed in Czechoslovakia after an absence of forty years, and the audience went wild. The evening concluded with Beethoven's Ninth Symphony, conducted by Leonard Bernstein.

Afterward, I went to Bernstein's dressing room, where a few of his other friends had already gathered. When he saw me, Bernstein cried, "Jarmila, what are you doing here?"

I laughed and answered, "I am home."

Appendix

Performances and Recordings

Film and Television Roles

Countess Jacinta, *Vyznavači Slunce* (The Sun Worshipers). Václav Binovec, director. Prague, 1926.

The Prima Donna, *Brand in der Oper* (Fire in the Opera House). Carl Fröhlich, director. Berlin, 1930.

Laura, *Der Bettelstudent* (The Beggar Student). Victor Janson, director. Berlin, 1931.

Marie, *Die verkaufte Braut* (The Bartered Bride, after Smetana's opera). Max Ophüls, director. Munich, 1932.

Frau Thormaelen, *Die Nacht der großen Liebe* (The Night of Great Love). Géza von Bolváry, director. Berlin, 1933.

Maja Zemanova, *Skřivánci Píseň* (Song of the Lark). Svatopluk Innemann, director. Prague, 1933.

Frasquita, *Frasquita* (after Lehár's operetta). Karel Lamač, director; Franz Lehár, conductor. Vienna, 1935.

Vera Starchenska, *Der Kosak und die Nachtigall* (The Cossack and the Nightingale). Phil Jutzi, director. Vienna, 1935.

Countess Vera Lizavetta Opalinsky, *The Last Waltz* (after Oscar Straus's operetta). Gerald Barry, Leo Mittler, directors, 1936. The French version of this film, *La dernière Valse,* was produced simultaneously, with Novotná again appearing as the Countess.

Mrs. Malik, *The Search.* Fred Zinnemann, director. 1948.

Maria Selka, *The Great Caruso.* Richard Thorpe, director. 1951. Also starring Mario Lanza, Ann Blyth, and Dorothy Kirsten.

Prince Orlofsky, *Die Fledermaus* for the *Omnibus* television series. William Spier, producer. New York, 1953. Also starring Brenda Lewis, Charles Kullman, and John Brownlee. Eugene Ormandy, conductor.

Nina Carson, "Rendezvous," an episode of the *Studio One in Hollywood* television series. Paul Nickell, director. New York, 1953.

Unknown character name, "Evening Star," an episode of the *Armstrong Circle Theatre* television series. Ed Roberts, director. 1954.

Mother, "The Bridge," an episode of *The Elgin Hour* television series. Daniel Petrie, director. 1955. Also starring Kim Stanley and John Ireland.

Unknown character name, "Thunder on Troy Street," an episode of the *Justice* television series starring Gary Merrill. 1955.

Mme. Baranska, *The Great Waltz,* television film. Bill Hobin, Max Liebman, directors. 1955. Also starring Patrice Munsel, Keith Andes, and Bert Lahr.

Dame Brinker, *Hans Brinker or the Silver Skates,* television film. Sidney Lumet, George Schaefer, directors, 1958. Also starring Tab Hunter, Peggy King, Basil Rathbone, Florence Anglin, and Dick Button.

Guest appearances on such television programs as *The Ed Sullivan Show, The Colgate Comedy Hour* (starring Bud Abbott and Lou Costello), *The Arthur Murray Party*, and *Live from the Met.*

Stage and Operatic Roles

Stage Roles

Hela, *Malérečka* (Dubňanská), Prague, 1922.

Apprentice, National Theater, Prague, 1922–1925. Roles include: a Page, *Saint Joan* (Shaw); the Actress, *Six Characters in Search of an Author* (Pirandello); Ziva, *Radúz a Mahulena* (Zeyer); et al.

Lydia, *Frühlingsstürme* (Weinberger). Theater im Admiralspalast, Berlin, 1933.

Schönheit (Beauty), *Das große Welttheater* (Hofmannsthal, after Calderón's *El gran teatro del mundo*). Max Reinhardt, director. Theater am Kurfürstendamm, Berlin, 1933.

Rosalinde, *La Chauve-souris* (Die Fledermaus) (J. Strauss II). Max Reinhardt, director. Théâtre Pigalle, Paris, 1933.

Helen, *Helen Goes to Troy* (Offenbach/Korngold, after *La Belle Hélène*). Herbert Graf, director; Léonide Massine, choreographer. Alvin Theater, New York, 1944.

Irene Adler, *Sherlock Holmes* (O. Rathbone). Reginald Denham, director. New Century Theatre, New York, 1953.

Operatic Roles (with year of role debut by city)

Girl, *Lucifer* (Mach). Prague, 1921.

Mařenka/Marie, *Prodana Nevésta/Die verkaufte Braut/The Bartered Bride* (Smetana). Prague Pištěk Theater, 1922. Prague National Theater (house debut), 1925. Warsaw, Berlin Vienna, 1925. Bělehrad, Lublaň, 1939. New York Met, Baltimore, Cleveland, Chicago, Boston, Seattle, St. Louis, San Antonio, Dallas, Cincinnati, 1941. Michigan City, 1945.

Girl, *Betlém* (Wenig). Prague Vinohrad Theater, 1922.

Rosina, *Il Barbiere di Siviglia* (Rossini). Louny, Prague Estates Theater (house debut), Berlin, 1925.

Violetta, *La Traviata* (Verdi). Louny, Prague National and Estates Theaters, Berlin, Brno, 1925. Bělehrad, Bucharest, San Francisco, 1939. San Francisco, New York Met, 1940. Dallas, Seattle, Chicago, Hollywood Bowl. Boston, 1942. Buenos Aires Colón, Rio de Janeiro, Santiago, 1943.

Ariel, *Bouře* (The Tempest) (Fibich). Prague National Theater, 1925.

Tatyana, *Eugene Onegin* (Tchaikovsky). Prague National and Estates Theaters, Vienna, 1925.

Queen of the Night, *Die Zauberflöte* (Mozart), Prague National Theater, Berlin, 1925.

Jitka, *Dalibor* (Smetana). Prague National Theater, 1926.

Lenka, *Mistr Jíra* (Vogel). World premiere, Prague National Theater, 1926.

Mlada, *Šárka* (Fibich). Prague National Theater, 1926.

Madelon, *Preciézky* (Les Précieuses Ridicules, after Molière) (Zich). World premiere, Prague National Theater, 1926.

Ännchen, *Der Freischütz* (Weber). Prague, 1926.

Frasquita, *Carmen* (Bizet). Prague National Theater, 1926.

Mimì, *La Bohème* (Puccini). Prague National and Estates Theaters, Berlin, Vienna, Basel, Plzeň, Olomouc, 1926. New York Met (house debut), 1940. Albany, Puerto Rico, 1941. Buenos Aires Colón, 1943. Boston, Montreal, 1944.

Camille, *Louise* (Charpentier). Prague National Theater, 1926.

Priestess, *Aida* (Verdi). Prague National Theater, 1926.

Princess, *Dědův Odkaz* (Novák). Prague National Theater, 1927.

Nannetta, *Falstaff* (Verdi). Prague National Theater, 1927.

Gilda, *Rigoletto* (Verdi). Prague National Theater, Verona, Vienna Staatsoper (house debut), Berlin, 1927. Santiago, 1943.

Adina, *L'Elisir d'Amore* (Donizetti). Naples Teatro San Carlo, 1929.

Concepción, *L'Heure espagnole* (Ravel). Berlin Kroll (house debut), 1929.

Tamar, *Das Leben des Orest* (The Life of Orestes) (Krenek). Berlin Kroll, 1930.

Madelon, *Le Preciose Ridicole* (Les Précieuses Ridicules, after Molière) (Lattuada). Berlin, 1930.

Woman, *Das glückliche Hand* (Schönberg). World premiere, Berlin Kroll, 1930.

Cherubino, *Le Nozze di Figaro* (Mozart). Berlin, Florence, Vienna, 1931. Salzburg, Cannes, 1937. Monte Carlo, Schveningen, 1939. New York Met, Philadelphia, 1940. Dallas, Richmond, 1941. Buenos Aires Colón, Chicago, 1943. Boston, 1944. Cleveland, Milwaukee, 1945. San Francisco, Los Angeles, 1946.

Cio-Cio-San, *Madama Butterfly* (Puccini). Berlin, Vienna, Prague National Theater, 1931. Bucharest, San Francisco (U.S. debut), 1939. Newark, 1942.

Manon, *Manon Lescaut* (Puccini). Berlin, 1931.

Helena, *Die schöne Helena* (*La Belle Hélène*) (Offenbach). Berlin, 1931.

Antonia, *Les Contes d'Hoffmann* (Offenbach). Berlin, Vienna, Florence, 1931. Rio de Janeiro, New York Met, Philadelphia, 1943. Los Angeles, 1949.

Marguerite de Valois, *Les Huguenots* (Meyerbeer). Berlin, 1932.

Karolina, *Dvě Vdovy* (Two Widows) (Smetana). Prague National Theater, 1933.

Giuditta, *Giuditta* (Lehár). Vienna, Paris, 1934.

Fiordiligi, *Così Fan Tutte* (Mozart). Vienna, Salzburg, 1935.

Octavian, *Der Rosenkavalier* (R. Strauss). Vienna, 1935. Salzburg, Amsterdam, Berlin, 1937. New York Met, Boston, Cleveland, 1942. Philadelphia, 1945. San Francisco, Los Angeles, 1946. Atlanta, Memphis, New Orleans, 1948. Salzburg, 1949.

Countess, *Le Nozze di Figaro* (Mozart). Salzburg, Vienna, 1935.

Euridice, *Orfeo ed Euridice* (Gluck). Vienna, 1935. Salzburg, 1936, 1937, 1949. New York Met, 1940. Boston, 1942.

Olympia, *Les Contes d'Hoffmann* (Offenbach). Vienna, 1936.

Giulietta, *Les Contes d'Hoffmann* (Offenbach). Vienna, Rio de Janeiro, 1936. San Francisco, 1946. New York Met, 1955.

Frasquita, *Corregidor* (Wolf). Vienna, Salzburg, 1936.

Alice Ford, *Falstaff* (Verdi). Milan La Scala, 1937. Buenos Aires Colón, 1943.

Pamina, *Die Zauberflöte* (Mozart). Vienna, Salzburg, 1937. New York Met, 1941. Baltimore, 1942. Chicago, 1943. Cleveland, Minneapolis, 1946.

Rusalka, *Rusalka* (Dvořák). Prague National Theater, Plzeň, 1939.

Sonia, *The Merry Widow* (Lehár). Los Angeles Civic Light Opera, San Francisco Light Opera Co., 1940.

Manon, *Manon* (Massenet). New York Met, New Orleans, Puerto Rico, Cincinnati, 1941. Santiago, 1943.

Donna Elvira, *Don Giovanni* (Mozart). New York Met, Philadelphia, Boston, Hartford, 1941. Cleveland, Dallas, 1942. Chicago, 1943. San Francisco, Los Angeles, 1949.

Marguerite, *Faust* (Gounod). Puerto Rico, 1941. Cincinnati, 1942. Knoxville, 1950.

Lucia, *Lucia di Lammermoor* (Donizetti). Santiago, 1943.

Freia, *Das Rheingold* (Wagner) New York Met, 1944.

Mélisande, *Pelléas et Mélisande* (Debussy). New York Met, 1945.

Olga, *The Great Waltz* (J. Strauss I, J. Strauss II). Los Angeles Civic Light Opera, New York, 1950.

Count Orlofsky, *Die Fledermaus* (J. Strauss II). New York, Baltimore, Philadelphia, Boston, Cleveland, Atlanta, Dallas, Des Moines, Minneapolis, Bloomington, Chicago, Rochester, 1951.

Madame Pompadour, *Madame Pompadour* (Fall). Vienna Volksoper, 1957.

Notable Symphonic Concert Repertory

Beethoven, Symphony No. 9 in C Minor, op. 125. Soprano soloist.

Berlioz, *La Damnation de Faust,* op. 24. Marguerite.

Brahms, *Ein Deutsches Requiem,* op. 45. Soprano soloist.

Debussy, *La Demoiselle élue.* Soprano soloist.

Honegger, *Jeanne d'Arc au Bûcher* (U.S. premiere, 1948). Marguérite.

Mozart, "Great" Mass in C minor, K. 427 (417a). Soprano soloist.

Provaznik, *Psalm 117.* Soprano soloist.

Ravel, *Shéhérazade.* Soprano soloist.

Discography

"Caro nome," *Rigoletto* (Verdi, in Czech translation) [3:20]. With orchestra. Prague, 1925. 78, Columbia J 1422 (1925); LP, Supraphon DV 6296 (1966).

"È strano . . . Di quell'amor," *La Traviata* (Verdi, in Czech translation) [3:45]. With orchestra. Prague. 1925. 78, Columbia J 1421 (1925).

"Ah! Je ris," *Faust* (Gounod, in Czech translation) [3:35]. With orchestra. Prague, 1925. 78, Columbia J 1421 (1925).

"Die Hölle rache," *Die Zauberflöte* (Mozart, in Czech translation) [3:05]. With orchestra. Prague, 1935. 78, Columbia J 1422 (1925).

"Zelení hájové—Hlas za scénou," *Psohlavci* (Kovařovic) [3:04]. With orchestra. Prague, 1926. 78, HMV 273059, AM 418 (1926); CD, Supraphon 11 1491-2201 [1] (1992).

"Hlásej, ptáčku," *Hubička* (Smetana) [2:57]. With orchestra. Prague, 1926. 78, HMV 273060, AM 418 (1926); LP, Pearl GEMM 261 (1983); CD, Pearl GEMM 9467 [1] (1990); CD, Supraphon 11 1491-2201 [2] (1992).

"Les oiseaux dans la charmille," *Les Contes d'Hoffmann* (Offenbach, in German translation) [2:41]. With orchestra. From the film *Brand in der Oper.* Berlin, 1930. LP, Supraphon 11 1086-1601 (1990); DVD, Supraphon SU 7005-2 (2003); CD, Supraphon SU 4158-2 [7] (2014).

"È strano . . . Ah fors'è lui," *La Traviata* (Verdi, in German translation) [3:20]. With the Orchestra of the Staatsoper Berlin, Erich Orthmann, conductor. Berlin, 1931. 78, Electrola EH 689, 62-903 (1931).

"Follie! . . . Sempre libera," *La Traviata* (Verdi, in German translation) [3:20]. With the Orchestra of the Staatsoper Berlin, Erich Orthmann, conductor. Berlin, 1931. 78, Electrola EH 689, 62-905 (1931).

"È strano! . . . Di quell'amor," *La Traviata* (Verdi, in Czech translation) [3:15]. With the Orchestra of the Staatsoper Berlin, Erich Orthmann, conductor. Berlin, 1931. 78, HMV/Electrola 72-780, AN 682 (1931); LP, Pearl GEMM 261 (1983), CD, RY 6 [2] (1995).

"Follie! . . . Sempre libera," *La Traviata* (Verdi, in Czech translation) [3:15]. With the Orchestra of the Staatsoper Berlin, Erich Orthmann conducting. Berlin, 1931. 78, HMV/Electrola 72-781, AN 682 (1931); LP, Pearl GEMM 261 (1983); CD, RY 6 [2] (1995).

"Ich bin ein glücklicher junger Mann"; "Ja, ein Traum," *Die schöne Helena* (Offenbach, arr. Korngold) [3:20]. With Gerd Niemar, tenor; Ernst Römer, conductor. Berlin, 1931. 78, Electrola EG 2326, AM 3603, 60-1624 (1931); LP, Pearl GEMM 261 (1983); CD, RY 6 [1] (1995).

"Herz entbrennt, doch nein!"; "Es ist ein Traum," *Die schöne Helena* (Offenbach, arr. Korngold) [3:20]. With Gerd Niemar, tenor; Ernst Römer, conductor. Berlin, 1931. 78, Electrola EG 2326, AM 3603, 60-1625 (1931); LP, Pearl GEMM 261 (1983); CD, RY 6 [1] (1995).

"Ave Maria" (Bach/Gounod, in Czech translation) [2:45]. With Arpád Sándor, piano. Berlin, 1931. 78, HMV/Electrola 70-2188, AM 3784 (1931); LP, Pearl GEMM 261 (1983).

"La Paloma" (Yradier, arr. Karel Balling, in Czech translation) [2:50]. With Arpád Sándor, piano. Berlin, 1931. 78, HMV/Electrola 70-2187, AM 3784 (1931).

"Die letzte Rose," *Martha* (Flotow) [3:05]. With Arpád Sándor, piano. Berlin, 1931. 78, HMV/Electrola 70-2185, AM 3783 (1931).

"Mám zlaté vlásky," *Rusalka* (Dvořák) [2:58]. With Arpád Sándor, piano. Berlin, 1931. 78, HMV/Electrola 70-2186, AM 3783 (1931), Pearl GEMM 261 (1983); LP, Supraphon 1016 3742 (1983); CD, Pearl GEMM 9467 [2] (1990); CD, Supraphon 11 1491-2201 [3] (1992).

Marie (Mařenka), "*Die verkaufte Braut*" (*Prodaná Nevěsta/The Bartered Bride* in German translation), film [77:00]. Theo Mackeben, conductor and arranger; Max Ophüls, director. Berlin and Munich, 1931. VHS, Bel Canto BCS-0671 (1995); DVD, Triad Productions (2008).

Songs from this soundtrack released on disc:

—"Wenn du gehst, ich will nicht klagen," "Gerne will ich dir vertrauen" [2:18]. CD, RY 80 [13] (1995).

—"Diese Rast von Wiederscheiden," "Nur in Lust und Leide" [2:08]. With Willi Domgraf-Fassbaender, tenor. CD, RY 80 [11] (1995).

—"An die Stunden mit dir zu sein," "Ach, welche Qual" [1:41]. with Domgraf-Fassbaender. CD, RY 80 [12] (1995).

"Nehmt euch ihr Männer vor Frauen in Acht," *Frühlingsstürme* (Weinberger) [3:12]. Berlin Stadtoper Orchester, Franz Schönbaumsfeld, conductor. Berlin, 1933. 78, Electrola EG 2727, 60-2203 (1933).

"Sitzt man Nachts mit einer Frau beim Tee," *Frühlingsstürme* (Weinberger) [3:32]. Berlin Stadtoper Orchester, Franz Schönbaumsfeld, conductor. Berlin, 1933. 78, Electrola EG 2727, 60-2202 (1933).

"Frühling in der Mandschurei," *Frühlingsstürme* (Weinberger) [3:05]. With Marcel Wittrisch, tenor; Berlin Stadtoper Orchester, Franz Schönbaumsfeld, conductor. Berlin, 1933. 78, Electrola 60-2198, EG 2725, AM 4171 (1933).

"Blau, himmelblau traumversunken, liebestrunken," *Frühlingsstürme* (Weinberger) [2:45]. With Marcel Wittrisch, tenor; Berlin Stadtoper Orchestra, Franz Schönbaumsfeld, conductor. Berlin, 1933. 78, Electrola

60-2199, EG 2725, AM 4171 (1933); CD, The Record Collector, Vol. 40, Singers 1995 TRC 6 [23] (1996).

"Una voce poco fa," *Il Barbiere di Siviglia* (Rossini, in Czech translation) [4:06]. With orchestra; from the film *Skřivánčí Píseň* (Song of the Lark). Prague, 1933. CD, Supraphon SU 4158-2 [1] (2014).

"Schön wie die blaue Sommernacht," *Giuditta* (Lehár) [3:14]. With Richard Tauber, tenor; Vienna Philharmonic, Franz Lehár, conductor. Vienna, 1934. 78, Odeon RO 20291, PO 167 (1934); AmD 20343, 196272, B 501, 0-4537a, 0-26316; LP, World Record Club SH 122; CD, Pearl GEMM 9310 (1987); CD, Bel Age 103.352 (1995); CD, RY 6 [5] (1995); CD, ORF CD32 LC5130 (1995); CD, Preiser PR 90 150 (1999); CD, EMI Classics 7 54838 2-567 (1993); CD, Flapper FLA PAST 7042 (1990s, date unverified); CD, LV 89401-3 (1994); CD, Preiser 90802 (2012).

"Meine Lippen, sie küssen so heiß," *Giuditta* (Lehár) [3:25]. With Vienna Philharmonic, Franz Lehár, conductor. Vienna, 1934. 78, Odeon RO 20291, PO 167 (1934), AmD 20343, 196272, B 501, 0-4537b; 0-26316; CD, Pearl GEMM 9310 (1987); CD, Bel Age 103.352 (1995).

"Meine Lippen, sie küssen so heiß," *Giuditta* (Lehár) [3:55/4:07]. With the Vienna Philharmonic and the Men's Chorus of the Vienna Staatsoper, Franz Lehár, conductor. Vienna, 1934. LP, EJS 532 "Potpourri, No. 23"; CD, Koch Schwann 3-1451-2B [14] (1994); CD, RY 6 [12] (1995); CD, Pearl GEMM 9255 (1991); CD, Koch Schwann 3-1834-2 [15] (2001).

Frasquita, *Frasquita* (Lehár) film [89:000]. Franz Lehár conductor; Karel Lamač, director. Vienna, 1934. VHS, 319; DVD, 871.

Songs from this soundtrack released on disc:

—"Liebe wird immer sich finden" [2:02]. With Hans-Heinz Bollmann, tenor. CD, VA 0066-2 [3] (1997).

—"Schatz, ich bitt dich," "Wenn der Sekt im Glasse springt" [4:21]. With Hans-Heinz Bollmann, tenor. CD, VA 0066-2 [4] (1997).

—"Wüßt ich wer Morgen mein Liebster ist" [3:13]. CD, VA 0066-2 [2] (1997).

—"Lala; Weisst du nicht?" [4:24]. CD, VA 0066-2 [5] (1997).

Vera Lizavetta, *The Last Waltz* (Straus) film [74:00]. Allan Gray, conductor; Leo Mittler, director. Paris, 1934. VHS, Bel Canto BCS-0671 (1995); DVD (2002).

Songs from this soundtrack released on disc:

—"Love we made not alone/When the swing is highly swinging" [4:24]. With Pamela Randal, Betty Huntley Wright, sopranos; Harry Welchman, tenor. CD, VA 0066-2 [9] (1997).
—Cossack Dance [2:03]. CD, VA 0066-2 [10] (1997).
—"Come, let us dance/Before we say goodbye" [2:45]. With Harry Welchmann, tenor. CD, VA 0066-2 [11] (1997).

"Humoresques," op. 101, B. 187 (Dvořák, arr. Taus) [2:46]. With unidentified orchestra, Alexander von Zemlinsky, conductor; Vienna, 1934–1935. 78, Odeon RO 20293, 0-25387 (1935), RA 161600; CD, Supraphon 11 1491-2201 [4] (1992); CD, LV 89956 [8] (1998).

"Poème" (Fibich, arr. with text by Karel Balling) [3:13]. With unidentified orchestra, Alexander von Zemlinsky, conductor; Vienna, 1934–1935. 78, Odeon RO 20293, 0-25387 (1935), RA 161600; LP, Pearl GEMM 261 (1983); CD, Pearl GEMM 9467 [3] (1990); CD, Supraphon 11 1491-2201 [5] (1992); CD, RY 6 [4] (1995); CD, LV 89956 [9] (1998); CD, OPD 8011 (2002).

"Mir ist die Ehre," *Der Rosenkavalier* (Strauss). With Elisabeth Schumann, soprano; Vienna Philharmonic, Josef Krips, conductor. Vienna, 1936. LP, EJS 332 B; Celebrity Record Co. (1960s, date unverified).

"Hab mir's gelobt," *Der Rosenkavalier* (Strauss). With Lotte Lehmann, Elisabeth Schumann, sopranos; Vienna Philharmonic, Josef Krips, conductor. Vienna, 1936. LP, EJS 332 B; Celebrity Record Co. (1960s, date unverified).

"Ist's ein Traum," *Der Rosenkavalier* (Strauss). With Elisabeth Schumann, soprano; Vienna Philharmonic, Josef Krips, conductor. Vienna, 1936. LP, EJS 332 B; Celebrity Record Co. (1960s, date unverified).

Pamina, *Die Zauberflöte* (Mozart): complete opera in live performance from the Salzburg Festival, July 30, 1937 [155:35]. With Alexander Kipnis, Helge Rosvaenge, Willi Domgraf-Fassbaender; Chorus of the Vienna Staatsoper, Vienna Philharmonic, Arturo Toscanini, conductor. Film, Selenophone 8 mm; Omega Angel Archive 483; Omega Opera Archive 1806. 3 LP, Cetra ATS 1025-27; 2 CD, Melodram 37040 (1988); CD, FTO 321.22 (1995/96); 2 CD, Grammofono 2000 AB 78017.25 (1994); 2 CD, Grammofono 2000 AB 78528/29 (2000); 2 CD, CACD 5.00273 (2002).

Songs from this performance released on disc:

—"Bei Männern" [2:32]. With Domgraf-Fassbaender. LP, Pearl GEMM 261 (1983); CD, Pearl GEMM 9467 [6] (1990); CD, RY 6 [10] (1995); CD, Orfeo C 394 101 B [10] (1995); CD, HI 20.30801 (1990s, date unverified).

—"Ach, ich fühl's" [3:30]. LP, Pearl GEMM 261 (1983); LP, Supraphon 11 1086-1601 (1990); CD, Pearl GEMM 9467 [7] (1990); CD, RY 6 [8] (1995); DVD, Supraphon SU 7005-2 (2003); CD, Supraphon SU 4158-2 [2] (2014).,

—"Soll ich dich, teurer, nicht mehr seh'n?" [2:41]. With Kipnis, Rosvaenge. LP Pearl GEMM 261 (1983); CD, RY 6 [9] (1995).

Cherubino, *Le Nozze di Figaro* (Mozart): complete opera in live performance from the Salzburg Festival, August 19, 1937 [156:22]. With Ezio Pinza, Esther Réthy, Mariano Stabile, Aulikki Rautawaara; Chorus of the Vienna Staatsoper, Vienna Philharmonic, Bruno Walter, conductor. Omega Opera Archive 4657; 3 CD, Eklipse Records EKR 43 (1995); 2 CD, Arkadia 50004 (1997); 3 CD, Andante 3981 (2003).

Song from this performance released on disc:

—"Voi che sapete" [3:01]. CD, Orfeo C 394 101B [18] (1995); CD, HI 20.30801 (1990s, date unverified).

Cio-Cio-San, *Madama Butterfly* (Puccini): radio broadcast of the San Francisco Opera, November 23, 1939 [93:30]. With Herta Glaz, Michael Bartlett, George Cehanovsky; San Francisco Opera Orchestra and Chorus, Gennaro Papi, conductor. 2 LP, EJS UORC 116 [12-1353/54] (1972), ASCO 116.

Soprano soloist, Ninth Symphony (Beethoven): radio broadcast from New York, December 12, 1939 [61:43]. With Kerstin Thorborg, Jan Peerce, Nicola Moscona; NBC Symphony Orchestra, Arturo Toscanini, conductor. 2 LP, ATS 1119; CD, Legato LCD 136 (1988); CD, Nuova Era 2248 (1990s, date unverified); CD, Relief REL CR 1893 (1991); CD, Naxos Historical AAD 8.811024 (1998); CD, Music & Arts B00DJSU074 (as part of a complete "Toscanini Conducts Beethoven" collection on 5 discs).

Euridice, *Orfeo ed Euridice* (Gluck): Metropolitan Opera radio broadcast of January 20, 1940 [102:07]. With Kerstin Thorborg, Marita Farrell;

Metropolitan Opera Orchestra and Chorus, Erich Leinsdorf, conductor. 2 CD, Walhall WHL 32 (1996); 2 CD, Guild GHCD 2317/18 (2005).

Cherubino, *Le Nozze di Figaro* (Mozart): Metropolitan Opera radio broadcast of March 9, 1940 [159:23]. With Ezio Pinza, Elisabeth Rethberg, Bidù Sayão, John Brownlee, Irra Petina; Metropolitan Opera Orchestra and Chorus, Ettore Panizza, conductor. 3 LP, EJS 118; 3 CD, Music & Arts 646 (1990).

Soprano soloist, *La Demoiselle élue* (Debussy): radio broadcast from New York, April 13, 1940 [20:09]. With Herta Glaz, mezzo-soprano; Women's Chorus of the Schola Cantorum, NBC Symphony Orchestra, Arturo Toscanini, conductor. CD, Naxos 8.110811-2 [I/3] (1998).

WGN Radio broadcast, New York, August 25, 1940. With Maurice Abravanel, conductor.

Songs from this performance released on disc:

—"Addio del passato," *La Traviata* (Verdi) [2:34]. LP, Supraphon 11 1086-1601 (1990); DVD, Supraphon SU 7005-2 (2003); CD, Supraphon SU 4153-2 [13] (2014).

—"Vilja," *The Merry Widow* (Lehár, in English translation) [3:01]. CD, VA 0066-2 [6] (1997).

Cherubino, *Le Nozze di Figaro* (Mozart): selected scenes. With Elisabeth Rethberg, Licia Albanese, Ezio Pinza, John Brownlee, Salvatore Baccaloni; Metropolitan Opera Orchestra and Chorus, Ettore Panizza, conductor. LP, EJS 228.

Songs from this performance released on disc:

—"Non so più" [2:44]. LP, Pearl GEMM 261 (1983); CD, Pearl GEMM 9467 [4] (1990); CD, RY 6 [6] (1995); CD, MET 24 (2001).

—"Voi che sapete" [3:16]. LP, Pearl GEMM 261 (1983); CD, Pearl GEMM 9467 [5] (1990); CD, RY 6 [7] (1995).

Violetta, *La Traviata* (Verdi): Metropolitan Opera radio broadcast of November 29, 1941 [122:04]. With Jan Peerce, Lawrence Tibbett; Metropolitan Opera Orchestra and Chorus, Ettore Panizza, conductor. 2 CD, MYTO Records 2 MCD 933.80 (1993); 2 CD, Walhall 0343 (2011); 2 CD, 82640.

Songs from this performance released on disc:

—"È strano . . . Sempre libera" [8:45]. With Peerce. LP, Supraphon 11 1086-1601 (1990); CD, MYTO Records MCD 941.94 (1994); DVD, Supraphon SU 7005-2 (2003); CD, Supraphon SU 4158-2 [12] (2014).

—"Teneste la promessa . . . Addio del passato" [4:30]. LP, Pearl GEMM 261 (1983); LP, Supraphon 11 1086-1601 (1990); CD, Pearl GEMM 9467 [8] (1990); CD, RY 6 [15] (1995); DVD, Supraphon SU 7005-2 (2003).

Donna Elvira, *Don Giovanni* (Mozart): Metropolitan Opera radio broadcast of March 7, 1942 [154:33]/[153:15]. With Ezio Pinza, Rose Bampton, Charles Kullman, Bidù Sayão, Alexander Kipnis, Norman Cordon, Mack Harrell; Metropolitan Opera Orchestra and Chorus, Bruno Walter, conductor. 3 LP, EJS 119; LP, Cetra LO 27.3; 3 CD, Nuova Era 2275-77 (1989), Memoires HR 4225-27 (1990); 2 CD, Great Opera Performances G.O.P. 798 (1996), Nuova Era PH 5081/83 (1996); 2 CD, Arkadia 50001 (1997); 2 CD, Naxos 8.110013-4 (1997).

Songs from this performance released on disc:

—"Ah, chi mi dice mai" [2:53]. With Pinza, Kipnis. LP, Supraphon 11 1086-1601 (1990); DVD, Supraphon SU 7005-2 (2003); CD, Supraphon SU 4158-2 [5] (2014).

—"Fuggi, il traditor" [1:39]. LP, Supraphon 11 1086-1601 (1990); DVD, Supraphon SU 7005-2 (2003); CD, Supraphon SU 4158-2 [6] (2014).

Guest appearance, "Radio Treasury Hour," with Alfred Wallenstein, conductor; New York, April 13, 1942.

Songs from this performance released on disc:

—"Ach, jaký žal; Ten lásky sen," *Prodaná Nevěsta* (Smetana) [5:26]. LP, Pearl GEMM 262 (1983); LP, Supraphon 11 0125-1912 (1990), 11 1490-1201 (1992); CD, Pearl GEMM 9467 [17] (1990); CD, Supraphon 11 1490-2201 [19] (1992); CD, Supraphon SU 4158-2 [18] (2014).

—"Doch der Vertrauter . . . Meine Lippen, sie küssen so heiß," *Giuditta* (Lehár) [3:49]. CD, VA 0066-2 [1] (1997).

Songs of Lidice (traditional, arr. Masaryk). Victor Studio, New York, 1942. With Jan Masaryk, piano. 78, RCA Victor M-936; LP, Victrola VIC 1383 (1969); LP, Pearl GEMM 262 (1983); LP, Supraphon 11 1490-1201 (1992); CD, Pearl GEMM 9467 (1990); CD, Supraphon 11 1491-2201 (1992); DVD, Supraphon SU 7005-2 (2003).

Individual songs from this album released on disc:

—"Zelení hájové"[2:16]. CD, Supraphon 120010-2911 (1992).
—"Ach synku, synku" [2:03]. CD, Supraphon 120010-2911 (1992).
—"Teče voda, teče" [2:02]. CD, Supraphon 120010-2911 (1992).

Pamina, *Die Zauberflöte* (Mozart): Metropolitan Opera radio broadcast of December 26, 1942 [158:19]. With Charles Kullman, John Brownlee, Ezio Pinza, Josephine Antoine; Metropolitan Opera Orchestra and Chorus, Bruno Walter, conductor. 3 LP, EJS MJA 5000; 2 CD, Walhall Records WHL 2 (1994).

Brindisi, *La Traviata* (Verdi) [1:09]. With orchestra, Morton Gould, conductor. 1943. CD, Supraphon SU 4158-2 [11] (2014).

"Sì, mi chiamano Mimì," *La Bohème* (Puccini): guest appearance on "Radio Treasury Hour," New York, March 13, 1943 [4:30]. With orchestra, Alfred Wallenstein, conductor. LP, EJS 295 "Potpourri No. 18"; LP, Supraphon 11 1086-1601 (1990); DVD, Supraphon SU 7005-2 (2003); CD, Supraphon SU 4158-2 [15] (2014).

Donna Elvira, *Don Giovanni* (Mozart): Metropolitan Opera radio broadcast from Chicago, April 3, 1943 [144:29]. With Ezio Pinza, Zinka Milanov, James Melton, Bidù Sayão, Salvatore Baccaloni, Norman Cordon, Mack Harrell; Metropolitan Opera Orchestra and Chorus, Paul Breisach, conductor. LP, EJS 229; 2 CD, Walhall Records WHL 28 (1996).

Portions of this performance released on disc:

—"Ah, fuggi!" and Act I finale. CD, Music & Arts 646 (1990).

Cherubino, *Le Nozze di Figaro* (Mozart): Metropolitan Opera radio broadcast of April 17, 1943 [214:12]. With Ezio Pinza, Bidù Sayão, John Brownlee, Eleanor Steber, Salvatore Baccaloni, Herta Glaz; Metropolitan Opera Orchestra and Chorus, Paul Breisach, conductor. 3 LP, Omega Opera Archive 3; 3 CD, NYM 1022; 3 CD, Guild GHCD 2203/4/5 (2002).

Songs from this performance released on disc:

—"Non so più" [2:48]. LP, Supraphon 11 1086-1601 (1990); DVD, Supraphon SU 7005-2 (2003); CD, Supraphon SU 4158-2 [3] (2014).
—"Voi, che sapete" [3:23]. CD, Supraphon SU 4158-2 [4] (2014).

"Voi che sapete," *Le Nozze di Figaro* (Mozart): from the Metropolitan Opera Radio Broadcast of January 29, 1944 [3:04]. LP, Supraphon 11 1086-1601 (1990); DVD, Supraphon SU 7005-2 (2003).

Guest appearance, WABC Radio, with André Kostelanetz, conductor, February 13, 1944.

Songs from this performance released on disc:

—"Love has found my heart" (Kálmán) [2:25]. LP, EJS 532 "Potpourri No. 23."
—"Vilja," *The Merry Widow* (Lehár) [2:40]. LP, EJS 532 "Potpourri No. 23."

Antonia, *Les Contes d'Hoffmann* (Offenbach): Metropolitan Opera radio broadcast of February 26, 1944 [140:00]. With Raoul Jobin, Ezio Pinza, Martial Singher, Mack Harrell, Patrice Munsel, Lily Djanel, Margaret Harshaw; Metropolitan Opera Orchestra and Chorus, Thomas Beecham, conductor. 2 CD, MYTO Records; 2 CD, 941.94 (1994); 2 CD, RY 2 CD 19/20 (1995); 2 CD, Opera Magic OM 24106 (2000).

Songs from this performance released on disc:

—"Elle a fui, la tourterelle" [4:47]. LP, Pearl GEMM 262 (1983); LP, Supraphon 11 1086-1601 (1990); CD, Pearl GEMM 9467 [15] (1990); DVD, Supraphon SU 7005-2 (2003).
—"Voyez l'étrange fantaisie . . . C'est une chanson d'amour" [3:49]. With Jobin. LP, Pearl GEMM 262 (1983); LP, Supraphon 11 1086-1601 (1990); CD, Pearl GEMM 9467 [16] (1990); DVD, Supraphon SU 7005-2 (2003); CD, Supraphon SU 4158-2 [10] (2014).
—"Tu ne chanteras plus?" With Pinza, Harshaw. LP, Pearl GEMM 262 (1983).

"Every Dream that Rustles the Trees," *Helen Goes to Troy* (Offenbach/ Korngold) [2:36]. With Erich Wolfgang Korngold, conductor. New York, 1944. (Note: While *Helen Goes to Troy* is based on Offenbach's *La Belle Hélène,* this number is interpolated from his *Les Contes d'Hoffmann,* with new lyrics for "Belle nuit, ô nuit d'amour," the Barcarolle.) LP, Supraphon 11 1086-1601 (1990); CD, RY 6 [11] (1995); DVD, Supraphon SU 7005-2 (2003).

Guest appearance, "Metropolitan Opera Presents," WJZ Radio, New York, December 10, 1944. With the Metropolitan Opera Orchestra, Wilfred Pelletier, conductor.

Songs from this performance released on disc:

—"Když mne stará matka" (Songs My Mother Taught Me) (Dvořák) [2:05]. LP, Supraphon 11 1490-1201 (1992).

—"Vissi d'arte," *Tosca* (Puccini) [3:10]. LP, Supraphon 11 1086-1601 (1990); DVD, Supraphon SU 7005-2 (2003); CD, Supraphon SU 4158-2 [17] (2014).

—"Hej, Slované!" (Unknown, traditional) [1:30]. LP, Supraphon 11 1490-1201 (1992); CD, Supraphon 11 1491-2201 [14] (1992).

—"Ah! Je ris," *Faust* (Gounod). LP, EJS 532 "Potpourri No. 23."

Arias by Johann Strauss II and Jacques Offenbach. With the Victor Orchestra, Frieder Weissmann, conductor. Victor Studio, New York, 1945. Produced but evidently not released as an album.

Songs from these sessions released on disc:

—"Wer uns getraut," *Der Zigeunerbaron* [Timing unavailable]. LP, Victrola VIC 1383 (1969).

—"Elle a fui, la tourterelle," *Les Contes d'Hoffmann* [3:59]. 78, Victor 11-9263; LP, Victrola VIC 1383 (1969); CD, LV 89956 [5] (1998); CD, Supraphon SU 4158-2 [9] (2014).

—"Belle nuit, ô nuit d'amour," *Les Contes d'Hoffmann* (originally released as "Barcarolle") [3:52]. 78, Victor 11-9263; LP, RHEIN-NIXEN (1872) Club 99 CL 110; CD, Club 99 CL 511 [20] (1989); CD, LV 89956 [4] (1998); CD, Supraphon SU 4158-2 [8] (2014).

—"Love Waltz," *Liebeslieder* (J. Strauss II, Op. 114, with English text) [Timing unavailable]. LP, Victrola VIC 1383 (1969).

—"Schatz-Walzer," *Der Zigeunerbaron* (with English text) [Timing unavailable]. Master D5 RD 511-1; JD 30.

—"Gypsy Song," *Der Zigeunerbaron*. LP, Victrola VIC 1383 (1969).

"Umrem, umrem" [2:12]. Radio broadcast, 1945. LP, Pearl GEMM 262 (1983); CD, Pearl GEMM 9467 [19] (1990); LP, Supraphon 11 1490-1201 (1992); CD, Suprahon 11 1491-2201 [12] (1992).

"Když mne stará matka" (Songs My Mother Taught Me) (Dvořák) [1:44]. NBC TV, New York, 1945. LP, Supraphon 11 1490-1201 (1992).

"With All My Heart, I Call for You" (J. Strauss II) [2:19]. NBC TV, New York, 1945. CD, VA 0066-2 [13] (1997).

"A ty, mé robě; Hajej můj andílku," *Hubička* (Smetana) [4:41]. With Victor Orchestra, Frieder Weissmann, conductor. Victor Studio, New York, 1945. 78, Victor 11-9153; LP, Victrola VIC 1383 (1969); LP, Supraphon 11 1490-1201 (1992); CD, Supraphon 11 1491-2201 [20] (1992); CD, LV 89956 [6] (1998); CD, Supraphon SU 4158-2 [19] (2014).

"Když mne stará matka" (Songs My Mother Taught Me) (Dvořák) [3:44]. With Victor Orchestra, Frieder Weissmann, conductor. Victor Studio, New York, 1945. 78, Victor 11-9153; LP, Victrola VIC 1383 (1969); CD, Supraphon 11 1491-2201 [18] (1992); CD, LV 89956 [7] (1998).

"Love, love, can it be love," *Der Graf von Luxemburg* (Lehár, in English translation) [3:06]. CBS Radio broadcast, 1945. CD, VA 0066-2 [8] (1997).

Octavian, *Der Rosenkavalier* (Strauss): Metropolitan Opera Radio broadcast of February 16, 1946 [174:30]. With Irene Jessner, Emanuel List, Nadine Conner; Metropolitan Opera Orchestra and Chorus, Georg Szell, conductor. 3 CD, OOA 1114; 3 CD, NYM 1078; 3 CD OP 215,7; 3 CD, Walhall 0331 WLCD 3331 (2011).

Mimì/Marcello duet, Act III, *La Bohème* (Puccini) [4:42]. With Martial Singher, baritone; Donald Voorhees, conductor. *Bell Telephone Hour*, WEAF Radio, 1946. LP, Supraphon 11 1086-1601 (1990); DVD, Supraphon SU 7005-2 (2003); CD, Supraphon SU 4158-2 [16] (2014).

"While we're swaying to the playing" (*Merry Widow* waltz) (Lehár) [2:53]. Unknown orchestra and venue, 1946. CD, VA 0066-2 [7] (1997).

Cherubino, *Le Nozze di Figaro* (Mozart): Metropolitan Opera radio broadcast of March 15, 1947. With Ezio Pinza, Hjördis Schymberg, John Brownlee, Eleanor Steber; Metropolitan Opera Orchestra and Chorus, Fritz Busch, conductor. Omega Angel Archive 486+658.

Mrs. Malik, *The Search* [1:44], film. With Montgomery Clift, Aline MacMahon, Ivan Jandl; Fred Zinnemann, director. DVD, WB Archive Collection B003156IKW (2009).

Musical excerpts from the film *The Search* (1948): "Aby nás Pán Bůh miloval" [2:32] and "Když se večer stmívá (Má hvězda)" [1:53] (both arr. Robert Blum). LP, Supraphon 11 1490-1201 (1992); CD Supraphon 11 1491-2201 [16] (1992).

Marguérite, *Jeanne d'Arc au Bûcher* (Honegger). With Vera Zorina, Nadine Conner; Westminster Choir, New York Philharmonic, Charles Munch, conductor. New York, 1948. Omega Angel Archive 1205.

"Umrem, umrem"/"I Saw My Country Die" [4:56]. *We, the People* radio program, 1948. CD, Supraphon 11 1491-2201 [13] (1992).

Cherubino, *Le Nozze di Figaro* (Mozart): Metropolitan Opera radio broadcast of January 8, 1949 [157:25]. With Italo Tajo, Bidù Sayão, John Brownlee, Eleanor Steber, Salvatore Baccaloni, Claramae Turner; Metropolitan Opera Orchestra and Chorus, Fritz Busch, conductor. 2 CD, WLCD 0093 (2005).

"When I Grow Too Old to Dream" (Romberg) [2:40]. ABC broadcast, 1949. With Sigmund Romberg, conductor. CD, VA 0066-2 [21] (1997).

Octavian, *Der Rosenkavalier* (Strauss): complete opera in performance at the Salzburg Festival [181:40]. With Maria Reining, Jaro Prohaska, Hilde Güden, Helge Rosvaenge; Chorus of the Vienna Staatsoper, Vienna Philharmonc, Georg Szell, conductor. LP, Omega Angel (Records) Archive 285+541; 4 LP, Cetra LO 69/4; 3 CD, ARL A46-A48 (1996); 3 CD, Dante LYS 184-186 (2000); 3 CD, Arioso AR 1004 (2003); 4 CD, Andante AND 3985 (2003); 4 CD, Cantus Classics 500654-500655 (2005).

"Love Is Just a Game," *Apple Blossoms* (Kreisler) [3:40]. With James Melton, tenor. U.S. venue and orchestra unknown, 1949–1950. CD, VA 0066-2 [18] (1997, incorrectly attributing the song to Rodgers and Hammerstein).

"Hello, Young Lovers," *The King and I* (Rodgers and Hammerstein) [2:41]. U.S. venue and orchestra unknown, 1949–1950. CD, VA 0066-2 [19] (1997).

"Falling in Love with Love," *The Boys from Syracuse* (Rodgers and Hart) [2:59]. Unknown orchestra, U.S. venue, date. CD, VA 0066-2 [16] (1997).

"Wien, Wien, nur du allein" (Sieczyński) [5:27]. Unknown orchestra, U.S. venue, date. CD, VA 0066-2 [24] (1997).

"Parigi, o Cara," *La Traviata* (Verdi) [4:58]. With James Melton, tenor; Frank Black, conductor, "Harvest of Stars" radio program, WNBC, New York, 1950. LP, Supraphon 11 1086-1601 (1990); CD, Supraphon SU 4158-2 [14] (2014); DVD, Supraphon SU 7005-2 (2003).

Cherubino, *Le Nozze di Figaro* (Mozart): Metropolitan Opera radio broadcast of February 11, 1950. With Italo Tajo, Bidu Sayão, John Brownlee, Eleanor Steber; Metropolitan Opera Orchestra and Chorus, Fritz Reiner, conductor. Omega Opera Archive 674.

Sigmund Romberg concert at the Hollywood Bowl. Songs from *The New Moon* and *Maytime*. With Walter Galjour, baritone; Los Angeles Orchestra, Sigmund Romberg, conductor. Los Angeles, 1950. CD, VA 0066-2 [22] (1997).

"Heja, heja, I was born in father's Gypsy land," *Die Csarasfürstin* (Kálmán in English translation) [2:30]. Orchestra and U.S. venue unknown, 1951. CD, VA 0066-2 [14] (1997).

"Wonder of the thousand wonders," *Die Csardasfürstin* (Kálmán in English translation) [1:52]. With Gordon MacRae, baritone. Orchestra and U.S. venue unknown, 1951. CD, VA 0066-2 [15] (1997).

Freia, *Das Rheingold* (Wagner): Metropolitan Opera radio broadcast of January 27, 1951 [135:55]. With Hans Hotter, Margaret Harshaw; Metropolitan Opera Orchestra, Fritz Stiedry, conductor. 2 LP, EJS UORC 276; 2 CD, NYM 900; CD, Gebhardt JGCD 0038-11 (2001).

Octavian, *Der Rosenkavalier* (Strauss): Metropolitan Opera radio broadcast of February 24, 1951. With Eleanor Steber, Fritz Krenn, Erna Berger; Metropolitan Opera Orchestra and Chorus, Fritz Reiner, conductor. Omega Opera Archive 164.

"To zní nad Prahou (Pražské zvony)" ("The Bells of Prague") (Stelibský) [1:45]. With Josef Stelibský, piano. "Crusade for Freedom" radio program, 1952. CD, Supraphon 11 1491-2201 [15] (1992.)

"L'Amour, toujours l'Amour" (Friml) [2:55]. Orchestra and location unknown, 1953. CD, RY 6 [13] (1995); CD, VA 0066-2 [17] (1997).

Orlofsky, *Die Fledermaus* (J. Strauss II): Metropolitan Opera radio broadcast of January 23, 1954. With Eleanor Steber, Patrice Munsel, Charles Kullman, John Brownlee; Metropolitan Opera Orchestra and Chorus, Tibor Kozma, conductor. Omega Opera Archive 1069+786; 2 CD, IP 597.

"If I were on the stage . . . Kiss me again," *Mademoiselle Modiste* (Herbert) [4:20]. CBS broadcast, "Opera goes to Hollywood," 1955. LP, Star Tone Records ST 211; CD, RY 6 [14] (1995); CD, VA 0066-2 [20] (1997).

Olga Baranska, *The Great Waltz* (J. Strauss I, J. Strauss II) [79:00]. Television film with Patrice Munsel, Keith Andes, Bert Lahr; Charles Stanford, conductor; Max Liebman, director. 1955. VHS, VAI 72002 (1993).

Song from this soundtrack released on disc:

—"The Ending of a Love Affair" [1:48]. CD, VA 0066-2 [12] (1997).

"Měsíčku na nebi," *Rusalka* (Dvořák) [5:13]. With Gibner King, piano. 1955. LP, Pearl GEMM 262 (1983); CD, Pearl GEMM 9467 [18] (1990); LP, Supraphon 11 1490-1201 (1992); CD, Supraphon 11 1491-2201 [21] (1992); CD, Supraphon SU 4158-2 [20] (2014).

Dame Brinker, *Hans Brinker or the Silver Skates* (Martin) [50:00]. *Hallmark Hall of Fame* television film with Tab Hunter, Peggy King, Basil Rathbone, and Dick Button; Franz Allers, conductor; Sidney Lumet, George Schaefer, directors. NBC Television, 1958. Soundtrack album, with Irwin Kostal and Fred Katz, conductors: LP, Dot Records DLP 9001 (1958); CD, Sepia Records B001HY3ALE (2008).

Notes

Introduction

1. Jarmila Novotná, *Byla jsem šťastná* (I Have Been Happy) (Prague: Melantrich, 1991); revised edition (Liteň, Czech Republic: Zamek Liteň, 2014).

2. See Figure 18.

3. For examples of some of the cigarette cards, as well as examples of "movie cards," see http://www.virtual-history.com/movie/person/892/jarmila-novotna/photographs.

4. Full-page advertisement for Rheingold beer, *New York Daily Mirror,* Dec. 8, 1952.

5. "Meine Lippen, sie küssen so heiß," lyrics by Paul Knepler, translated by William V. Madison.

6. Downes, "De Luca Returns as Elder Germont," *New York Times,* Feb. 9, 1940.

7. Novotná made her screen debut before the sound era, in a silent film, *The Sun Worshipers* (1926).

8. Long available commercially in the United States only on VHS made from a badly damaged print, *Die verkaufte Braut* is currently posted on YouTube, from a superior print, with English subtitles. See https://www.youtube.com/watch?v=5M3E7E3q9Iw.

9. *Frasquita*'s only truly "stagy" sequences are the overture and the finale, conducted by Lehár himself in the orchestra pit of a Viennese theater.

10. Most European audiences in 1935 would have recognized the name Frasquita as that of a supporting role in Bizet's *Carmen.* Novotná sang the part onstage in Prague in 1926.

11. As of October 2016, the movie could be found on YouTube, in German without subtitles. The reels are not entirely in consecutive order, but the plot is easy to follow. See https://www.youtube.com/watch?v=TAhnepDYdpM&t=5219s.

12. It would be difficult for even the most accomplished writer to describe the weight of Novotná's wartime concerns while simultaneously describing the glittering parties, opera galas, and bucolic family holidays that occupied so much of her day-to-day life in America. Yet her fears for her homeland loomed constantly in the background.

13. That same glamour is abundantly represented in *The Great Caruso* and in many of Novotná's European films, such as *Die Nacht der großen Liebe* (1933), *Der Kosak und die Nachtigall* (1935), and even *Frasquita.*

14. The rough equivalent of $10,000 in 2017.

15. See Figure 45.

16. Taken together, the three "trouser" roles of Octavian (*Der Rosenkavalier*), Cherubino (*Le Nozze di Figaro*) and Orlofsky (*Die Fledermaus*) account for half of her appearances at the Met.

17. Lanfranco Rasponi, *The Last Prima Donnas* (New York: Knopf, 1982). Not coincidentally, Rasponi was Novotná's longtime publicist. He probably helped her to write her recital-lectures.

18. Will Crutchfield, "Classical Music: Once the Voice Was Melody Itself. In Fact, It Still Is," *New York Times,* March 7, 1993. Crutchfield is a distinguished American conductor and musicologist.

19. Ibid.

20. Today even many of those dinner companions' children are dead: the Metropolitan Opera general manager Anthony Bliss, to cite one notable example; or the actor Robert Montgomery's daughter, the television star Elizabeth Montgomery.

21. Letter from Jarmila Novotná to William V. Madison, dated Aug. 17, 1990; collection of William V. Madison, quoted with permission from George Daubek. Naming a planet is a multistep process: the planet Jarmila Novotná was given a permanent number, 5897, in April 1994, and the name was finalized in April 1997.

22. I confirmed this with President Havel himself, during a break in his interview with Dan Rather of CBS News in 1994.

23. See Figure 60.

1. Europe, 1907–1939

1. Gleich (1900–1976) would sing again in *The Bartered Bride* opposite Novotná, at the National Theater in 1946.

2. Smetana was principal conductor of the Prozatímní divadlo (Provisional Theater), which became part of the National Theater when the National opened in 1881; at that point, Smetana had already retired.

3. See Figure 4.

4. One of the most acclaimed actor-directors of his time, Gründgens (1899–1963) was the model for the protagonist of Klaus Mann's novel *Mephisto.* István Szábó's film adaptation (1981) won the Academy Award for best foreign film.

5. Ophüls may have changed the character Hans's job from farmer to postilion in order to facilitate one of the film's more exciting scenes, a chase on horseback, as Kezal the marriage broker (played by Otto Wernicke) pursues Hans.

6. Early in his career, Bertolt Brecht was a member of Valentin's company; the playwright cited the comic as an important influence on his work.

7. Berry (1883–1951) was one of the most prolific film actors in France at the time. American audiences may know him best from Jean Renoir's *Le Crime du Monsieur Lang* (1935) and Marcel Carné's *Le Jour se lève* (1939) and *Les Visiteurs du Soir* (The Devil's Envoys, 1942).

8. The czardas is a traditional Hungarian dance; it is also the name given to a challenging aria sung by Rosalinde in *Die Fledermaus.*

9. After World War II, the Mendelssohn family's extensive art collection became an object of years-long contention between the family and the Austrian government. The government ultimately denied the family's demand for restitution.

10. Korda's filmography as producer and/or producer-director includes *The Third Man* (1949), *The Thief of Baghdad* (1940), and *The Private Life of Henry VIII* (1933). Beecham conducted the score for Michael Powell and Emeric Pressburger's *The Tales of Hoffmann* (1951); Korda introduced Powell to Pressburger.

11. Timeline: Tomáš Garrigue Masaryk stepped down as President of Czechoslovakia on Dec. 14, 1935. Edvard Beneš succeeded him.

12. Felix Salten (1869–1945) is best remembered as the author of *Bambi*, source of the Disney film (1942). Plays by Ferenc Molnár (1878–1952) were adapted for films such as William Wyler's *The Good Fairy* (1935, screenplay by Preston Sturges), Rodgers and Hammerstein's *Carousel* (1956), and Billy Wilder's *One, Two, Three* (1961).

13. Werfel (1890–1945) did not live to see the publication of his "second biography" of Verdi, in 1973. He also wrote *The Song of Bernadette*, source of the 1943 movie.

14. See Figure 17.

15. By this time, Reinhardt had already directed his best-known film, *A Midsummer Night's Dream* (1935), for Warner Bros.

16. Schuschnigg returned to Austria after retiring from Saint Louis University in 1967. He died in 1977.

17. Timeline: On March 14, President Hácha was summoned to Berlin to meet with Hitler, who a few hours later told him that Germany was invading Czechoslovakia as they spoke. Following the Nazi takeover, Hácha retained some power (albeit under the administration of a German "Protector of Bohemia and Moravia") and the title State President of the Protectorate of Bohemia and Moravia. He remained in office until May 1945.

2. In America during the War

1. In addition to a distinguished operatic career, Stevens (1913–2013) was Bing Crosby's costar in *Going My Way* (1944) and a popular guest on television variety shows.

2. The Metropolitan Opera began its annual tours in 1898 and ceased touring in 1986.

3. *Flotsam* (1939), Erich Maria Remarque's novel about European refugees, was adapted for the screen as *So Ends Our Night* (1941), starring Fredric March.

4. The longest such affiliation in broadcast history, Texaco's sponsorship of the Saturday afternoon broadcasts from the Metropolitan ended in 2004.

5. *The Bluebird of Happiness The Memoirs of Jan Peerce* (New York: Harper Collins, 1976).

6. Jan Masaryk, liner notes, *Songs of Lidice*, RCA Victor, New York, 1942.

7. The New Opera Company presented operettas on Broadway from 1941 to 1944, notably the hit *Rosalinda* (1942–1944), an adaptation of *Die Fledermaus;* and *The Merry Widow* (1943–1944) starring Jan Kiepura and his wife, Marta Eggerth.

8. Hubert Renfro Knickerbocker (1898–1949), Pulitzer Prize–winning reporter for the *New York Evening Post* (now called the *New York Post*), the *Philadelphia Public Ledger,* and WOR radio.

9. Vyacheslav Mikhailovich Molotov (1890–1986), Stalin's foreign minister.

10. Novotná's songs during her June 26, 1945, appearance on NBC television were Dvořák's "Songs My Mother Taught Me" and a Johann Strauss II aria in English, "With All My Heart, I Call for You." See the Discography section of the Appendix.

3. After the War

1. Announcing the German surrender at his factory at nearby Brunnlitz, Oskar Schindler urged his Jewish workers to "Thank the Daubek Mill [i.e., the Brněnec mills], whose energetic support improved your nutrition, often beyond the realm of the possible." Schindler saved some 1,200 Jews from the Holocaust. His speech is displayed at Yad Vashem, Israel's Holocaust museum.

2. James Melton (1904–1961), a tenor, sang both popular music and opera.

3. An identical scene appears in the finished film. It is unclear whether Novotná is describing that scene, or whether a similar incident during the filming inspired the scene.

4. The character to have been played by Novotná, Lilli Vanessi, is the only one to retain an Austrian-sounding name. Patricia Morison originated the role.

5. Falkenburg (1919–2003), an actress, and McCrary (1910–2003), a journalist, pioneered the talk show on radio and television, combining celebrity interviews with serious discussions of world events. *The Search* would have been ideally suited to their program.

6. According to her son, Novotná did not donate the painting; she sold it to the National Gallery "for a pittance."

7. "Bal de Tête" is a play on the French phrase *bal de fête,* a holiday dance. *Tête* means "head."

8. Clift was bisexual. It is impossible to know whether either Novotná or Daubek was aware of this.

9. Elizabeth Montgomery, later the star of television's *Bewitched*, was a bridesmaid at Jarmila Daubek Packard's wedding.

4. The Happiest Times

1. Ambassador Humes disliked the Manon portrait and commissioned John Winslow to paint her as Violetta. Today neither portrait is on display in Founder's Hall, most of the paintings having been replaced by 8-by-10 photos of hundreds of Met artists, Novotná among them.

2. Tatiana Daubek has pursued a musical career; she is now an accomplished violinist who, with her husband, oboist Gonzalo X. Ruiz, has formed the ensemble House of Time, performing on period instruments.

3. The estate at Liteň was sold after Novotná's death and is now in private hands; the museum was moved to the former home of the village pastor, where it remains.

Index